Patterns of Experience
in Autobiography

Patterns of Experience
in Autobiography

by Susanna Egan

The University of North Carolina Press

Chapel Hill and London

© 1984 The University of North Carolina Press

Manufactured in the United States of America

Library of Congress Cataloging in Publication Data

Egan, Susanna, 1942–
   Patterns of experience in autobiography.

   Bibliography: p.
   Includes index.
   1. Autobiography. I. Title.
CT25.E36 1984   808'.06692   83-12508
ISBN 0-8078-1581-0

For Kieran,

Michael, Catherine, and David

Contents

Preface ix

Abbreviations xiii

Introduction 3

Chapter 1. The Inevitability of Fiction 14

Hale White and Moore: From Autobiographer to
Fictive Narrator 23

Newman and De Quincey: The Evolution of
Narrative Pattern 40

Chapter 2. Childhood: From Innocence to Experience 68

Rousseau and Wordsworth: Metaphors of Innocence 79

Aksakoff, Gorky, De Quincey, and Hudson: Innocence
Lost but Memory Regained 95

Chapter 3. Youth: The Heroic Journey and the
Process of Art 104

Carlyle: Fabrication of Self 112

Wordsworth: Revelation of Poetic Spirit 119

Rousseau: A Maze of Self-Knowledge 127

Moore: Redemption of Self through Art 131

Chapter 4. Maturity: Conversion or Descent
into the Underworld 137

Mill: A Crisis of Identity 147

Wordsworth: Nurture of the Creative Soul 155

Carlyle: From Crisis to Rebirth 163

Chapter 5. Confession: The Hero Tells His Story 169

Saint Augustine, Petrarch, Bunyan 178

Rousseau and the Nineteenth-Century
Confessional Novel 185

Conclusion 196

Notes 203

Selected Bibliography 213

Index 223

Preface

This work began in a seminar on fictions conducted in 1973 in the English Department at the University of British Columbia by professors John F. Hulcoop and Ira B. Nadel. Our texts spanned many decades and several languages; our purpose was to describe the nature and value of fictions. In heated discussion in this very lively gathering I first asked myself whether autobiography did not have to be true in order to mean anything at all. The year 1973 is a long time ago in the history of the discussion of autobiography. Most of what has been important to my work had not yet appeared in print. My tortuous thinking was greatly helped by the criticisms I received from John Hulcoop, Ira Nadel, and Michael Goldberg, who set me some very specific problems to deal with.

That I began by resolving them in terms of nineteenth-century texts was less a deliberate than an inevitable matter. I was working on nineteenth-century fiction with specialists in that period and the nineteenth century is so rich a source of autobiographies that I felt little temptation to look elsewhere. A problem of period only arose when it became clear that my solutions were increasingly archetypal in form, that I was maybe asking nineteenth-century men in particular to represent Man in general. I have thought about this, however, and really do not believe that I am asking them to do any such thing. And if I were, they are far too determinedly individual to comply. Rather, having approached their autobiographies in search of individual revelations of truth and found so many elements of stereotypical stories, I have reached the conclusion that they do provide the personal truths that I am looking for but present them, for reasons that I hope my argument makes clear, in these typical forms. I was discovering all over again, in other words, that archetypal forms serve as efficient purveyors of personal meaning. Fiction is true because it truly expresses aspects of human nature and experience. Autobiography is fictive in its turning to these forms in order to say whatever is more than commonplace. And the idiosyncratic nineteenth-century autobiographer becomes particularly interesting because he is the one who is so determined to tell us all and who resorts again and again to what I can only call fictive forms of narrative in order to tell us anything at all.

If some of my helpful critics raised their eyebrows as nineteenth-century texts fell so happily into the archetypal patterns that long reading, thinking, and discussion assured me made sense, others took umbrage at my omission of female autobiographers. Certainly, I have not set out to exclude women. My explanation here lies partly, I think, with the evolution of female autobiography, which deserves a study of its own. Harriet Martineau and Beatrice Webb, for example, are so "manly" in explanation of their hard-won dignity, purpose, and achievement that they do not lend themselves to a study of what is essentially Romantic autobiography, which, deliberately or inadvertently but very definitely, describes the inner self. And part of the answer lies in the merging in the nineteenth century of autobiography with the novel. The Brontës and George Eliot would provide rich material for a topic like the present one if novels rather than autobiography were the prime focus.

The nineteenth-century focus, then, and the inattention to women are two areas in which this work "just growed." If adherence to this kind of growth is a weakness, it is mine alone. I have hoped that the interest I have felt in the thesis and in these particular texts might be of more value than any attempt to make the work encompass its many and rich possibilities.

Developing as it has over a fairly long period of time, this book quite obviously owes an enormous debt to the criticism and theory that have appeared in the last ten years. Such impersonal though keenly felt debts are impossible to list. From the many who do not even know that they have helped me, I should like to isolate those who must know the indebtedness I feel. I must thank James Olney for the great value to me of his contributions to this field and for his personal criticism, guidance, and very kind support. Karl J. Weintraub has read the work at least twice with generous care; his detailed criticism has contributed much to the book's final value. The fact that he takes issue with much of what I want to say makes me particularly grateful for the supportive nature of his criticism. My husband, Kieran Egan, whose own writing has contributed so largely to mine, has also read and talked and listened with constant generosity.

For many years now the Canada Council has provided the means that enable me to work; I am grateful for the moral as for the financial nature of such support. I would like to thank the kind editors at the University of North Carolina Press who have worked as vigilantes on this text. My thanks also to Irene Hull, who transformed a chaotic manuscript into an impeccable typescript. With so much very excellent help, this book should be better than it is. In the final analysis, however, and to the relief, no doubt, of all whose help I so gratefully acknowledge, I must call it a poor thing because it is my own.

Abbreviations

Ab.	William Hale White, *The Autobiography of Mark Rutherford*
CEOE	Thomas De Quincey, *Confessions of an English Opium-Eater*
Confessions	Jean-Jacques Rousseau, *The Confessions*
EL	William Hale White, *The Early Life of Mark Rutherford (W. Hale White) By Himself*
HF	George Moore, *Hail and Farewell*
JSM	John Stuart Mill, *Autobiography of John Stuart Mill*
Letters	John Henry Newman, *Letters and Correspondence of John Henry Newman*
Prelude	William Wordsworth, *The Prelude*, ed. Selincourt
SR	Thomas Carlyle, *Sartor Resartus*
Tristram	*John Henry Newman*, ed. Henry Tristram

Patterns of Experience
in Autobiography

Introduction

People commonly perceive their lives as containing certain distinct stages. Whether persuaded by the rigorous attempts of scholars like Jean Piaget and Erik Erikson to classify the developing forms of mental life or by the more general comments of a popular book like *Passages*, by the simplifying effect of personal memory, or by the constraints that language imposes on any attempt to relate experience, we learn to summarize crucial and multiform activities and happenings under headings like "childhood," "adolescence," and "mid-life crisis."

Such verbal reductionism also affects the autobiographer, who approaches the more formidable task of writing his life as a narrative. He, too, describes his life in terms of certain distinct stages, like childhood, youth, maturity, and old age. The autobiographer, furthermore, describes these stages according to more elaborate literary conventions than the conversationalist, not only in terms of summary titles but also in terms of certain narrative patterns.

This study explores the nature of some dominant narrative patterns that are common in autobiography. It does not attempt to catalog them nor to identify them through an exhaustive list of autobiographies. Nor does it seek to refine distinctions between fiction and fact or between the work of imaginative literature and the imaginative product that is also empirically verifiable. Rather, by drawing on a varied sampling of written lives, it scans the epistemologically grey area where autobiographical novel and poem overlap with the formal autobiography in order to characterize certain autobiographical patterns in some detail and to suggest both how and why they work.

Why, for example, does Rousseau describe his childhood in terms of a paradise whose golden gates have closed behind him? The particular answer might lie in the many happy months that Rousseau spent with the Lamberciers in the country. But even if paradise can provide a plausible metaphor to describe a period of Rousseau's childhood, why should Gorky, whose story is so different, adhere to the same narrative pattern? Gorky's autobiography opens with his father's dead body and continues in the squalor and brutality of his grandparents' house. Yet he describes a paradisal sanctuary that he creates for himself; he isolates a period of peace, safety, and rich sensations of beauty before he is forced out into the world.

Similarly, why should "journey" provide a recurring metaphor for autobiographers who write about their youth? In autobiographical narratives as different as *The Prelude*, *Hail and Farewell*, *Sartor Resartus*, and *Great Expectations*, journey or quest describes a significant aspect of youth. It becomes the metaphor that extracts and demonstrates some common meaning from very different events in different individual lives.

Then again, both the religiously devout Cardinal Newman and the atheist John Stuart Mill describe central crises in their lives in terms of "conversion." The narrative patterns for conversion can be found in spiritual autobiography, as in *The Confessions of Saint Augustine*, in an autobiographical poem like *The Prelude*, in an autobiographical novel such as *The Portrait of the Artist as a Young Man*, or even in so unliterary and unselfconscious an autobiography as that of the South American naturalist, W. H. Hudson.

Finally, "confession" is a very common form adopted by the autobiographer who writes late in life. Like the narrative forms that describe "paradise," "journey," and "conversion," "confession" adheres to certain formulas that make it clearly recognizable whether the nature of the confession is religious or not.

The existence of such formulas or narrative patterns has been long and substantially established in literature. It can be asserted with confidence that the stories of paradise lost, of the journey or quest, of conversion and confession are literary conventions that serve, like iambic pentameter or first-person narrator, to define particular parameters for literary narrative. The question here, however, is not whether such patterns are so familiar as to be conventions but rather why they are so common in autobiography. When the poet, the novelist, and the historian have access to numerous conventions and yet turn to these particular patterns when their work is autobiographical, the question becomes: What sense do these patterns make out of many different lives? How and why do they work?

These stages of the written life, deriving the language of the representative hero from the epic and the language of private experience from religion, can of course be traced through the traditions and conventions of Western literature. In order to demonstrate their fundamental value to the autobiographer, however, I hope to show in each case how they also derive from the psychological imperatives that determine man's perception of himself and of his world. They are part of what Yeats has called our simplifying image. The autobiographer, in other words, has more than a literary convention neatly to hand; he has what I shall call a myth that is capable of describing the quality of his secret and inner experience both because it acts as an emotionally and generally accurate description of that experience and because it means much the same thing to him as it does to his reader.

I propose to devote a chapter to each of the four narrative patterns mentioned above in order to explore several ways in which they are effective tools for the autobiographer. It is worth noting that the narrative patterns or metaphors, rather than the texts, will be the main objects of study. I hope that the answers that make sense in one context will make sense also in another so that the result may be cumulative sense rather than disparate explorations. Certainly, the four patterns share one feature in common that should be examined now: they have very little to do with life as it is lived; they are all imaginative verbal constructs; all of them are fictions.

Despite its disparaging connotation of fabrication or lies, fiction making is an inevitable human process connected as much with the way the mind works as with the need to entertain an audience. In order to discuss the specific and elaborate fictions commonly used in autobiographies, we need to look at fiction making both in relation to human perception and as it serves to translate lived events into literary events. In chapter 1 I shall begin by exploring quite briefly why and how fictions in general translate experience into a readily comprehensible verbal form. Because the fictionalizing process is fundamental to establishing why and how certain patterns work, it seems worthwhile to elaborate this theoretical discussion into practical examination of why and how it works in a few specific autobiographies. Therefore, chapter 1 will move from theoretical discussion to look first at the creation of a narrator in William Hale White's *Autobiography of Mark Rutherford* and in George Moore's *Hail and Farewell*. It will then turn to the evolution of narrative pattern in two earlier autobiographies, Cardinal Newman's *Apologia Pro Vita Sua* and De Quincey's *Confessions of an English Opium-Eater*. Newman's account of his sickness in Sicily, a nodal point of the *Apologia*, is traced as closely as possible from an event in his life through correspondence and journal entries into the fictional form that serves his narrative purpose in the autobiography that he intended most simply and adequately to represent the truth about himself. Newman's quotidian jottings are interesting in their own right and because they add up to a fascinating picture of Newman. They are useful here, however, only insofar as they illustrate the apparently unconscious or at least insidious transformation of quotidian phenomena into a narrative pattern closely related to that described here as conversion. Similarly, De Quincey's autobiographical essays, written and revised over a wide span of time, can be seen in the process of probably quite conscious and deliberate transformation into the narrative pattern of his revised *Confessions*. Newman and De Quincey, both essentially essayists, both absorbed and fascinated by their own experience, translate the transient into the paradigmatic and demonstrate the artistic process by which this is done. Interestingly enough, each of the patterns that I shall examine contains some consciousness of the written life as an art form in process.

Chapter 1, in other words, explores why and how "contingent reality," to use Frank Kermode's term for life as it is lived,[1] is transformed into literary events, the autobiographer into a character in a book, and an essentially shapeless life into a life of shape and meaning. It examines the mechanics of that fictionalizing process that provides direction for random events and generally accessible meaning for originally subjective experience. Having clarified some of the mechanics of this process in chapter 1, I shall then move on to consider my four chosen patterns in some detail.

The stages of the written life begin with childhood, which is discussed in chapter 2. Childhood moves from innocence to experience. It relies on memory and may be controlled by nostalgia. Psychology provides certain clear and common facts about the maturing process of the small child that help to explain why the Edenic paradigm is so useful for understanding and describing this period of life. Rousseau and Wordsworth are my main exemplars for use of this myth of Eden in autobiography, though I shall turn for further exemplification to works by George Moore, Serge Aksakoff, Maxim Gorky, W. H. Hudson, and Thomas De Quincey.

Youth, the subject of chapter 3, brings a journey, maybe a search for a promised land. In religion this journey is a pilgrimage. In epic it is a quest. In either case, the relevant abstraction for the autobiographer is that all men are engaged in a search, either for lost time, or for their identity, or because they need *rerum cognoscere causas*. Both psychology and sociology support the relevance of this narrative pattern to this stage of life. In autobiography, of course, as in fiction, the journey provides a sustained metaphor for the artist in the process of creation. In this terminology, autobiography represents the activity of the quest and, if it is successful, it becomes the answer that was sought:

> We shall not cease from exploration
> And the end of all our exploring
> Will be to arrive where we started
> And know the place for the first time.[2]

The journey provides a significant metaphor in Carlyle's *Sartor Resartus*, Wordsworth's *Prelude*, Rousseau's *Confessions*, and George Moore's *Hail and Farewell*.

Maturity, the subject of chapter 4, often involves a crisis in which the past and the future are transformed in the light of some overwhelming and special knowledge. Saint Augustine describes "[his] miserable heart overcharged with most gnawing cares, lest [he] should die ere [he] found the truth."[3] In religious terms, this crisis is conversion. For the epic hero it entails descent into the underworld, a trial of the spirit that brings knowledge and wisdom and the power to guide others. And here, once again, psychological studies support my notion that such a crisis takes a specific form in the human character before finding its typical form of expression. For the epic hero as for the religious convert, descent into death and ascent into rebirth provide a central experience on the journey or quest. This experience, however, and the story that derives from it, are so distinct that they can best be described and discussed in a separate chapter from the journey. Carlyle and Wordsworth both describe "conversion" as central to their journey, and to these accounts we shall add discussion of Rousseau, William Hale White, and John Stuart Mill.

Old age, discussed in chapter 5, involves confession for the convert. For the hero it entails the telling of his story. Louis Dudek has remarked on the stereotypical quality of this most personal form that offers a range of intimacy wide enough to include both *The Waste Land* and Shelley's bleeding among the thorns of life.[4] Unlike the myths of Eden, the journey, or even conversion, however, confession as a narrative pattern derives from no clear or single origin. We cannot point to creation myths or to widely known epics or folktales as the source of this form in literature. Like the novel, moreover, confession depends more heavily on internal signals than on identifiable form for its character. It becomes necessary, accordingly, to alter my approach to the subject; whereas I hope to be able to show here, as for each of the other narrative patterns, the psychological underpinnings that give it its element of necessity, I also need to describe the historical evolution of the internal signals that constitute the "form."

For this purpose it seems sensible to look briefly at the works of Saint Augustine, Petrarch, and Bunyan before turning to the autobiographical flowering of confession in the writings of Rousseau, Goethe, and the nineteenth-century novel. William Spengemann's use of Saint Augustine and his successors is rather different from mine, but he is helpful in describing Saint Augustine's *Confessions* as setting the problems for all successive autobiographers, providing three solutions, and, indeed, rehearsing "the entire development of the genre from the Middle Ages to the modern era."[5] Prompted by the lack of any precise or single origin for confession, I propose to follow Spengemann's lead and trace the evolution of this form, which differs further from the others in that it describes in part the very act of autobiography.

Having described the stages of life as childhood, youth, maturity, and age, and having suggested that mythology, classical literature, and the Christian religion contribute to the terms in which we can describe these stages and, further, that sociology and psychology seem to support an element of necessity in these particular metaphors, I should add that the very notion that there are such stages is, of course, a fiction in itself. In Louis Renza's words, I am almost certainly fictionalizing the object about which I am theorizing.[6] I am not, however, asking for any suspension of disbelief but simply assuming an ironic consciousness that can accept form as form and that can acknowledge certain forms as useful without finding them either arbitrary or inevitable. Not all autobiographers categorize their lives in these terms. Of those that do, not all use all the forms. Of those that use some forms, not all use them exhaustively; in some cases internal metaphors merely point to the fictional form that has remained latent and has not directed the narrative to any significant degree.

Having said so much to limit the operation of these narrative patterns, I should describe the textual limits within which they may be seen at work in detail. This study will concentrate for the most part, but not exclusively, on nineteenth-century texts in English. In an essay entitled "Conditions and Limits of Autobiography," Georges Gusdorf suggests as a precondition for autobiography that "humanity must have emerged from the mythic framework of traditional teachings and must have entered into the perilous domain of history."[7] It is, of course, no coincidence that the rise of autobiography should occur simultaneously with a movement toward scientific historiography. In both autobiography and historiography we see the development of a new historical consciousness, a sense that events are best explained by describing their history, that meaning is established by describing the process that precedes and causes an event. Whether or not we are satisfied with this inheritance of what may be called excessive historicism, clear alternative ways of fixing meaning have yet to be established. Formalism and structuralism, for example, represent modern attempts to transcend the grip of historical consciousness, but their success in escaping the requirements of historicism is neither established nor convincing.[8] It is no part of my intention to argue this case in detail, especially when structuralists themselves are doing so.[9] The point is worth making here simply to explain in part why so many of the best and most interesting autobiographies were written in the nineteenth century and why it seems both permissible and fruitful to examine them as exemplars of a mode of making sense of experience that has not been transcended.

This is not to say that earlier and later autobiographers do not use the narrative patterns that I propose to study. Indeed, apart from the service to which Saint Augustine, Petrarch, and Bunyan are pressed, there are many possibilities for discussion that would take us outside the nineteenth century. If these particular patterns derive from ancient and persistent psychological imperatives, it should be possible to trace them at work in the autobiographies of any period in time. However, my interest in their function in nineteenth-century autobiography is quite specific.

"Time allows for repetition and recognition, for the diffusion of activities to a broader population, thereby taking off the edge of idiosyncracy and innocence."[10] The nineteenth century sees autobiography, in Elizabeth Bruss's terms, finally "distinguished from other illocutionary acts,"[11] become, indeed, "an almost banal literary event."[12] In competition with the lyric and the novel, avowed autobiography moves away from memoir or narration of public, externally verifiable events into the far more difficult narration of hidden experience. Spengemann explains how earlier autobiographers found some fixed point external to themselves, a center of reality in God, Reason, or Nature as their cultural climate allowed. But for the nineteenth-century autobiographer, stripped of external securities (Gusdorf's "mythic framework of traditional teachings"), that center, "the point where all things have their true, eternal being, where nothing is lost and everything can be truly known," resided in himself, "deep within dark cavern of the individual psyche." Autobiography under these circumstances can be seen "as the prime instrument of Romantic knowledge."[13]

Montaigne had sought such knowledge. So did Rousseau, whom I must nudge into the nineteenth century to serve his turn. It is surely impossible to exclude him from any discussion of the autobiographer's attempt to find and reveal his inner self. But it is this late development in autobiography that particularly interests me, when autobiography proliferates, is recognized as a distinguishable art form, and even spills over into other "forms" such as the poem and the novel, when the writer, his own analyst and best authority, investigates the truths discernible to no one else and expresses them with such frequency in terms of these narrative patterns. For if the nineteenth-century autobiographer intends an authoritative account not only of personal but also of specifically subjective experience, is it not a contradiction in terms that he should so very frequently resort to what appear to be formal literary conventions in order to describe long stretches of that experience? Indeed, my wish to understand such an apparent contradiction provided the initial energy for this study.

Any temptation to examine a large number of texts across national and temporal boundaries has been further counteracted by an urgent sense that the case I am trying to make for the fictionalizing process in autobiography can best be made by relatively detailed analysis of a small core of texts. The case for the function of these four narrative patterns in autobiography could possibly be made from a very small core of texts indeed. Rousseau, Wordsworth, and Carlyle, for example, offer material enough to explain the function and purpose of paradise, journey, conversion, and confession in the written life. Exclusive concentration on such a core would certainly absolve one from the charge of random sampling to suit an arbitrary purpose. It would also suggest, however, an absolute and inescapable quality in these narrative patterns that is not at all part of my claim. I hope, therefore, that repeated use of a few autobiographies as basic exemplary material may demonstrate in detail both how and why these patterns work and how they accumulate and overlap within particular texts to enrich the meanings of the narrative. Extensions of national and temporal boundaries may then provide further instances of the same patterns in less detail and purely as random sampling.

Each literary form examined here represents a translation of life into literature that is, for the most part, the result of conscious artistry. Where such translation is not actually deliberate, it results from a perspective on the past during which a possibly unconscious subscription to these patterns has had time to affect the autobiographer's perceptions. It has therefore seemed sensible not to include letters and diaries, autobiographical as these most certainly are, particularly when they are collected over a substantial period of time. The patterns of perception that could be demonstrated from diaries and letters would reveal something about the tendency toward such pattern making in the reader but could not be very helpful in revealing the artistic function of such pattern making on the part of the writer. I have tried to demonstrate the inevitability of some sort of artistic pattern making in my discussion of the fictionalizing process in chapter 1. When this is established, my only concern is with the why and how of the narrative patterns as they exist not in process but in the completed autobiographical text.

All the texts included here are referred to in translation except for two works by Rousseau for which no translation is readily available.

1. The Inevitability of Fiction

It seems fair to assume that the autobiographer begins his work with a clear sense of himself to which he would like to be true. Who he is matters more, in the long run, than the things that have happened to him even if he describes who he is by means of the things that have happened to him. His individuality is his birthright and he will not sell it, unless he is incompetent, for a mess of facts.

However, even if he intends to write about his life as directly as possible, the activity of writing interferes between his past and the written word that he creates. "To speak is to act," Sartre writes. "[A]nything which one names is already no longer quite the same; it has lost its innocence."[1] Or, as Roman Jakobson puts it: "La propriété privée dans le domaine du langage, ça n'existe pas."[2] The autobiographer may summon memory to his aid, amended and corrected by data such as letters and diaries, and begin to write about himself, but his muse, Mnemosyne, is an artist, his data are inadequate, his peception is partial, his role is essentially that of interpreter and coordinator, and his "actual events" become "virtual events" in the process of writing. Fiction, in other words, ensnares reality from the beginning. The fact of this ensnaring is a commonplace of criticism. How it is achieved is accounted for variously by various critics. As my theme involves the ways in which fictional patterns help to establish meaning in autobiographies, it will be useful to refine this commonplace in the context of fictionalizing in autobiography.

Susanne Langer's definition of the difference between actual events and virtual events, or events in literature, may describe the kind of truth that autobiographers feel that they can tell. Virtual events have a double duty to perform that distinguishes them from actual events: they must convince and they must contain an emotional factor. They are qualitative in their very constitution and have no existence apart from values, from the emotional import which is part of their appearance. They are contained, for example, more significantly in a madeleine cake or a Vinteuil sonata than in the registry of births and deaths. As autobiography is a written record, the events it includes, regardless of their basis in fact, must perform double duty as virtual events, and will be effective, indeed true, only insofar as they portray an emotional reality.

Anthony Trollope, for example, who produced only one official, relatively dry and specifically businesslike autobiography, wrote numerous accounts of the lonely, incompetent hobbledehoy in London subjected to the control of corrupt and greedy landladies, tempted and trapped by unworthy women, falling into debt and its correlative despair, but protected from afar by the benign influence of good women and an eccentric but kindly uncle. We are forced to believe him when he says that the man of letters is in truth ever writing his autobiography. Charley Tudor of *The Three Clerks* (1858) bears a strong likeness to Johnny Eames of *The Small House at Allington* (1864) and to the young Anthony Trollope of the *Autobiography* of 1883. The events in the lives of these three young men clearly relate to Trollope's actual life even though they may, in all three versions, be fictional in detail or specifics. In each case, however, the written event both exists and convinces because of "the emotional import which is part of its appearance."[3] As with the "blacking warehouse" section of *David Copperfield* or the beating of little Ernest Pontifex, such events are true to an emotional reality. Bruss makes much the same point with her illustrations from various Nabokov works that use the same material for different purposes. "Form and function," she writes, "are not isomorphic; several functions can be and usually are allotted to the same structure, and most functions are capable of being realized through more than one form."[4] Trollope needed to convey the essence of his own youth in London. Whether Johnny Eames or Charley Tudor or Anthony Trollope portrayed that quality most sharply for him, he was able to convey it at all only by creating virtual events.

Bruss, of course, deriving her terms from Austin, describes autobiography as an "illocutionary act," thus drawing attention both to the conventions that establish meanings and to the potential gaps between intentions and their fulfillment. Her discussion, based on linguistic clues, of the ways in which autobiographers have tried to construct their experiences from the inside, as she puts it, takes its energy from her interest in change, from the "progressive articulation of the autobiographical act."[5] Given changing conventions and cultural and literary contexts, she explores the ways in which this genre that we call autobiography continues to modulate, evolve, and exist. In contrast to Bruss, however, I am interested essentially in the *un*changing ways in which private experience finds its generic expression; I subordinate act to form. This is not a perverse and impossible avoidance of the changes that do take place. I am not hoping, Canute-like, to discountenance the realities of context, culture, time, and change. Rather, assuming such realities as given, I should like to concentrate on certain aspects of the translation from experience to art that are least affected by mutability. Among these, before any word is written, is the transformation of reality resulting from the very activity of perception.

E. H. Gombrich suggests that "there is no rigid distinction . . . between perception and illusion."[6] He agrees with Kermode that it is necessary to posit a contingent reality or world of actual events, but he argues persuasively that contingent reality is completely unamenable to reproduction; only comparisons, analogues, or metaphors can possibly work. After centuries of visual art, Constable could only see a landscape in terms of a Gainsborough, who saw it in terms of the Dutch masters, and so on. Similarly, Northrop Frye finds "no such thing as self-expression in literature."[7] Each work, after all, conforms not to reality but to its own laws established by the tradition within which it exists. Schemata evolve to guide perception, which is accordingly largely affected by expectation. According to Gombrich, "all thinking is sorting, classifying. All perceiving relates to expectations and therefore to comparisons."[8] Neither size nor color, for example, makes any sense on its own but only within a context that provides relationships. For the artist these relationships are determined by his medium. (Gombrich is writing about visual art, but literary or musical form also provides determining media.) "If this is true—and it can hardly be gainsaid—the problem of illusionist art is not that of forgetting what we know about the world. It is rather that of inventing comparisons which work."[9]

Gombrich, like the structuralists, like Piaget, finds his original schemata not in the actual world but in the perceiving mind of man. He disposes of Ruskin's "innocent eye" as a "myth" and presents overwhelming evidence for what structuralists call the innate patterning qualities of the mind. Rembrandt, in other words, for all his sixty-two self-portraits, never *saw* himself, either as a physical actuality or as others saw him, but only as an illusion, a distortion in a looking-glass. He was able, however, to transform his perception of himself, indistinguishable from illusion, into a comparison that worked for himself and for other people. The closer a copy of reality comes to reality itself, the more it loses its own identity (one reason why photography has had to struggle to assert itself as an art). Or, as Langer puts it, the difference between a life-mask and a portrait is the *deathlikeness* of the former. "To bring anything really to life in literature," Frye writes, "we can't be lifelike: we have to be literature-like."[10] Frye is writing about the function of literary conventions, but the point he is making overlaps with Langer's discussion, especially when she refers to the absence of James's "air of reality" in so many newspaper articles and suggests that the " 'livingness' of a story is really much surer, and often greater, than that of actual experience."[11] It may indeed be necessary to modify R. D. Laing's statement that even facts become fictions without adequate ways of seeing the facts and say that facts cannot be grasped at all until they have been transformed into fictions.

Undoubtedly, Rembrandt's friends recognized his self-portraits, yet they would have been forced to admit that the portraits represent many degrees of removal from reality through illusion to invention, though they might have expressed themselves more simply and said he looks *as if* he were alive. According to Hans Vaihinger, thought distinguishes between things-in-themselves and the world of *as if*: it "creates for itself an exceedingly artificial instrument of enormous practical utility for the apprehension and elaboration of the stuff of reality."[12] In basic agreement but more stirring language, Carlyle remarks: "Of this . . . sort are all true works of Art: in them . . . wilt thou discern Eternity looking through Time; the Godlike rendered visible" (*SR*, 3:223). Carlyle is describing the wondrous agency of symbols that conceal and yet reveal the reality from which they derive, Vaihinger the logical process whereby abstract thought, scientific procedures, and ethical behavior become possible. He thus concludes:

> The fictive activity of the mind is an expression of the fundamental psychical forces; *fictions* are *mental structures*. The psyche weaves this aid to thought out of itself; for the mind is inventive; under the compulsion of necessity, stimulated by the outer world, it discovers the store of contrivances that lie hidden within itself.
> . . . With an instinctive, almost cunning ingenuity, the logical function succeeds in overcoming . . . difficulties with the aid of . . . accessory structures.[13]

The autobiographer, in other words, shares his resources with the artist, the writer, and the common man alike; each derives his fictions originally from the very way in which the mind works. Each one thinks by means of metaphor. James Olney, discussing autobiography's "impulse to order," describes metaphor in this context as "essentially a way of knowing."[14] Or, as Jerome Bruner explains: "If it is the case that art as a mode of knowing has precisely the function of connecting through metaphor what before had no apparent kinship, then . . . the art form of the myth connects the daemonic world of impulse with the world of reason by a verisimilitude that conforms to each."[15]

If we equate Bruner's verisimilitude with Vaihinger's accessory structures in his world of *as if*, and with Gombrich's illusion created by comparisons that work, we can describe metaphor as the crucial and inescapable means of perceiving our world and of explaining what we perceive. Metaphor creates a virtual event and, crucially for autobiography, it creates a virtual life. "Even the personality called 'I' in an autobiography," Langer reminds us, "must be a creature of the story and not the model himself. 'My' story is what happens in the book, not a string of occasions in the world."[16] Similarly, she continues, "[l]iterary events are *made*, not reported, just as portraits are painted, not born and raised."[17]

Such distinctions between life and art, which sound like platitudes in the discussion of art in general, become crucial in discussion of autobiography, where the temptation constantly exists to equate or identify the narrator with the author. Metaphor conceals and reveals the original, the model, by creating a comparison that works, a likeness, a virtual character. Metaphor of this kind represents what psychologists call displacement, what Eliot meant by an objective correlative, the projection of an inner reality onto any external form that can bear and describe it.

As a child, for example, Carl Jung made a little man, placed him on a stone, and hid him in a pencil case in the attic.[18] The safety of his life, he felt, depended on that secret manikin hidden with the stone in the pencil case. He gave shape, in other words, to a secret that was the secret of his own identity. Working with patients many years later, Jung found that therapy began in every case with the story that is not told, the hidden stone. Determined to confront his own unconscious, to find his own story or myth, he built himself a town with building blocks. He describes how he found it necessary to differentiate himself from the contents of his own unconscious by personifying them and bringing them into consciousness. He detaches all the pieces of his own persona from himself, like the building blocks, partly for experimental reconstruction, essentially because his thinking and feeling are at their very core metaphorical. Jung is an exemplary model for the necessity and value of metaphor as a mode of achieving that conscious cognition, of creating previously unapprehended relationships between a man and the fictions that he creates. Jung is an exemplary model, but all autobiographers, of necessity, by the very act of autobiography, reconstruct themselves in some form or another with building blocks or bring out from their attic that hidden pencil case.

Jung, like Bruner, describes myth as a significant metaphor, "the natural and indispensable intermediate stage between unconscious and conscious cognition,"[19] connecting, in Bruner's words, "the daemonic world of impulse with the world of reason." Just as metaphor enables the autobiographer to project himself in such a way that he both understands himself and elicits understanding, so myth-as-metaphor also serves to condense experience into a narrative of tellable length. It works as narrative shorthand for the autobiographer and ensures the accessibility of his story to his audience.

For the autobiographer takes one final step and stoops, in E. M. Forster's words, to story, "that low atavistic form."[20] Only within a story can events of any kind sort their bewildering variety into a determinate meaning. The narrative of autobiography manipulates the bewildering variety of lived experience by imposing on it a beginning, a middle, and an end. Tzvetan Todorov, in fact, describes the ideal narrative as beginning "with a stable situation which is disturbed by some power or force. There results a state of disequilibrium; by the action of a force directed in the opposite direction, the equilibrium is reestablished; the second equilibrium is similar to the first, but the two are never identical."[21]

The autobiographer, of course, may begin where he likes (Wordsworth begins [...] and he may [...] ipulate his narrative structur [...] adopts (Stephen Dedalus beg [...] oo-cow story and its teller); b [...] e to the narrative pattern des [...] tured out-line parallels the mos [...] h, life, and death. It is com [...] is not explicit, to read of a l [...] nind or a soul or the discover [...] a safer given than his life, for which the end is not known at the time of writing, the autobiographer can narrate his life in terms of a basic plot formula: anticipation, recognition, and fulfillment. A frequent teleological determinism derives from techniques whereby what was foreseen is fulfilled. According to Gusdorf:

> The difficulty is insurmountable: no trick of presentation even when assisted by genius can prevent the narrator from always knowing the outcome of the story he tells—he commences, in a manner of speaking, with the problem already solved. Moreover, the illusion begins from the moment that the narrative *confers a meaning* on the event which, when it actually occurred, no doubt had several meanings or perhaps none. This postulating of a meaning dictates the choice of the facts to be retained and of the details to bring out or to dismiss according to the demands of the preconceived intelligibility.[22]

The narrator gains control and authority, and the reader a sense of order and understanding.

The theme that any autobiographer chooses provides a shape for his narrative. It also provides a meaning. The formula of anticipation, recognition, and fulfillment is matched by the formula for separation, initiation, and return borrowed from rites of passage and described by Vladimir Propp as part of the total action of every folktale.[23] Joseph Campbell calls this formula the "nuclear unit of the monomyth."[24] The two formulas are as basic to narrative form and to self-perception as birth, life, and death to the body. They are fictions in their creative ability to ignore or exploit particular actions in order to achieve universal meanings, to convey, as Frye translates Aristotle, not what happened but *what happens*.

It is unlikely, of course, that any autobiographer has ever sat down to his task consciously determined to write "a nuclear unit of the monomyth." It is likely, however, that his readers would acquire a more intimate sense of him from his letters, sonnets, diary entries, or conversations than from the finished product called the story of his life. More intimate, but less coherent. The distinction that needs to be made between the lyric, the letter, or the diary entry and the autobiography is not one of value but rather one of kind. We can learn nothing more intimate than the cry of the lover who would that his love were in his arms and he in his bed again. We can learn nothing more coherent than the story of a man who would "give the true key to [his] whole life,"[25] who would "tell [his] personal myth,"[26] or who knows that "three passions . . . have governed [his] life."[27] The distinction is that of time and retrospect. The autobiographer does not sit down to write a monomyth, but he does sort the variety of his moments' meanings into the meaning that he ascribes to his life.

For most men, it is safe to say, the final meaning is likely to transcend all others. Few men write great lyrics or letters. Many, however, have made sense of their lives by transforming them into very fine autobiographies, which, by virtue of their fictive nature, cannot be translated back into the actual world. Susan Sontag observes that "the knowledge we gain through art is an experience of the form or style of knowing something, rather than a knowledge of something (like a fact or a moral judgement) in itself."[28] The chaos of actual events is common to all experience, but the artist excels at transformation of such chaos essentially into a meaningful form that is accessible to all. Francis Cornford cites examples of this process of transforming multitudinous facts into coherent fictions. He concentrates on "the moulding of a long series of events into a plan determined by an *art form*."[29] *The Peloponnesian War*, he finds, is a tragedy, for although "Thucydides, like Descartes, thought he had stripped himself bare of every preconception," his work, like that of Descartes, "shows that there was after all a residuum wrought into the substance of his mind and ineradicable because unperceived."[30] Everyone, after all, takes his own habits of thought for granted and perceives his bias only by contrast. For the historian the book of how-it-was is inevitably sealed; reflected from the narrator's mind, we can discover only the fictive form in which it will be remembered, not as a sequence and overlap of many events but as a tragedy that ruined Athens.

The autobiographer, too, subordinating the historical activity of describing what happened to the poetic activity of conveying what happens, incorporates his facts into a "mythic" narrative. Frye draws an important analogy between mythos, the typical action of poetry, and the significant actions that men engage in because they are typical and recurring. Myth is the verbal imitation of such rituals. "Such plots," Frye writes, "because they describe typical actions, naturally fall into typical forms."[31] Or, as Jung puts it: "There are as many archetypes as there are typical situations in life. Endless repetition has engraved these experiences into our psychic constitution, not in the form of images filled with content, but at first only as *forms without content*."[32] What happened, in all its complexity, does not lend itself easily to narration. Life, in that sense, "is not susceptible perhaps to the treatment we give it when we try to tell it."[33] At so basic a level as this, when the rhythms of life are to be comprehended and translated into narrative, myth and ritual provide paradigmatic forms that make sense. They provide the narrative metaphors, the comparisons that work.

Hale White and Moore: From Autobiographer to Fictive Narrator

The autobiographer who begins with a clear sense of himself that he would like to convey through his life story faces particular problems in the creation of his narrator. We have glanced at the critic's danger of too close identification of narrator with author, yet this identification is part of the author's intention. He is not simply creating a fictitious character who must appear lifelike; he is creating a likeness, a self-portrait, which he intends should convince us of its likeness to him. The author of the third-person autobiographical work encounters fewer problems in this area; no statement of the identification that he feels or that others may perceive needs to be explicit in the text. Stephen Dedalus, like Rachel Vinrace or Paul Morel, or even like the Overton-Pontifex mixture, can come into a life of his own as a fictive character by virtue of the objectivity established by mere use of the third person. His identity and the meaning of his story are cushioned and contained by the controlling narrator who is distinct and apart from him. The first-person narrator, on the other hand, faces the problems of creating and controlling his narrative onstage, so to speak. He needs to establish his authority, his viewpoint, and his narrative techniques so that we believe that he is who he claims to be but also so that his story can carry conviction. "I," an author in the world of contingent reality, has to translate into "I," the narrator, a fiction and part of fictive events without forfeiting credibility or disturbing our suspension of disbelief.

Autobiographical works use numerous devices for overcoming these problems of hero-narrator identification. Young Ernest Pontifex, for example, is presented through the sympathetic, mature vision of the paternal Overton, the young self seen by the older self, but neither one explicitly identified with Samuel Butler. Stephen Dedalus moves from third to first person, from past to present tense in order to achieve a similar distinction between the then of remembered times and the now of the narrator's viewpoint. Tone may do much to establish both authority and personality. An autobiographer may color his narrator with the inflection of his language and with the choices he makes, particularly with his initial material for self-presentation. I propose here to look at just two examples of the autobiographical narrator in order to see in more detail how and with what benefits to the work as a whole the autobiographer in the world transforms himself into a character in a book. For an unusual form of third-person narration, I shall look at William Hale White's *Autobiography of Mark Rutherford*, and for a tour de force of first-person narration, George Moore's *Hail and Farewell*.

William Hale White demonstrates very clearly the value of metaphor for representation of the hidden man. He creates a persona called Mark Rutherford, whose turbulent, painful *Autobiography* appeared in 1881. Nearly thirty years later, Hale White writes in his own person some autobiographical notes entitled *The Early Life of Mark Rutherford*. These notes, "not written for publication, but to please two or three persons related to me by affection" (*EL*, p. 91), are a remarkable achievement. They translate an emotionally turbulent youth into less than one hundred small pages of untroubled, pellucid prose. Like his own father, who admired Cobbett, and like the Mary Mardon whom Mark Rutherford admires in the *Autobiography*, White was able to act on the belief that "if the truth is of serious importance to us we dare not obstruct it by phrase-making" (*EL*, p. 30). Or, in Burlitt's words, "'painted glass is very beautiful, but plain glass is the most useful as it lets through the most light'" (*EL*, p. 31). "A good deal of [his early life] has been told before under a semi-transparent disguise," he continues, "with much added which is entirely fictitious. What I now set down is fact" (*EL*, p. 5).

A comparison between this "factual account" and the earlier *Autobiography of Mark Rutherford*, where the facts are disguised and amplified, can clarify some of the benefits that accrue to the autobiographer who fictionalizes his hero and rejects explicit identification of the hero with himself. *The Autobiography of Mark Rutherford* covers the same ground but is over twice as long as *The Early Life*. It was written at "extraordinary high-pressure," his second wife writes in *The Groombridge Diary*. "He was then at work every night at the House of Commons, and he wrote in the mornings, 4:30. He ought," she adds affectionately, "to have had more sleep."[34] Significantly, too, Hale White did not claim the *Autobiography* for many years. He made it his manikin, and he hid behind it. Rutherford is a metaphor for Hale White, and Rutherford's fictions describe Hale White's suffering in metaphorical terms. The events and the characters that Rutherford alters or adds did not, we must believe, happen in Hale White's life. But only because they happen in fiction can we grasp the emotional realities that explain the significance of each simple fact or event. The disguise and fiction, then, achieve a basic purpose of autobiography; they convey a quality of truth for which the "facts," certainly as they stand in *The Early Life*, are inadequate.

Most of the events in the *Autobiography* correspond exactly with those in *The Early Life*. Rutherford describes his Calvinist background, his conversion that was meant to be Pauline, the irrelevance of the theological college, the brief attempt at schoolmastering, and the work for Chapman, now called Wollaston. The only purely fictitious interpolation among these events is Rutherford's actual assumption first of a Calvinist and then of a Unitarian ministry. His experience as a minister serves the useful purpose of elaborating what-might-have-been; it develops the meaning of "the great blunder of my life, the mistake which well-nigh ruined it altogether" (*EL*, p. 55); but it does not account for the more than doubled length of the text or its increased complexity.

The Autobiography of Mark Rutherford is about the painful erosion of faith, the fear of death, and the longing for friendship. It is also about the maturing of the man who learns to live with the inadequacies of the essentially mortal soul stripped of hope and comfort. Each character, each incident furthers some aspect of these complex themes.

The erosion of faith, for example, begins with the new capacity for what Rutherford calls inner reference as distinct from religious obedience, a capacity awoken in him by the *Lyrical Ballads*. Yet only by stressing the rigid theology of the college where a question is a heresy and the rigid character of both Calvinist and Unitarian parishioners can Rutherford make clear the loneliness of his own condition and his difficulty in improving it. He writes of a sermon he gave while still at college on the meaning of atonement and of the president's caution that his personal interpretation was inappropriate, which fell on him afterwards "like the hand of a corpse" (*Ab.*, p. 53). He gives a sermon early in his ministry on Christianity as the religion of the lonely and unknown, and finds no response at all. "Nobody came near me but my landlord, the chapel-keeper, who said it was raining, and immediately went away to put out the lights and shut up the building" (*Ab.*, p. 75). He goes home to his cheerless supper of bread and cheese and beer in front of an empty grate, hysterical that his own creed cannot stand stress. "Towards morning I got into bed, but not to sleep; and when the dull light of Monday came, all support had vanished, and I seemed to be sinking into a bottomless abyss" (*Ab.*, pp. 75–76). This scene, whether it derives from fact or not, finds no counterpart in *The Early Life*. Clearly, it represents an internal event, but unlike the habit of melancholia born on his one night as a schoolmaster, which is recorded in both texts, this scene makes a dramatic statement about his inner development. This is, after all, a spiritual history. Rutherford describes his fear of insanity as a reptile with its fangs driven into his very marrow, getting up with him in the morning, walking about with him all day, and lying down with him at night. He uses a variety of fictional and metaphorical devices in order to give loneliness and fear a local habitation and a name.

Attached to his loss of faith is Rutherford's fear of death. So common is this fear that he offers it as an exemplary justification for assuming that a record of his sufferings may help others. For the man with a strong faith, death offers at least such abstractions as redemption and life everlasting. For Rutherford, who uses terms like "adrift" and "abyss," it means extinction of personality. Both texts contain the incident in which he overcomes his fear of drowning by an exercise of will. The *Autobiography*, however, also elaborates his fear of alcohol. Taken only for awhile and, it would seem, quite temperately, alcohol relieves his fears of insanity, but it threatens an imprisonment and dependence greatly to be feared if loss of identity is equivalent to death. Rutherford learns to wait for the depression to lift. Patience, like will, is necessary for the survival of a strong person.

The erosion of faith and the fear of death are equaled only by the loss of a perfect friend in the person of Jesus. Rutherford must transfer his need for friendship, like his seach for meaning and purpose, to the world around him. His search is made quite explicitly in terms of the value derived from its religious origins:

I longed to prove my devotion as well as to receive that of another. How this ideal haunted me! It made me restless and anxious at the sight of every new face, wondering whether at last I had found that for which I searched as if for the kingdom of heaven. (*Ab.*, p. 55)

Much later in the *Autobiography*, he writes: "The desire for something like sympathy and love absolutely devoured me" (*Ab.*, p. 204). If his hunger and thirst have abated by the time he writes, it is only because time heaps ashes on every fire. He has been repulsed into self-reliance and reserve, and warns his readers never to reject such advances as he made for friendship; such devotion as he had to offer is simply the most precious thing in existence. "Had I found anybody who would have thought so," he concludes, "my life would have been redeemed into something which I have often imagined, but now shall never know" (*Ab.*, p. 206).

The middle section of the book is devoted to people who in one way or another represent such human possibilities. Rutherford devotes a chapter to Mardon, a chapter to Miss Arbour, a chapter to Ellen and Mary. The specific narrative that runs just beneath his loss of faith recounts his doubts about marrying Ellen and his wish to marry Mary, Ellen being a simple girl of the old faith, Mary a clear-headed skeptic of the new. These two girls, like Mardon, represent moral polarities at the fictional level even if they find their origins in White's life. They are clarified by fiction into opposites, and Miss Arbour, with her harrowing tale of her miserable marriage, arbitrates between them. For each character, like each situation, represents a possibility of growth for the young man who is learning the cloudy terms of inner reference. Rutherford's indecision is given in terms that are familiar to readers of fiction; just as his descriptions of hysteria and calm resort to metaphor, so he turns here to the pathetic fallacy, projecting onto the landscape the despair in his own mind:

I went on and on under a leaden sky, through the level, solitary, marshy meadows, where the river began to lose

itself in the ocean, and I wandered about there, struggling for guidance. (*Ab.*, p. 115)

Miss Arbour offers more than a glass of water. She offers the
example of her own life as a lesson to save the young minister
from something worse than death—self-degradation.

Similarly, the butterfly catcher offers himself as an example,
also in story form: "'It will be twenty-six years ago next
Christmas,' said he, 'since I suffered a great calamity'" (*Ab.*, p.
198). The pursuit of butterflies, which attracted him accidentally, drew his attention specifically to the world around him
and so helped him to overcome his fears of no existence beyond the grave. Rutherford has long since recognized that
there is "no Saviour for us like the hero who has passed trium-
phantly through the distress which troubles *us*" (*Ab.*, pp. 95–
96).

The only parallel given by *The Early Life* between people in
Hale White's life and these significant fictional characters encountered by Rutherford is that between George Eliot and
Theresa (an appropriate pseudonym!). Of George Eliot,
White writes in *The Early Life* no more than his admiration
for her ("I did know what she was worth," p. 83) and his
regret that he did not pursue his friendship with her. "She
took the kindest notice of me, an awkward creature not accustomed to society" (*EL*, p. 84). Rutherford, by contrast,
creates a whole character in Theresa, her walk, her stance, her
look, her methods of dispute, her perceptions about people
and emotions, and most important, her redemption of the
absent-minded, incompetent Rutherford both from a practical mistake and from self-contempt. "It was as if . . . some
miraculous Messiah had soothed the delirium of a fever-
stricken sufferer, and replaced his visions of torment with
dreams of Paradise. . . . I should like to add one more beatitude to those of the gospels and to say, Blessed are they who
heal us of self-despisings. Of all services which can be done to
man, I know of none more precious" (*Ab.*, pp. 242–43).

Theresa as a healing saint offers an entirely plausible translation of the young Marian Evans. In this instance, she also demonstrates Rutherford's need to transform all the important people in his life, whether or not they existed in White's life, into correlatives for emotions or needs, or embodiments of attitudes in his inner conflict. Just as Jung reconstructs his inner man in building blocks, so Rutherford uses people and events to represent aspects of his search for a confident identity and purpose.

Having stressed the representative quality of Rutherford's characters, it is maybe necessary to clear him of the charge of oversimplicity. Deacon Snale may stand in Heep-like contrast to Mardon, whose eyes were "perfectly transparent, indicative of a character which . . . would not permit self-deception" (*Ab.*, p. 91); but Deacon Snale stands also in contrast to Miss Arbour, whose serene face and orderly precision are like grass and flowers growing on volcanic soil, and to Mrs. Lane (who is based in part on an aunt of Hale White's). She fetches both her moral authority and her religious inspiration from her own conscience; notably, her "conversation was lifted out of the petty and personal into the region of the universal" (*Ab.*, p. 192). And just as Miss Arbour and Mrs. Lane represent the same doctrinal school as Snale, so Mardon is paralleled by but contrasted with Wollaston. Both are skeptical freethinkers, the one chiseling at Rutherford's faith through conversation, the other interviewing him for a job on the grounds of his skepticism. Wollaston, however, has ossified in his freethinking as clearly as Snale ever did in his religious faith. His ideas, acquired long ago, have never been further explored, have never fructified in him. They are like hard stones that he rattles in his pocket.

Such contrasts elaborate Rutherford's acceptance of the need for light and shade in the world. He discovers, for instance, that Mardon is more familiar with sentiment than his strict skepticism would prepare one to believe. He may refuse to follow an argument into the clouds, but he silently acknowledges that "the poorest and the humblest soul has a right to the consolation that Jesus was a man of sorrows and acquainted with grief" (*Ab.*, p. 171). At the end of one visit,

Mary sings from the *Messiah*. "I seemed to be listening," Rutherford writes, "to the tragedy of all human worth and genius. . . . I looked round, and saw that Mardon's face was on the table, buried in his hands" (*Ab.*, pp. 171–72).

Hale White ends *The Early Life*, which is essentially a pleasant, anecdotal account of earlier times, with an optimistic, upbeat clarion call to the Victorian age. In contrast, Rutherford's *Autobiography* ends with a tentative, exploratory solution for Rutherford's overwhelming fear of death. It evolves the stoical gospel of endurance and even joy that Rutherford later promulgates in Drury Lane, a gospel qualified and enhanced by the limitations of individual capability. Mary and Rutherford watch by Mardon's deathbed as dawn changes to sunrise over the ocean. The day becomes stormy later as the two of them recognize their grief, but the beautiful sunrise at the death of an atheist echoes an earlier instance in which Rutherford feels depression lifting like a reminder that somewhere the sun shone. "At times," Rutherford concludes, "we are reconciled to death as the great regenerator, and we pine for escape from the surroundings of which we have grown weary; but we can say no more, and the hour of illumination has not yet come" (*Ab.*, p. 252).

The Early Life deals with no emotion deeper than nostalgia. The narrator, explicitly identified with the author, addresses his readers like a wise father addressing attentive children. On the other hand, the *Autobiography*, which tells the same story under semitransparent disguise, provides more complex situations, more profound and personal emotions, a more complex voice. It raises many disturbing issues but offers little by way of resolution. For Rutherford's spiritual record, unlike Hale White's memoir, a period piece filled with amusing incidents, is of "a commonplace life, perplexed by many problems I have never solved; disturbed by many difficulties I have never surmounted; and blotted by ignoble concessions which are a constant regret" (*Ab.*, p. 13). White's second wife first read the *Autobiography* in 1904 and endorsed this "antifictional" view:

> Here you got the *commonplace*, not the sham common-
> place which rises perpetually *out* of the commonplace
> into the regions of the *remarkable* (so that your "plain"
> heroine has, you infer, magnificent eyes, and your
> "mean" hero a mighty heart) but real commonplace
> which is nothing more than it professes to be, and
> moves only in circumscribed spheres.[35]

Reuben Shapcott, supposed editor of the *Autobiography*
and *Mark Rutherford's Deliverance*, opens the latter by explaining that Mark Rutherford is no hero and is not meant to
be: "He was to me a type of many excellent persons whom
this century troubles with ceaseless speculations, yielding no
conclusions and no peace."[36] But the form in which this commonplace is given is nonetheless familiar in fiction. Teufelsdröckh, Robert Elsmere, and Ernest Pontifex, to name only a
few, face the same problems and evolve their own solutions.
And White, through the voices of Rutherford and Shapcott, is
here presenting another fiction. It is not fiction because facts
are semidisguised or altered but because disguise and alter-
ation and shape have all worked to body forth truths that
facts cannot describe, to show "that unknown abysses, into
which the sun never shines, lie covered with commonplace in
men and women, and are revealed only by the rarest opportunity" (*Ab.*, p. 136).

From the single decision to create a manikin, to describe
himself by means of a metaphorical character, White is able to
enrich his whole text with the emotional and psychological
truths that he was unable to exhibit through a first-person
narrator explicitly to be identified with the author. The narrator of *The Early Life* is impersonal, without inner life. He can
talk about his life and times, but nowhere does he come close
to the "inner reference" that distinguishes his alter ego, Mark
Rutherford. It is possible to describe the effect of the characterization of the narrator-hero on the autobiography as a
whole by saying *le texte, c'est lui*. The manner in which the
narrator is transmuted from a man in the world to a character

in a book affects the entire manner in which he can tell his life story.

George Moore achieves a rather different form of metaphor that enables him to overcome Hale White's problems and pose as his own narrator. He opens his trilogy, *Hail and Farewell*, with a remarkable discussion that could well be entitled "the nature of truth as told in metaphorical terms." He finds an analogy for the Irish renaissance in the Pre-Raphaelite movement. In the process of making the analogy, he demonstrates his particular method for first-person narration. At the outset of his story, in order to describe the affinity of the Pre-Raphaelite movement with the Irish renaissance, he translates the complex historical data on the foundation of the Pre-Raphaelite movement into one crisp image. According to Moore, Dante Gabriel Rossetti, Holman Hunt, and John Millais stand up one evening in the studio in Newman Street to make a unanimous declaration of faith in nature and the purity of fifteenth-century art. What he achieves in this translation is clear fiction, an unambiguous relationship with his reader perhaps best described by Proust:

> And then she [Odette] would say quite simply, without taking (as she would once have taken) the precaution of covering herself, at all costs, with a little fragment borrowed from the truth, that she had just, at that very moment, arrived by the morning train. What she said was a falsehood; at least for Odette it was a falsehood, inconsistent, lacking (what it would have had, if true) the support of her memory of her actual arrival at the station. . . . In Swann's mind, however, these words, meeting no opposition, settled and hardened until they assumed the indestructibility of a truth so indubitable that, if some friend happened to tell him that he had come by the same train and had not seen Odette, Swann would have been convinced that it was his friend who had made a mistake. . . . These words had never appeared to him false except when, before hearing them,

he had suspected that they were going to be. For him to believe that she was lying, an anticipatory suspicion was indispensable. It was also, however, sufficient.[37]

Moore takes a recognizable piece of history, the start of the Pre-Raphaelite movement, and translates it into simple (but not simplistic) narrative in order to demonstrate his authorial voice, to establish the authenticity of the Irish movement and the manner in which he is a reliable historian for it. He also establishes his own aesthetic by this sleight of hand as a translator of fact into fiction, thereby preventing any anticipation of falsehood on the part of his reader, clarifying the manner and therefore the nature of the truth of his arrival at the station.

For Moore's work, as for that of the Pre-Raphaelites, nature is the source and inspiration. Nature dictates the work; the artist transcribes from her dictation. Nature, for Moore, represents the world of contingent reality; his task as artist is to translate the world of contingent reality into the world of art. His whole book discusses this complicated process explicitly and continuously. What he establishes in his introductory analogue is maintained throughout. It becomes possible, accordingly, to understand the development of the Irish Agricultural Organization Society in these same terms. Clearly what happens is that Plunkett comes back from America with lofty ideas for cooperation and all the courage of his platitudes. Clearly, Plunkett and Anderson go off together and preach and preach, and return together to Dublin and know that something is lacking. Plunkett looks in Anderson's eyes. Anderson looks into Plunkett's eyes. Their body of Ireland has not come to life, so they begin to chant. Plunkett chants the litany of the economic man and the uneconomic holding, and his chant is taken up by Anderson with the litany of the uneconomic man and the economic holding. These chants do not bring the body to life, but they do bring out of the brushwood a tall figure with a long black cloak and a manuscript sticking out of his pocket who wants to know what they are doing. Trying to revive Ireland, they say. But Ireland is deaf to their economics, the newcomer tells them, because they do not know her folktales and cannot croon them by the fireside. This, of course, is Yeats, who goes off in search of Æ, who rides around Ireland on his bicycle until all the people are captivated by the tune of his pipes; gradually the body forms on the Plunkett-Anderson skeleton and begins to come to life.

Similarly, the piper must pipe with many voices:

> And every Thursday evening the columns of *Sinn Fein* were searched, and every lilt considered, and every accent noted; but the days and the weeks went by without a new peep-o-peep, sweet, sweet, until the day that James Stephens began to trill; and recognising at once a new songster, Æ put on his hat and went away with his cage, discovering him in a lawyer's office. A great head and two soft brown eyes looked at him over a typewriter, and an alert and intelligent voice asked him whom he wanted to see. Æ said that he was looking for James Stephens, a poet, and the typist answered: I am he. (*HF*, 3:170)

Again, an indubitable piece of life translates into the direct action of a children's story, but this time the story moves from fairy-story language to biblical. One clear advantage of an avowed authorial voice is the scope it provides for inflecting and combining connotations implicitly in the very formation of phrases.

From the outset, then, Moore is a distinct narrator of his autobiography. He is also a conscious creator of "fictional" characters. His characters, like his story, originate with nature; the hieratic Yeats, the esurient Edward Martyn, and (the interpreter's voice struggles for an adjective) the maieutic Æ form a "trilogy, if ever there was one, each character so far above anything one meets in fiction" (*HF*, 1:xii). Yet "[a] story would be necessary to bring Edward [Martyn] into literature, and it would be impossible to devise an action of which he should be part" (*HF*, 3:191). "I wish I could remember his words," he writes later of his father; "the sensation of the scene is present in my mind, but as soon as I seek his words they elude me" (*HF*, 2:225). Of his degenerate relative, Dan, however, he writes that: "It will be difficult to get him on to paper. . . . for, though I may transcribe the very words he uttered, they will mean little on paper unless I get his atmosphere" (*HF*, 1:17). It is inevitable that his friends should all be actors in the unwritten plays that amuse him on his walks. It is also inevitable that they should to some extent reflect their author himself. "In these memories of Æ," he admits, "there must be a great deal of myself, it sounds indeed so like myself, that I hesitate to attribute this sentence to him" (*HF*, 2:57). As aspects or reflections of Moore, nature's characters run a danger of unreality. "But, why is one person more unreal than another? I asked myself [of nature's creation, Lewis], deciding that a man without a point of view always *conveys the impression of unreality*" (*HF*, 3:70, my italics). Moore's characters, like Rutherford's, accordingly take representative stances, thus accounting for the adjectives needed for identification. Edward Martyn is the devout Catholic for whom art becomes impossible. The Colonel, Moore's brother, is the Catholic parallel for the author, inheritor of the same past, only progenitor of the family future. Yeats and Æ represent the hieratic, pagan energies that contrast so effectively with the Catholic present, Æ in particular wearing the air of one who has lived before and will live again, a Lohengrin come to fight the battle of others.

Catholicism pervading life and obstructing art becomes increasingly integral to Moore's own identity. In these terms, he must see himself as a messiah. He hears a mysterious voice telling him: "Order your manuscripts and your pictures and your furniture to be packed at once, and go to Ireland. . . . So the summons has come, I said—the summons has come" (*HF*, 1:282). (He is mistaken, of course, for this voice echoes the injunction that Mary and Joseph should flee into Egypt to protect the infant Jesus, and this correct interpretation of the voice is true to Moore's final understanding of his own role.) If he needs proof that he is God's instrument in Ireland's cause, it comes with his opportunity to undermine an English offensive in the Boer War by publication of its treachery. But the Messiah in Ireland belongs to the Catholic church, and the middle volume centers on Moore's discovery that Catholicism is an intellectual desert, that dogma draws a circle around the mind, and that the mind petrifies within the circle drawn around it.

A renaissance, on the other hand, represents a rearisen kingdom of earth. Rather than sacrifice himself, therefore, for the bubble that is literature in Catholic Ireland, Moore casts himself as Siegfried, parallel to Æ's Lohengrin. Christian Messiah and pagan hero are metaphors for Moore's fictional attitude. In this case, they involve mixed metaphor for action: if one sacrifice of a lifetime is for a bubble, then the other is for the making of that bubble into something worthy and substantial; Siegfried's task is to reforge the sword that lies in broken halves in "Mimi's" cave.

A pagan hero provides a more satisfactory metaphor than a messiah because character and action develop most naturally in terms of a love story. Just as nature's story sends Moore to Ireland, so art can immortalize his love for Cathleen ni Houlihan, his flight from her charms, her call, and her bondage. Proust describes the value of transferring into art the emotions given by nature:

> He told himself that, in choosing the *thought of Odette* as the inspiration *of his dreams of ideal happiness*, he was not, as he had until then supposed, falling back, merely, upon an expedient of doubtful and certainly inadequate value, since she contained in herself what satisfied the utmost refinement of his taste in art. . . . The words "Florentine painting" were invaluable to Swann. They enabled him (gave him, as it were, a legal title) to introduce the image of Odette into a world of dreams and fancies which, until then, she had been debarred from entering, and where she assumed a new and nobler form. . . . [His] misgivings . . . were swept away and [his] love confirmed now that he could re-erect his estimate of her on the sure foundations of his aesthetic principles.[38]

Like Swann, Moore finds his love surprising, many-sided, confusing. Love brings home to Moore his own identity and particularly his failings, as it does to Swann. Moore loves his mistress, who is English and an artist. Through her he discovers his own impotence. Cathleen ni Houlihan presents the same problem. She is represented first by the old woman at Mount Venus who wears laborer's boots and coarse grey petticoats. He even returns to London to escape from such bondage as this to "the hag whom I could see wrapped in a faded shawl, her legs in grey worsted stockings, her feet in brogues" (*HF*, 1:223). Yet at Mount Venus, this same woman has a portrait of herself as a young girl, and "she seemed so startlingly like Ireland that I felt she formed part of the book I was dreaming, and that nothing of the circumstances in which I found her could be changed or altered" (*HF*, 1:6). She fascinates the artist rather than the man: "I invented story after story to explain her as I returned through the grey evening in which no star appeared, only a red moon rising up through the woods like a fire in the branches" (*HF*, 1:12–13).

The English Stella embodies Moore's love. This strange Cathleen provides his dream of love. She is both old and young. She mystifies and attracts him, rising at one point from the very landscape of the Burran mountains and sinking into his heart. Together, these loves that are real and ideal enjoin a notion of love as emotion that passes through life, or indeed passes with life, rather than love as a stable present. The young lover becomes elderly and impotent. The young woman becomes an old hag. This Siegfried, in other words, enjoys no "happy, happy love . . . / For ever panting, and for ever young," but, quite literally, the transient, human equivalent

> That leaves a heart high-sorrowful and cloy'd,
> A burning forehead, and a parching tongue.

On feeling he is not the predestined hero for whom Cathleen ni Houlihan had been waiting through the centuries, he might well fall to sighing, not for Cathleen ni Houlihan's sake but for his own (*HF*, 1:29).

Moore finds himself inadequate as a lover. As a hero, it is his cause that disappoints him. He has been called to Ireland to redeem her from the bonds of Catholicism by raising to life an excellent Irish literature. He realizes, however, in the middle of the middle volume, that Irish literature is a bubble. "We have gone through life together," he writes of Edward Martyn, "myself charging windmills, Edward holding up his hands in amazement" (*HF*, 2:157). The hero who sees a windmill where he thought there was a giant, or a bubble in place of a life's glorious mission, can only renounce his fantasy and die. Yet Moore's sense of calling does not leave him. Some sacrifice is demanded of him, by whom or for what he does not know, but he feels he must leave his native land and his friends for the sake of the book that he is writing. He divines it to be a work of liberation from ritual and priests, a book of precept and example, a turning point in Ireland's destiny. He prays to be spared the pain of writing, to be allowed, perhaps, the comforts of a wife and son in the Clos St. Georges. But no man escapes his fate. Moore leaves Ireland on a grey and windless morning in February, the extent of his loss, and accordingly his sacrifice, being measured by his paraphrase of Catullus: "Atque in perpetuum, mater, ave atque vale."

Moore's book is his life writing. He cannot love in perpetual youth or combat real giants like the ideal hero of myth or art, yet "since the day I walked into my garden saying: Highly favoured am I among authors, my belief had never faltered that I was an instrument in the hands of the Gods" (*HF*, 3:210). He merely wonders what means he has been given for accomplishing God's holy purposes:

> I had begun to lose patience, to lose spirit, and to mutter, I am without hands to smite, and suchlike, until one day on coming in from the garden, the form which the book should take was revealed to me. But an autobiography, I said, is an unusual form for a sacred book. But is it? My doubts quenched a moment after in a memory of Paul, and the next day the dictation of the rough out-

> line from the Temple to Moore Hall was begun, and
> from that outline, decided upon in a week of inspira-
> tion, I have never strayed.   (*HF*, 3:210)

The book, then, like all life, is a process of gestation. He is
no longer Christ or Siegfried but the mother to whom God
has spoken, giving life from his own life because he is filled
with the Holy Ghost. He conceives immaculately and mag-
nificently of his own life as a work of art, a savior, consciously
transforming the passage of time into a constant present and
the elusiveness of people and emotions, including his own
person and his own feelings, into attitudes, gestures, and
comic stereotypes that tell his story for him.

   Moore describes his mission and achievement as the redemption of Ireland from the church by means of art. In terms
of the problems of self-presentation and narrative technique
that beset the autobiographer, one can say that his redemption is of the self from mortality and decay. Unlike William
Hale White, Moore claims explicit identity with his narrator.
Whereas Hale White allows Mark Rutherford to speak in the
first person under the editorial eye of Reuben Shapcott,
Moore creates his fiction out in the open and through his
explicit identification with his narrator. The narrator explains
his terms of reference, interprets his metaphors, and expounds
the technique, indeed makes a book out of the technique,
whereby he translates nature's story into a work of art. Once
again, as with Hale White, the technique whereby the narrator is realized affects the nature and quality of his
autobiography.

Newman and De Quincey:
The Evolution of Narrative Pattern

Just as narrative devices serve to translate the autobiographer
into a credible and authoritative fictive narrator, so his narration makes sense of events in his life by translating them into a
mythic shape. We have described the ideal narrative that lends

itself to such translation according to Todorov's definition: it begins in equilibrium, is disturbed by disequilibrium, and moves into a new equilibrium. Todorov's pattern accords with Campbell's analysis of myth and Propp's work with folktales. Propp and Campbell both describe a pattern of separation, initiation, and return. These overlapping patterns, we have suggested, correspond to a plot formula that is very common to autobiography, that of anticipation, recognition, and fulfillment.

These patterns are mythic first in the sense that they provide the typical forms for coherent fictions, second because they provide the original content or myth that the autobiographer uses when he translates the events of his life into a paradigmatic pattern. He may, like Thucydides, create a tragedy, in which case his narrative pattern is mythic in the first sense, or he may describe his childhood in terms of his loss of paradise, in which case his story is mythic in both senses.

The purpose of such myth making in the narrative life of an autobiographer is essentially that of translating the unique and inexplicable into the universal, of making sense out of one life for others to understand. To explore the process of such translation, we shall look first at Newman's sickness in Sicily and then at De Quincey's flight from boarding school. By following the various accounts that each writer has given of a particular cluster of events, we can trace the evolution in each case of a narrative pattern that is mythic in both senses of the word; it makes particular narrative sense out of events that would otherwise be incoherent, and it explains the events in terms of a mythic paradigm. For Newman, this paradigm is "conversion," for De Quincey, "confession." In each case, the use of such a paradigm makes sense in terms of the total theme on which the autobiographical work is based.

Beginning, then, as close to the lived events as possible, we can assume from letters and journals that John Henry Newman went abroad with his friend Hurrell Froude and Froude's father in December 1832. After touring the Mediterranean and visiting Naples and Rome, Newman decided, against the advice of his friends, to visit Sicily. At one point, he mentions the possibility of a companion, but that project must have fallen through (*Letters*, 1:342). On 9 April 1833 he set off for Naples on his own. In Naples he bought provisions, hired or bought three mules, and engaged the services of one Gennaro as a servant. On 19 April he left Naples by sea and reached Messina on the twenty-first.

Newman's tour of Sicily seems to have been successful despite some bad weather, some rather primitive inns, his inability to climb Etna, and his discovery that the chestnut trees of Trecastagne were nothing more than roots cut level with the ground. If he had never fallen ill, he might have remembered only the scenery, of which his letters are full, and the historical enthusiasm that had fired his visit and that he fueled by rereading Thucydides. One valley in particular inspires him with its serene beauty (*Letters*, 1:397). There he feels a truly religious spirit, justifying the hope earlier expressed from Rome in a letter to his sister Jemima: "Spring in Sicily! It is the nearest approach to Paradise of which sinful man is capable. I set out on Easter Monday" (*Letters*, 1:377–78).

In later years, however, it was his illness that made Sicily memorable. It figures in the *Apologia* of 1864, thirty-one years later, as the spiritual "crisis" immediately preceding his involvement in the Oxford movement. The meaning he ascribes to it can be traced from the earliest accounts that Newman wrote in 1833 to his friends, Frederic Rogers and Robert Wilberforce, to this definitive account given in the *Apologia* in 1864. He began a private journal account of his illness in August 1834. He wrote this in pieces until 1840. He then reread and edited it in 1842, 1855, 1874, and 1876, before finally handing it over to Anne Mozley for publication.

In 1869 Newman saw his illness as one of three that had marked his life at important points. Tristram quotes from his journal entry for 25 June 1869:

> Another thought has come on me, that I have had three great illnesses in my life, and how have they turned out! The first keen, terrible one, when I was a boy of fifteen, and it made me a Christian—with experiences before

and after, awful and known only to God. My second, not painful, but tedious and shattering, was that which I had in 1827, when I was one of the Examining Masters, and it too broke me off from an incipient liberalism, and determined my religious course. The third was in 1833, when I was in Sicily, before the commencement of the Oxford Movement. (Tristram, pp. 119–20)

Newman always denied any significance in his own participation in the movement, so the Sicilian illness here, as in the *Apologia*, is not directly connected with the Oxford movement. In the *Apologia*, however, the connection is one of dramatic placing, which creates its own fictional causality. Here one has to consider it as the third of three important illnesses and look back to the opening statement—"and how have they turned out!"—to find the causality operating in Newman's fictionalizing mind.

Newman's illness was undoubtedly serious. He suffered prolonged high fever in a primitive inn, far from family and friends, tended by one servant. He gave Froude's address in Oxford to Gennaro so that news of his death would reach his family. Recently mobile again, but still very weak, Newman writes to his pupil, Frederic Rogers, from Palermo on 5 June, explaining his delayed return: "I have *not* been weatherbound or shipless, taken by Barbary pirates, or seized as propagandist for Liberalism. No; but, you will be sorry to hear, confined with a very dangerous fever in the very centre of Sicily for three weeks" (*Letters*, 1:404–5). He explains that the weather has been unusually wet for the time of year, that Sicily has suffered an epidemic of fever, and that he himself has suffered hardships that some extra expense could have avoided:

> From my return to Catania I sickened. When the idea of illness first came upon me I do not know, but I was obliged on May 1 to lie down for some time when I had got half through my day's journey; and the next morning I could not proceed. This was at Leonforte, above one hundred miles from Palermo. Three days I remained

> at the inn there with the fever increasing and no medical
> aid. On the night of the third day I had a strange (but
> providential) notion that I was quite well. So on the
> next morning I ordered the mules, and set off to
> Girgenti, my destination. I had not gone far when a dis-
> tressing choking feeling (constriction?) of the throat and
> chest came on; and at the end of seven miles I lay down
> exhausted in a cabin near the road. Here, as I lay on the
> ground, after a time, I felt a hand at my pulse; it was a
> medical man who by chance was at hand, and he pre-
> scribed for me, and enabled me by the evening to get to
> Castro Giovanni (the ancient Enna).   (*Letters*, 1:407)

Even here, within days of his recovery, Newman regulates
his prose so that his effects are created essentially by rhythm.
"Sickened" becomes dramatic as the final word of a short
sentence. The semicolon in the next weaving sentence sets off
the quiet announcement that he could not proceed. His distance from Palermo is important. Then there are biblical echoes, possibly quite unconscious, in the words and wordings:
"Three days I remained at the inn" and "on the night of the
third day." The lack of medical aid finds prominence at the
end of a sentence. The notion that he is well is strange but
providential, a point that he will develop later. He does not
approach the physically graphic until he questions the chok-
ing feeling, lies down exhausted, and is lying on the ground
when a hand appears at his pulse. Here and here only does he
become the subjective victim, and even here without any dramatic emphasis on the physical features of his bodily wretch-
edness. The doctor's proximity being not by habit but by
chance develops the providential note established earlier. One
wonders whether Castro Giovanni is identified as the ancient
Enna because Newman is too much a scholar to omit that
comparison or because he is conscious of the implications for
his own endangered state. This reference disappears after the
letter to Wilberforce. It provides a pagan allusion, after all,
which is perhaps inappropriate in so emphatically Christian a
paradigm.

At Leonforte Newman gave his servant Froude's address, yet "at the same time [expressed] to him a clear and confident conviction that I should *not* die. The reason I gave was that 'I thought God had work for me.'" It is curious that at this stage of Newman's telling, or maybe to this correspondent (who was, however, a lifelong friend), Newman feels the need to qualify such a statement: "I do not think there was anything wrong in this, on consideration." The rest of the letter to Rogers concerns his treatment and recovery at Castro Giovanni, more graphic in physical detail ("I could not raise myself in bed or feed myself") and more human ("I had all through the fever corresponded with the doctor in [really very good] Latin)." The letter ends on the much more conventional note of the traveler abroad, bearing one echo of his earlier expectations of Eden:

> And now you will say my expedition to Sicily has been a failure. By no means. Do I repent of coming? Why, certainly I should not have come had I known that it was at the danger of my life. I had two objects in coming— to see the antiquities and to see the country. In the former I have failed. . . . But . . . I did not know before nature could be so beautiful. It *is* a country. It passes belief. It is like the Garden of Eden, and though it ran in the *line* of my anticipations (as I say), it far exceeded them. (*Letters*, 1:408)

Within days of his illness, then, Newman is able to be flippant with a close friend, giving Barbary pirates and his propaganda for liberalism as equally absurd reasons for delay. The illness on which we have concentrated here provides only two paragraphs of a long letter. His travels, road conditions, inns, and scenery supply the rest. Only verbal echoes hint at religious connotations, and these could be part of the unconscious style of a learned and religious man. Even given the self-conscious, literary style of the letter, if Newman had written no more about his illness in Sicily, it would never have become an autobiographical event.

In July, however, Wilberforce wrote to congratulate Newman on recovery from the illness of which Wilberforce had heard indirectly. Newman replied with a brief account of the fever and then more fully on 4 August. Tristram notes that this more significant letter was ignored by Mozley in her collection but that Newman himself borrowed it from Wilberforce's widow in 1876 and "transcribed it himself, omitting the more ephemeral passages" (Tristram, p. 117). Part of the significance of this letter may be explained by the difference between Newman's relationship with Rogers and with Wilberforce, part by the particular letter to which he is in this case responding.

The account that Rogers had received eight or nine weeks earlier is now played down. It is briefer and receives less impetus from rhythm and connotation:

> I was taken ill first at Catania, after spending two nights (unwillingly) in the open air. When I got to Leonforte in the very heart of the country, I broke down. For three days I lay without any medical assistance. On the morning of the fourth [not the night of the third] a notion seized me [strange (but providential)] that my illness was all fancy; so I set out on my mule. After seven miles in great distress from a sort of suffocating feeling, I was forced to betake myself to a hut by the wayside, where I lay the greater part of the day. On a sudden I found fingers at my pulse; a medical man happened by chance to be in a neighbouring cottage, and they called him in. On that evening I got to Castro Giovanni, the ancient Enna, where I was laid up three weeks.

> Not till I got home could I persuade myself I was not in a dream; so strange has everything been to me. (Tristram, p. 118)

Wilberforce has asked Newman for "something of what passed in [his] mind during all [he had] gone through" (*Letters*, 1:412, 13 July). Newman devotes the rest of this letter to an analysis of why, though he gave his servant directions in case of his death, he did not feel he would die. "I hope it was not presumptuous," he begins, and explains that though he had to act as if he would die, he "could not help saying, '. . . I think God has work for me yet.'" Indeed, the inn was lonely and wretched and his mind was wandering, but he did receive a revelation that he was one of God's elect; that his own sins had "led God thus to fight against [him]"; that he had been willful in his determination to visit Sicily; that three years before to the day he had resigned his post as tutor in a manner that was, he now realized, hasty and impatient; that he had preached a university sermon against willfulness the very day before he left Oxford, thus seeming to predict his own condemnation; that he had maybe cherished resentment against the provost; that in him was fulfilled the text in 1 Corinthians 11:29–32:

> For he that eateth and drinketh unworthily,
> eateth and drinketh damnation to himself,
> not discerning the Lord's body.
>
> For this cause many are weak and sickly
> among you, and many sleep.
>
> For if we would judge ourselves, we should
> not be judged.
>
> But when we are judged, we are chastened
> of the Lord, that we should not be condemned
> with the world.

Above all, he had not run counter to any advice, so he had "not sinned against the light." He apparently repeated this line often at the time; it occurs in every account henceforth, but he is no longer able to explain it by 1864 and the writing of the *Apologia*. He decides he will walk in the way of God's commandments,

> putting myself in the *way* of His mercy, as if He would meet me (Isai. xxvi. 8). And surely so He did, as I lay in the hut; and though I have no distinct remembrance of the whole matter, yet it certainly seems like some instinct which He put within me, and made me follow, to

> get me to Castro Giovanni, where I had a comfortable
> room and was attended to most hospitably and kindly.
> (Tristram, pp. 118—19)

The account of the illness itself is comparatively condensed
and literarily insignificant, but parenthetical terms like "providential" are amplified. By August, in other words, Newman,
still suffering from hair loss and a slight cough, was able to
write of his illness in terms of God's punishment for his sins
and God's mercy and election for divine work. It is not surprising that a devout, self-conscious, and introspective man
should have seen a serious illness as a divine visitation. He
seems also to have had for a long while a keen sense of the
possibilities of martyrdom and of his own talents for messi-
anic leadership. As early as 1822 he had written in his
journal:

> Let me go through sickness, pain, poverty, affliction, re-
> proach, persecution, any thing of worldly evil, if it is to
> promote Thy glory. O save me from a useless life, keep
> me from burying my talent in the earth. (Tristram, p.
> 188)

Newman seems to have held himself in readiness, so to speak,
to have been prepared for the kind of adventure that would
clarify his purpose in life. His own perception of himself provides the "anticipation" needed for narrative.

The equilibrium from which his story starts may best be
described as psychological disequilibrium. Newman arrived
in Sicily at a particularly turbulent stage of his life. In the
spring of 1829, he, Wilberforce, and Froude, all Oxford tutors, had come into conflict with their provost about Peel's
reelection to Parliament. The tension at Oriel had been further
increased by conflicting assumptions about the responsibil-
ities of tutors to students; Newman, predictably, had seen in
his tutorial role a personal and religious mission. The conflict
had become intolerable. Newman had been deprived of pupils
and had resigned. In addition to these anxieties, so much a
part of his daily life, Newman was deeply concerned about the

Whig suppression of benefices. He went abroad with the Froudes, it is clear from his letters, far more intent on England than on the delights of the Mediterranean.

He writes to Rogers from Rome on 5 March: "I long to be back, yet wish to make the most of being out of England, for I never wish to leave it again" (*Letters*, 1:362). He then writes to his mother from Naples on 17 April: "My only loss is that of time, which I grudge . . . because I am impatient to get home" (*Letters*, 1:392). Describing the absurd appearance of his equipage to his sister Harriet, he writes from Catania on 25 April: "Nor had I any such exuberance of spirits as would bear me up against the ridiculousness of my exterior" (*Letters*, 1:396). Continuing the same letter from Syracuse on 27 April, he adds: "I never thought this expedition was to be one of pleasure only, for I wished to see what it was to be solitary and a wanderer" (*Letters*, 1:398). This reason is very different from the one given to Rogers on 5 June, after his illness, that he had come "to see the antiquities and to see the country."

These letters that precede the trip to Sicily contain many such hints that his expectation of pleasure is slight, that the journey is in some sense a duty, a ritual separation of the hero from society. In the same letter to Jemima in which he writes of spring in Sicily as a close approach to paradise, he also writes: "It will be far more delightful in retrospect than in actual performance" (*Letters*, 1:377). He repeats to Harriet on 25 April: "I was setting out on an expedition which would be pleasant in memory rather than in performance" (*Letters*, 1:396).

But Sicily was not out of the blue to become a trial of Newman's strength in solitude. He and Froude were both full of a sense of mission. "The state of the Church is deplorable," he writes to his mother from Naples on 28 February. "It seems as if Satan was let out of prison to range the whole earth again. . . . I begin to hope that England after all is to be the 'Land of Saints' in this dark hour, and her Church the salt of the earth" (*Letters*, 1:358). If the church was endangered by Whig suppression of benefices and by liberalism within its own ranks (Newman felt that his illness in 1827 broke him off "from an incipient liberalism"), these two felt that they could restore its strength and integrity. Together they worked on the "Lyra Apostolica." "It will commence (I hope) in May," he writes to J. F. Christie from Rome; "but of course be silent" (*Letters*, 1:370). He tells Rogers of the usefulness to others of verse that one can write without being a poet (and indeed he is not one!): "I am so convinced of the use of it, *particularly in times of excitement*, that I have begun to practice myself, which I never did before; and since I have been abroad, have thrown off about sixty short copies, which may serve a certain purpose we have in view" (*Letters*, 1:366, my italics). When he was writing the *Apologia* thirty years later, Newman remarked on the persistent vision through the "Lyra Apostolica," beginning with "Angelic Guidance," which he wrote at Whitchurch while waiting for the down mail to Falmouth to begin his trip abroad:

> Are these the tracks of some unearthly Friend,
> His foot-prints, and his vesture-skirts of light,
> Who . . .
>
>   . . . in dreams of night
> Figures the scope, in which what is will end?
> Were I Christ's own, then fitly might I call
> That vision real. . . .[39]

In Rome the two visionaries borrowed a Homer, and Froude chose as their motto "the words in which Achilles, on returning to the battle, says 'You shall know the difference, now that I am back again.'"[40] In the *Apologia*, too, Newman relates that he responded to Cardinal Wiseman's courteous invitation to return with the words that they had a work to do in England. It is here, too, that he explains: "Especially when I was left by myself, the thought came upon me that deliverance is wrought, not by the many but by the few, not by bodies but by persons."[41]

Much of the religious crisis that he saw so quickly in his illness can be attributed to Newman's preoccupation with problems at home and to his intense awareness of the truth of his own vision of his responsibility as a leader of the English church. Freedom from tutorial duties, extensive influence as a university preacher, and a fervent belief in his own talents for missionary work and for martyrdom revealed in his journal as early as 1822 would be enough to account for his need to test himself, Christlike, in the wilderness and, more importantly, to recognize after the event that that was what he had done.

But Newman was also, in the words of Abbé Bremond, "le plus autobiographique des hommes" (quoted by Tristram, p. 143). That is, he not only wrote about himself continuously in one form or another, but he also saw his life in terms of patterns and landmarks. His very perception of himself falls into fictive shapes. He honored certain days, for instance, such as 12 April, which was the date in 1822 when he was admitted to an Oriel fellowship, or 14 July, which was the date in 1833 of Keble's Assize sermon, which Newman saw as the notably single event that opened the Oxford movement. We have noted the significance that he found in 1869 for three illnesses suffered in his youth. The first led to his conversion, the third was followed immediately by the beginning of the Oxford movement, but the second served no clearer purpose than to save him from incipient liberalism. This was a vague enough achievement, surely, but "le plus autobiographique des hommes" sees the whole pattern; he sees liberalism as the road not taken, and he sees the specific and necessarily dramatic point at which the alternative route was chosen.

Tristram's collection of autobiographical writings includes also a revealing half-page begun when Newman was only eleven:

> John Newman wrote this just before he was going up to
> Greek on Tuesday, June 10th, 1812, when it only
> wanted 3 days to his going home, thinking of the time
> (at home) when looking at this he shall recollect when
> he did it. (Tristram, p. [5])

This early consciousness of the present as a significant portion of the about-to-be-past continues with the additions made over the years:

At school now back again.
And now at Alton . . . how quick time passes and
how ignorant are we of futurity . . . April 8th,
    1819 Thursday.
And now at Oxford . . . Friday February 16th, 1821—
And now in my rooms at Oriel college, a Tutor, a
Parish Priest and Fellow. . . . September 7, 1829.
Monday morning. ¼ past 10.
And now a Catholic at Maryvale and expecting soon
to set out for Rome. May 29, 1846.
And now a Priest . . . September 23, 1850.
And now a Cardinal. March 2, 1884.

Tristram calls this "An Autobiography in Miniature." It spans seventy-two years, and it deals in the present moment as potential memory.

The accuracy of such memory and its suitability for the audience that he soon thought of as inevitable seems to have preoccupied Newman for much of his life. Tristram notes that he began keeping a journal in 1820. Newman refers to it at the opening of the *Apologia* as "such recollections of my thoughts and feelings on religious subjects, which I had at the time that I was a child and a boy,—such as had remained on my mind with sufficient prominence to make me then consider them worth recording."[42]This journal he transcribed with additions in 1823 and continued until 1828. He retranscribed the whole during the Lent of 1840, this time with omissions. On 31 December 1872 (the end of the year is, of course, to the autobiographic mind another significant point at which to end and begin things), he began recopying, this time with even more omissions. All the superseded copies were carefully burned in 1874. It is hard for the casual diarist to understand how a journal entry can become superseded. The autobiographer, on the other hand, can decide that any material in his life is outdated by virtue of a superseding vision that creates coherences unsuspected at the time, because of his consciousness of his audience, and because of his wish to create the only acceptable reading of his life.

To this extent, then, Newman is false to his own constant insistence that a "life" can be composed only from letters and journals that minimize biographical interpretation and reveal, simply, the inner man. "Why cannot art rival the lily or the rose?" he asks in "The Last Years of St. Chrysostom." "Because the colours of the flower are developed and blended by the force of an inward life; while on the other hand, the lights and shades of the painter are diligently laid on from without. . . . even if the outline is unbroken, the colouring is muddy."[43] In the same brief discussion, however, he defines "Life" as "a narrative which impresses the reader with the idea of moral unity, identity, growth, continuity, personality":[44] in other words, with art. (We learn something of Newman's self-perception, by the way, from his devotion to Saint Chrysostom, the golden-throated orator and adherent of the true religion against the destructive powers of schism; these powers banish him from the center of the civilized world to the wilds of the Euxine!)

Newman is "le plus autobiographique des hommes" not only because he is introspective, self-conscious, and articulate but also because he is constantly exercising his own powers of interpretation, trying to keep the color vivid but showing more concern for the unbroken outline than for the lights and shades. Any autobiographical account that he has left therefore represents a palimpsest rather than a transparent chronicle. Even the entries in the autobiography in miniature are loaded with the self-consciousness of significant events within the given perspective of future memory. For an exercise in memory, however, we should turn to the special journal account of his illness in Sicily. It provides by far the longest and most graphic account of his illness. Internal dating establishes that Newman wrote this account at intervals from 31 August 1834 to 25 March 1840. He began writing after he had first seen the illness as significant rather than merely dramatic and continued through the most active and turbulent years of his life in the Anglican church. He then made further notes and changes, all scrupulously dated 1842, 1855, 1874, and 1876. In 1885 Newman sent a copy of the account to Anne Mozley for publication.

Interestingly enough, this account is more disjointed, more vivid, less self-conscious, and more revealing than the letters to Rogers and Wilberforce, which were written soon after the event. The dated revisions may provide explanations: "It struck me camomile would do me good (as being a tonic & stomachic. March 8 1840)." Or they may contain late flashes of memory: "(Febr. 6, 1843. We had a speculation about having a *litter* made, on which I might be carried to Palermo)." Or they are discreet: "diorrhea, costiveness, and retention of urine," for example, become "cholera" and "the other complaint." Otherwise, this account is less tailored than the others. Little or no distinction is made between the physically and the spiritually significant. More detail is given of people coming and going, of Newman's encounters with servants, doctors, beggars, and citizens. There is even a diagram of his room at Castro Giovanni. Clearly, Newman needed to keep his own memory alert for detail despite the overview that he was so speedily able to take.

This account also adds a few emphases that may be worth noting. As before, Newman attributes his illness to punishment for self-will but for the first time indicates that this notion is entirely subjective: "I felt I had been very self willed— that the Froudes had been agst my coming, so also (at Naples) the Wilberforces—perhaps the Neales & Andersons—I said to myself Why did no one speak out? Say half a word? *Why was I left now to interpret their meaning?*" (Tristram, pp. 124–25, my italics). He develops the ideas earlier suggested in the letter to Wilberforce that he had been insubordinate to his provost, that his own sermon on willfulness had foretold his own fate, and that he would now literally walk in God's way by leaving Leonforte for Castro Giovanni. But he has the advantage now of hindsight and can write of the devil's obstructing him, "I could almost think the devil saw I am to be a means of usefulness, & tried to detroy me" (Tristram, p. 122). For he can now point to the beginning of the Oxford movement and add: "Altogether my name, which was not known out of Oxford circles before I went abroad, is now known pretty generally" (Tristram, p. 123). A revealing passage follows in which he sees himself as a pane of glass, able to transmit heat though in fact cold, as having all the talents for a great religious leader but being at heart hollow. Undoubtedly his admirers imagine that they find here the humility of the saint, and his detractors a succinct statement of the truth. What is important in seeing this as an autobiographical document is to realize the self-torment that undoubtedly accompanies such degrees of introspection and the subjectivity of the judgment that the same man as artist can then fashion. In this case, as the conclusion of the journal account would suggest, a part of the fashioning, whether consciously or not, desires sympathy:

> The thought keeps pressing on me, while I write this, what am I writing it for? For myself, I may look at it once or twice in my whole life, and what sympathy is there in *my* looking at it? Whom have I, whom can I have, who would take interest in it? . . . This is the sort of interest which a wife takes and none but she—it is a woman's interest—and that interest, so be it, shall never be taken in me. . . . I willingly give up the possession of that sympathy, which I feel is not, cannot be, granted to me. Yet, not the less do I feel the need of it. Who will care to be told such details as I have put down above? Shall I ever have in my old age spiritual children who will take an interest such as a wife does?
>
> (Tristram, pp. 137–38)

It is for his spiritual children that Newman finally submits this manuscript for publication, long after the *Apologia* has regained him his wide influence with the British public and established his distinction in the Catholic church. By 1885 these details have become for all who may read them simply additional coloring for a picture whose clear outline the *Apologia* has already established. Realizing that he had this journal account complete by 1864, we can appreciate the rigorous elimination of detail that the narrative line and dramatic causality in the *Apologia* demanded.

"What I shall produce," Newman writes R. W. Church in April 1864, "will be little, but parts I write so many times over."[45] In May he tells Rogers: "It is not much in bulk, but I have to write over and over again from the necessity of digesting and compressing."[46] The story, the outline is important, the compression essential, for the *Apologia* is to be "the true key to my whole life; I must show what I am, that it may be seen what I am not, and that the phantom may be extinguished which gibbers instead of me. I wish to be known as a living man, and not as a scarecrow which is dressed up in my clothes. . . . I now for the first time contemplate my course as a whole."[47] The difference between the two accounts may be likened to the contrasts that Hardy effects in *The Dynasts* between uncomprehending, swarming humanity and the overview of the body of Europe taken by the spirits of the Pities, the Years, and so on.

Newman's account of his illness in the *Apologia* is the briefest of them all, yet in its context at the end of part 1 of the final 1865 version, the most dramatic. From the many possible details and interpretations Newman extracts only those that make sense in this particular narrative and adhere to the pattern that we call "conversion." The context is given with great care:

> We set out in December, 1832. . . . Exchanging, as I was, definite Tutorial labours, and the literary quiet and pleasant friendships of the last six years, for foreign countries and an unknown future [equilibrium and separation], I naturally was led to think [anticipation] that some inward changes, as well as some larger course of action, was coming upon me.[48]

Avoiding Catholics, apart from a few carefully noted instances, Newman is driven back upon himself and feels his "separation":

England was in my thoughts solely, and the news from England came rarely and imperfectly. The Bill for the Suppression of the Irish Sees was in progress, and filled my mind. I had fierce thoughts against the Liberals.[49]

He mentions the aggressive motto at the beginning of the "Lyra Apostolica"; his sense that deliverance is wrought by persons, not bodies; and the importance of the phrase "Exoriare aliquis!," an early favorite with him, and of Southey's "Thalaba":

I began to think that I had a mission. . . . When we took leave of Monsignore Wiseman, he had courteously expressed a wish that we might make a second visit to Rome; I said with great gravity, "We have a work to do in England." I went down at once to Sicily, and the presentiment grew stronger. I struck into the middle of the island, and fell ill of a fever at Leonforte.[50]

Newman's details provide the context for his story; they describe his anxiety and his sense of mission. The sense of mission is reinforced by the meeting with Wiseman and by literary allusions that emerge in his mind as appropriately as biblical texts to those seeking guidance. His isolation is suggested by the otherwise unnecessary detail that he had struck into the middle of the island. In the course of the fever, which is not detailed at all, his servant is mystified by the two key sentences: "I have not sinned against the light," and "I have a work to do in England" (disequilibrium, initiation, recognition). He does not need to discuss willfulness or even a struggle with Satan (he is, after all, underplaying his own leadership of the Oxford movement) so long as the sense of exalting mission emerges even from delirium. Had Newman assumed a more significant role as leader in the Oxford movement, his fever might have played a more significant part in this narrative as the source of inspiration from which his leadership derived. The context of this starkly abbreviated narration receives its closure, its purpose, its sense of spiritual causality,

and its new equilibrium in the hero's return and in the fulfillment of his anticipation at the end of this first part:

> At last I got off again, and did not stop night or
> day . . . till I reached England and my mother's house.
> My brother had arrived from Persia only a few hours
> before. This was on the Tuesday. The following Sunday,
> July 14th, Mr. Keble preached the Assize Sermon in the
> University Pulpit. It was published under the title of
> "National Apostasy." I have ever considered and kept
> the day, as the start of the religious movement of
> 1833.[51]

Walter E. Houghton describes Newman's theories of style
and of biography as starting from the same origin, the need to
produce the inner man. Newman himself, however, defines
style as "a thinking out into language," which may, in this
case, be paraphrased as the process of autobiography. That
serious fever suffered over thirty years earlier is no longer
merely an isolated event in the life of a highly self-conscious,
articulate man with a clear sense of his own talents. Its con-
comitant introspection, self-chastisement, and intimation of
divine election have provided the fictional "crisis" that alters
the life of the convert. In this crisis a mission is recognized and
out of it, with all the tensions and frustrations of delay on the
journey home, that mission is in retrospect realized. Whether
from a keen sense of devout modesty or because of the low-
key rhetoric with which he intends to convince his Protestant
readers that he, not Kingsley, is telling the truth, Newman
clearly underplays the potential of his narrative. We have seen
from letters and journal entries that his sense of ferment and
mission, followed by the gravity of his illness and the importance of his part in the Oxford movement, could well have led
to a major conversion story. However, despite the muted tones
and the underplaying of events that were of actual seriousness
and seen by him at the time as significant, Newman has created an emotional shape of anticipation-recognition-fulfill-
ment or separation-initiation-return, and in this paradigm his
illness plays a central part. By retaining and using the mythic

shape, in however muted a form, Newman lends weight to the seriousness of his concerns and a suggestion of inevitability to their consequences.

Whereas Newman takes major events in his life and buries their skeleton in his final story to create an almost subliminal persuasion of crisis, De Quincey begins with events seen at first as relatively insignificant but from which he elaborates a major fiction. Like Newman responding to Kingsley by describing the history of his religious opinions in order to demonstrate his love of truth, De Quincey writes his *Confessions of an English Opium-Eater* ad hominem, indignantly repudiating Coleridge's assertion that he had turned to opium as an adventurous voluptuary by elaborating those sufferings of his youth that made opium a necessary palliative. Both Newman and De Quincey have a particular concern. Both are anxious to be believed, and both of them elaborate fictions in order to attain credibility.

Like Newman, George Moore, and Hale White, De Quincey kept on telling the story of his life. De Quincey's problem in writing about his life, however, is one of continuity and narrative tension, of achieving a shape larger than an essay, of finding or enforcing a coherent vision of himself and his life story. Moore, who wrote five autobiographies, discusses the problem of writing for journals and finds that he "could not learn to see life paragraphically. [He] longed to give a personal shape to something, and personal shape could not be achieved in a paragraph nor in an article."[52] De Quincey's autobiography is a reworking of articles that had appeared in *Tait's Edinburgh Magazine* beginning in 1834, *Hogg's Instructor* in 1851, and *Blackwood's Magazine* in 1845. It fails as autobiography precisely because the essayist always wins.

De Quincey's brother called him "the prince of Pettifogulisers," a name that Virginia Woolf finds appropriate. She calls his autobiography "as dropsical and shapeless as each sentence is symmetrical and smooth," and remarks on how strange it is that "the sensibility which was on the alert to warn him instantly if a sound clashed or a rhythm flagged failed him completely when it came to the architecture of the whole."[53] De Quincey himself writes of his autobiography as a work "confessedly rambling . . . whose very duty lies in the pleasant paths of vagrancy,"[54] thereby justifying histories of the Female Infidel, two Irish rebellions, his brother Pink, eighteenth-century travel, and the customs of Oxford. Yet it also includes poignant essays on his early childhood that demonstrate his powers of controlled, subjective writing.[55]

As part of his constant efforts to write about his life, De Quincey also kept planning to record his opium dreams, but like the pleasure dome of Kubla Khan, nothing in fact ever got built. It is to childhood that he repeatedly returns. The explicit intention of the first edition of his *Confessions* (1822) is to tell the dreams induced by opium, but this intention is never realized. The *Confessions* include an extended account of De Quincey's childhood instead, on the grounds that this will create "some previous interest of a personal sort in the confessing subject, apart from the matter of the confessions, which cannot fail to render the confessions themselves more interesting" (*CEOE*, p. 349).

When De Quincey revised his *Confessions* in 1856, it might be assumed that he would add material at the end, in other words, finally write about his dreams. In fact, to Ian Jack's indignation, he does nothing of the sort but gives instead an even fuller account of his early years, thus throwing the work out of proportion, according to Jack, and moving closer to autobiography, which Jack insists is no part of his original intention. In the *Suspiria de Profundis*, which calls itself a sequel to the *Confessions*, De Quincey indulges once again not in dreams but in memories of childhood. Ian Jack and Esther Salaman agree that the revised *Confessions* of 1856 is in fact weaker than the 1822 version. Jack makes some close textual comparisons and stands on firm ground when he says that "there is a flabbiness about the 1856 version, when it is compared with that of 1822."[56]

The significance of the 1856 version, however, lies not in the garrulity of the veteran essayist but in his careful imposition of coherence and causality on the earlier text. Whereas childhood, for example, had earlier been introduced merely "[as] creating some previous interest of a personal sort in the confessing subject," it becomes "at present, and at this point . . . indispensable as a key to the proper understanding of all which follows" (*CEOE*, p. 113). De Quincey himself felt that here he had finally mastered a coherent narrative, its effects set in motion by clear and adequate causes.

Even in the 1822 version of his *Confessions*, De Quincey sees the potential narrative significance of his departure from Manchester Grammar School. "The morning came," he writes, "which was to launch me into the world, and from which my whole succeeding life has, in many important points, taken its colouring" (*CEOE*, p. 354). The early version, however, does not elaborate any causal connections between his leaving school against the wishes of his guardians and his subsequent dependence on opium. The reason for leaving school is slight. De Quincey feels that he is a better Grecian than the headmaster and wishes to go directly to the university. In the section of the autobiography called "At Manchester Grammar School" (1853), a title given by Masson to distinguish an episode that is embedded in an account of De Quincey's mother and uncle, De Quincey finds school tedious, suffers from bad health, and so returns home. In the revised *Confessions*, by contrast, the school itself receives its first detailed description, and the decision to leave school takes twenty-five pages, compared with two in 1822. The extra space is consumed not by flabby garrulity but by the need to make the event inevitable and to set in motion a chain of inevitable events that can explain the sufferings that followed. De Quincey accordingly weaves into his story a sense of sin and expulsion based on the Edenic paradigm. His flight from school is linked with war in Europe even before it takes place and with the familiar analogy of storm, with inevitable forces, in other words, larger than a mere boy. This whole passage is a special addition to the 1856 text:

> O, wherefore, then, was it—through what inexplicable growth of evil in myself or in others—that now in the

summer of 1802, when peace was brooding over all the land, peace succeeding to a bloody seven years' war, but peace which already gave signs of breaking into a far bloodier war, some dark sympathising movement within my own heart, as if echoing and repeating in mimicry the political menaces of the earth, swept with storm-clouds across that otherwise serene and radiant dawn which should have heralded my approaching entrance into life. (*CEOE*, p. 152)

An incompetent doctor, exacerbating De Quincey's bad health with bad medication, cooperates with other evil circumstances:

he . . . sealed and ratified that sentence of stormy sorrow then hanging over my head. Three separate persons, in fact, made themselves unintentional accomplices in that ruin (a ruin reaching me even at this day by its shadows), which threw me out a homeless vagrant upon the earth before I had accomplished my seventeenth year. (*CEOE*, p. 153)

The images of doom, expulsion, innocent youth, and contradicted hopes or expectations are far more evocative of paradise lost than of a bright and capable youth taking a unilateral decision to go home from school. True to the theology of the situation, De Quincey assumes his own responsibility for his fall but shares it with the doctor and the headmaster. To personal responsibility for the event is then added another cause, a direct metaphor for the inevitable; like the furious instinct that drives tribes of buffalo to the salt licks or locusts or lemmings on their mysterious path, no possible obstacle having power "to alter or retard the line of their inexorable advance" (*CEOE*, p. 159), he determines to run away.

In 1856, then, as by no means in 1822 or in any intervening essay, De Quincey takes considerable pains to establish the equilibrium for his narrative and its disruption; the separation, in Propp's and Campbell's terminology, of the hero from his fellows; and an anticipation of disaster whose fulfillment is common knowledge before he begins. We know, because that is where he starts, that he turns to opium after great suffering. We know, and this knowledge informs his story, that Adam and Eve endured great suffering when they were expelled from Eden.

In 1856, as in 1822, he comes then to the morning that is to launch him into the world, but this time the final, lingering look around the room is interrupted by a trance, "a frost as of some death-like revelation" (*CEOE*, p. 176). He finds renewed within him a hateful remembrance derived from a moment that he had long left behind. This deathlike revelation, this hateful remembrance, is of his visit to the Whispering Gallery at St. Paul's Cathedral, where his friend's whisper at the farther end reaches him "as a deafening menace in tempestuous uproars." Impressed by the history contained in St. Paul's and by the "solemn trophies of chance and change amongst mighty nations," he had been surprised then too by a trance in which he had been persecuted by the thought of the fatality that must attend an evil choice. De Quincey describes his visit to St. Paul's with Lord Westport in chapter 8 of the autobiography, which is called "The Nation of London." First written for *Tait's* in 1834 and then revised in 1853, this account contains no mention of the whisper that becomes so menacing. In 1856, however, in the context of the revised *Confessions*, De Quincey recognizes his Rubicon in this memory. A word once uttered cannot come back. A decision once acted on cannot be revoked. This time, when he leaves his room, the door closes forever.

This flight from school and from his guardians becomes the unpardonable folly that lays the foundation of De Quincey's lifelong repentance. It is further complicated by the letter containing money that has been incorrectly delivered to De Quincey and needs to be returned to the post office at Chester. Like the true significance of his departure from school and like the whisper at St. Paul's, this letter appears only in the revised version of the *Confessions*. It serves no other purpose here than to dramatize De Quincey's decision to leave school; it complicates the issue by imposing on it an appearance of real and immediate guilt. The burden of the letter determines De Quincey to turn to Chester rather than to the Lakes. He now carries a twofold burden, both the responsibility and, now that he is running away from school, the suspicion of a guilty connection between receipt of the money and his own evasion of authority. The letter is oppressive, and De Quincey longs "(like Christian in Bunyan's allegory) to lay down [his] soul-wearying burden at the feet of those who could sign [his] certificate of absolution" (*CEOE*, p. 183). When he manages to have the letter redelivered, he is "released—suddenly released and fully—from the iniquitous load of responsibility thrust upon [him]" (*CEOE*, pp. 190–91). The letter, however, is incidental, an event subservient to the pressures of the narrative. Release from this burden leaves De Quincey still with the knowledge "that the situation was one without hope. . . . in reality [he] had no palliation to produce" (*CEOE*, pp. 196–97).

De Quincey's original sin lies in his departure from school. He revises his description of this event in order to show how, like Adam and Eve, he is responsible for his choice and yet how, since Adam and Eve have long since fallen, his story allows him no choice because it is based on theirs. His outcast state is inevitable. Despite the closing of that door behind him as the sin is committed, we find recognition of the sin, the disequilibrium of his story, the initiation into his outcast state in his sojourn in the Welsh hills. To pursue the parallel, he knows he is naked, but he has not yet been cast out of Eden.

The hiatus is brief and tranquil, a lull before the final storm, the propulsion, again described as inevitable, that drives him to seek his fortune in London. It is as if "some overmastering fiend, some instinct of migration, sorrowful but irresistible, were driving [him] forth" (*CEOE*, p. 219). He leaves on a day of golden sunshine in November, the last brief summer of the year, like the lightening before death in sick patients. His farewell to Wales is his farewell to summer, to youth, and to peace. He contrasts the almost sepulchral stillness of that day with the raving and everlasting uproar of the metropolis. Staying in Shrewsbury, he falls into a trance as fierce winds roar through the night. His mind has been filled by the Welsh mountains, "[b]ut now rose London—sole, dark, infinite—brooding over the whole capacities of my heart" (*CEOE*, p. 227). The rhythm and the vowels are ominous; they echo that Miltonic spirit who

> with mighty wings outspred
> Dove-like satst brooding on the vast Abyss.[57]

More than ever, he feels, he stands on the brink of a precipice. His senses are sharpened by the storm and by his solitude in a large and lofty room: "Still, as I turned inwards to the echoing chambers, or outwards to the wild, wild night, I saw London expanding her visionary gates to receive me, like some dreadful mouth of Acheron" (*CEOE*, p. 228).[58]

He has, in fact, a plan, which is mentioned only when it can no longer interfere with the pressures of irresistible fate. He means to borrow money from a moneylender against the security of his patrimony. Sharing the moneylender's empty house, like Dick Swiveller, with a mistreated little servant-girl, he refers ironically to the cold, the gloom, the sad comfort they brought each other in terms evocative of the outcast state. "'The world was all before us,'" he quotes, "and we pitched our tent for the night in any spot we might fancy" (*CEOE*, p. 239).

Extreme suffering, physical and mental, fulfills, of course, the expectation aroused at the beginning of the narrative. It represents the equilibrium that was sought. Only in this revised version of the *Confessions*, however, has De Quincey created sufficient cause to explain that suffering, to render it comprehensible. Comparison of the revised edition with the 1822 version and with essays written in the intervening years shows how De Quincey marshaled whatever material he could find to create the coherent narrative form that distinguishes the *Confessions* of 1856. I am reluctant, however, to place Propp's and Campbell's framework on the narrative brought only to this point. De Quincey shows us the hero separated indeed from his fellow men and initiated through hellfire, but the return with glory on his wings remains for the end of the *Confessions* as a whole. De Quincey claims to write his *Confessions* in the first place for instruction. Just as George Moore offers the book containing his life story as a savior in the form of art to redeem Ireland from serfdom to its priests, so De Quincey's ability to tell his story, equaled by his gradual renunciation of opium, is the gift with which he returns to humanity. More important, however, than rigid application of narrative formulas is our appreciation through textual comparisons that De Quincey, like Newman, creates an elaborate fiction out of particular events in his life in order to extract from them a particular meaning.

Ending the *Confessions* with the claim that his opium addiction is virtually cured, De Quincey uses the biblical analogy again for one final effect. His sleep is still "tumultuous; and, like the gates of Paradise to our first parents when looking back from afar, it is still (in the tremendous line of Milton) 'with dreadful faces throng'd and fiery arms'" (*CEOE*, p. 327). In part the purpose of this reference is to close a book that is patently unfinished; he has created an impressive causality but still fails to develop the results that he originally promises, to record his opium dreams. In part it is a reminder of the paradigm on which his story is based. The 1856 *Confessions* differ so markedly from the 1822 version and from the intervening autobiographical sketches precisely by adhering to this mythic shape. We may be justified by the fact and the nature of these revisions in calling this last of De Quincey's attempts at autobiography a consummate work of fiction. In Shumaker's words, De Quincey has created a meaningful art form because he, like Newman, Moore, and Hale White, does more than submit to events. The events are still there, but they now receive a form that conveys a clear meaning.

I have called this chapter "The Inevitability of Fiction." I have discussed very briefly the roles played by perception and the written word to create a world of *as if*, a likeness to or comparison with contingent reality. Unable to lift *any thing* out of life and into art without transforming it, the autobiographer is faced with the task of finding comparisons with himself and with the events in his life that will convey a clear meaning to his readers. He creates, accordingly, a fictive self to narrate the events of his life and a fictive story to contain those events.

In order to explore the mechanics of this process to see how it can be done, I have looked at the means whereby Hale White and George Moore have created narrators for their autobiographical works. The manner of man who tells the story necessarily affects the kind of story that is told. A fictive narrator may be acquired by following rule-of-thumb techniques, but he tends to look *as if* he were alive, retaining therefore the individuality he derives from his author and imposing on his story the particular perceptions and emotions with which his author interprets his life.

Similarly, the process of translating events in any given life into a narrative need not lead to a mythic shape. As it so often does, however, and as these shapes will be the subject of further study, it has seemed sensible to examine the process whereby two particular autobiographers have revised their work in such a way as to achieve a mythic shape. The necessity becomes apparent from an artistic point of view. Both Newman and De Quincey improve their stories and strengthen their claim to our attention by revisions that bring events into the service of an overriding mythic narrative.

Having looked at narrators and their stories-in-process, it remains for us now to take one particular mythic shape at a time in order to see how and why it works in the completed autobiography.

2. Childhood: From Innocence to Experience

The Garden of Eden provides so familiar an analogue for childhood that the merest allusions to it set off chain reactions of comprehension. "[I]t was Adam and maiden," writes Dylan Thomas,

> The sky gathered again
> And the sun grew round that very day.[1]

"They had entered the thorny wilderness," George Eliot writes of Tom and Maggie Tulliver, "and the golden gates of their childhood had for ever closed behind them."[2] Rousseau, Wordsworth, and Leigh Hunt, to name only a few, echo Genesis or *Paradise Lost* as they set out into the world's wide spaces. Use of Eden and its loss to describe childhood can be documented ad infinitum. More to the point here, however, than such documentation, I propose to examine the particular characteristics of this myth that determine why it is so widely used. What kind of sense does it make of childhood?

The autobiographer who describes his childhood as Edenic, to whatever extent, is assuming more, whether consciously or not, than the usefulness of a very good yarn. He is assuming with some justification a sensible equation between the story of his life and that of humankind. The child's intellect and imagination, for example, have been described as developing along patterns that follow those of the development of the human race. Writing in the 1970s, Piaget adheres to the thesis of G. Stanley Hall, the American pioneer of child study, who wrote in 1909 that "infancy, childhood and youth are three bunches of keys to unlock the past history of the race."[3]

The fictions, furthermore, that men make to describe the process of child development are remarkably similar the whole world over. The nineteenth-century autobiographer, in other words, does not simply use the myth of Eden as a metaphor for childhood because this myth has been enshrined in the conventions of Western literature. Were he an East Indian, a Polynesian, or a Siberian, he might well use the same basic formula. It is not that all creation stories are the same but rather that they share certain crucial features, those particular features that make sense of the universally common aspects of early human development. What, then, are the main characteristics of the Edenic myth that are commonly shared with other creation myths that enable it to make sense of childhood?

Studying the primitive, myth-making mind, Claude Lévi-Strauss articulates an important aspect of primitive comprehension that the best children's story-tellers seem always to have known intuitively. He demonstrates how the primitive or childlike mind makes sense of experience by conceptualizing things in terms of polar opposites.[4] It then searches for mediating categories. It learns, for example, to conceptualize the temperature continuum in terms of the extremes of hot and cold. It then mediates between these extremes to form the category warm. It then mediates again between cold and warm and warm and hot, and so conceptualizes a continuum. Similarly, children most commonly learn the extremes of nature and culture and build their continuum with such anomalies as animals that talk and wear clothes. (Peter Rabbit, losing his coat and shoes in the hostile setting of Mr. McGregor's garden, flees for safety to the wild wood; there, however, his mother goes shopping, cooks supper, and tucks her bunnies up in bed.) Learning the unreality of the mediating category amounts to learning the discontinuity between nature and culture and acquiring a sophisticated, unchildish perception of "reality." (When rag dolls cease to talk, when imaginary friends are no longer real, when fairies and Santa Claus cease to visit in the night, the modern child, too, is preparing for more substantial knowledge; he is learning to lose Eden.)

Examining the Garden of Eden in structuralist terms, Edmund Leach argues convincingly and in detail that the story of creation poses a series of oppositions that are mediated, each in turn, to make sense along a continuum of experience. Water and dry land, for example, represent opposites, yet plants need both. Fish and birds mediate the opposition between sky and land, salt water and fresh. After the opposition of heaven and earth comes the opposition of man and garden and, within the garden, of the tree of life and the tree of knowledge, whose fruit brings certain death. The original creation theme, in other words, is extended. Isolated categories like man, life, one river, "occur only in ideal Paradise; in the real world things are multiple and divided; man needs a partner, woman: life has a partner, death."[5] Oppositions breed further oppositions that provide yet further explanations. Adam and Eve eat the forbidden apple (this experience mediated by the hermaphrodite, immortal, skin-sloughing serpent) and learn about sex and death. Sex, however, also brings life. Notably, Eve does not become pregnant in paradise.

Paradise belongs to a divinely comic vision of the world in which nothing essentially changes. The myth, in its varying forms, sets up these oppositions and their mediating categories; it provides the primitive and childish explanation of the facts of life, its origins, and its end. Sex, birth, and death, however, cannot take place in Eden. They belong to the troubled, changing wilderness beyond the garden. Wilderness and garden represent the final polar opposites of the paradigm; wilderness belongs to adults. Only children, green and golden, inhabit the garden; when they leave the garden, they leave their childhood behind.

Like this Judeo-Christian myth of creation, which is obviously of such importance to Western culture, other creation myths emphasize the same basic polar oppositions and demonstrate the same basic characteristics as the Eden story. Man and woman belong to and contrast with each other as do life and death, east and west, spring and winter, day and night, light and dark. Again and again, creation establishes man in a happy springtime that gives way to the richer and sadder experience of change. (Some Russian autobiographies exemplify this transition with painful clarity.)

In Siberia, for instance, Good and Evil contend even before

the world is made.[6] God creates Lonely Man in the very center of the world, where the moon and the sun shine together because time stands still and where the eternal cuckoo heralds eternal spring. God's creation, however, has been so damaged by the evil Erlik that man must now find a woman and continue creation on his own. Like Satan in Eden, Erlik enters a serpent and persuades Lonely Man and his woman to eat forbidden fruit, and so he brings about their nakedness, sickness, and death.

The Hindu creation also opposes gods and demons, light and dark, immortality and death. Yama and Yami, twin children of the sun, build a garden on earth where animals and birds may live in safety from the winter of the world. Here they agree to give birth to mortal men, and because men must die, Yama their father takes on himself the responsibility of dying first so that he can lead future generations from the unreal to the real, from darkness to light, from death to immortality. He knows that the springtime of his garden is not part of the human lot. As he dies, winter encroaches on the garden he has built.

The Norse creation, too, contrasts the golden age of men and gods with the Ragnarök that will end the world. Evil presents a constant force with which the gods must contend. With the death of Balder, god of the spring, comes a winter that destroys all hope. Two wolves swallow the sun and the moon. Brother murders brother. This is wind time and wolf time when no man is spared. Darkness covers the world and the final war of the gods brings an end to the whole of creation.

The polar oppositions in each account are emphatic. Each story develops from a stable springtime to a winter of change. The "promise" of youth gives way to sickness and death. Brother killing brother parallels the death of Abel at the hands of Cain and the sparing of no man is equivalent to the fallen generations that follow Adam and Eve. Two messages are common. The first is that death is inevitable. The African creation myths explain death simply by means of a mistaken message or the interference of a trickster. Nothing more elaborate is actually necessary when the message itself is so absolute. The second common message these stories share connects death with sex. Just as Adam and Eve discover their nakedness, so Yami's elaborate seduction of her twin brother, Yama, introduces change where there had been stability. It takes the story from spring to winter. It leads to both birth and death.

Perhaps most interesting because both metaphorical and graphically explicit, the Polynesian creation connects such impermanence with the loss of perfection. The godlike hero Maui, who harnesses the sun, fishes up land, and steals fire for men, tries also to cross the threshold of Night and Death to ensure that mankind need never cross it. He journeys to the west where Death lies sleeping on the ground with her legs spread apart. If he can cross the threshold of obsidian and greenstone between her thighs and travel through her body, he will destroy her and men will never die. He turns himself into a caterpillar for this last and most scandalous of his adventures, but a fantail explodes with laughter. The goddess wakes. She kills Maui in an instant and thereby ensures that all men will meet death by the way of rebirth.

These primitive and "childish" explanations of the universal paradise lost make profound, clear, and enduring sense not only because they explain everything in the world that most cries out for explanation but also because they illustrate an important aspect of every individual's maturation. Paradise and paradise lost describe the contrast that analysts of childhood have remarked upon between children's perception of the world as part of themselves and their relatively sudden realization of its otherness. All aspects of Eden are single, timeless, perfect, and unchanging. Similarly, the young child's absorption of his world allows room for only one creature to exist, himself. He has no concepts with which to distinguish the world's working from that of his own mind. Wordsworth's earliest memories, for example, derive much of their power from his sense of the natural world as an amazing extension of himself:

> Along his infant veins are interfused
> The gravitation and the filial bond
> Of nature that connect him with the world. . . .
> For feeling has to him imparted power
> That through the growing faculties of sense
> Doth like an agent of the one great Mind
> Create, creator and receiver both,
> Working but in alliance with the works
> Which it beholds.   (*Prelude*, 2:242–60)

He explores his world with a delight not unlike that of a baby's discovery of its own feet and fingers. Thomas Traherne is another who conveys this magic potency:

> The city seemed to stand in Eden, or to be built in
> Heaven. The streets were mine, the temple was mine,
> the people were mine, their clothes and gold and silver
> were mine, as much as their sparkling eyes, fair skins
> and ruddy faces. The skies were mine, and so were the
> sun and moon and stars, and all the World was mine;
> and I the only spectator and enjoyer of it.[7]

Dickens also captures this same monomania with Pip's sensation that the church jumps over its own weathercock when the convict holds him upside down.[8]

Loss of Eden coincides with an adult perception of the world as multiple and alien rather than as a single and stable extension of the self. "What came to me," writes Edmund Gosse, "was the consciousness of self, as a force and as a companion, and it came as the result of one or two shocks, which I will relate."[9] Notably, Gosse's first shock is his discovery that his father is not infallible and does not know everything. Separation of one's identity from the world results from shocks that reveal its impermanence, insecurity, and flaws. In terms of the universal myth, such separation results from discovery of the most alarming changes that man's mind can encompass, those of procreation, birth, and death.

The commonly shared features of creation myths describe and explain the working of the infant mind. They present the world as a permanent extension of the self and describe the discovery of its otherness. They present the innocent and healthy body that discovers both its own sexuality and the inevitability of its death. They use metaphors in common to describe both permanence and change, metaphors like spring and winter, day and night, heat and cold, which are paralleled by the moral and emotional oppositions that so essentially concern young children, oppositions like big and small, bad and good, love and hate. The autobiographer who uses the Edenic myth to describe his own childhood is not, then, simply turning to an appropriate literary convention; he is borrowing a tool that describes truths for himself that are true for every man. The distinct and individual events of his story make sense to himself and to his reader within a framework that renders their validity and gives them meaning. For the autobiographer describing his own childhood, in other words, this particular myth works by enhancing the personal in terms that are universally true and clear.

The autobiographer tends also to emphasize the salient features of his childhood paradise by the very process of attempting to recover it for his narrative. He turns to childhood, often in old age or after a serious illness, as a reviving act of memory. Such memory revives the elderly author both because it recaptures that green and golden time and because it too is sacred and unchangeable. George Moore reflects that

> the present is no more than a little arid sand dribbling through the neck of an hour-glass; but the past may be compared to a shrine in the coign of some sea-cliff, whither the white birds of recollections come to roost and rest awhile, and fly away again into the darkness. But the shrine is never deserted. Far away up from the horizon's line other white birds come, wheeling and circling, to take the place of those that have left and are leaving. (*HF*, 1:247)

Memory, like Eden, defies change and death.[10]

Then, too, memory of childhood recaptures a time of very keen, clear perception. W. H. Hudson recalls how his first sight of flamingos exceeds by many degrees of delight his experience on scores of later occasions. "Has heaven a more delectable scent," wonders George Moore, "than the *remembrance* of a syringa in bloom?" (*HF*, 2:263, my italics). Wordsworth and Rousseau both stress the accuracy of remembered feeling. "I may omit or transpose facts," writes Rousseau, "or make mistakes in dates; but I cannot go wrong about what I have felt" (*Confessions*, p. 262). Emotions are conveyed by precise particulars. Ruskin recalls the solitude in which his imagination fastened onto the inanimate, the squares and colors in a carpet, knots in the wood of the floor, the bricks in neighboring houses, "the sky, the caves, and pebbles, observable within the walls of Eden."[11] Joyce's very young Stephen Dedalus is entirely composed of such detailed and specific perceptions and sensations. Lawrence establishes the authenticity of the boy Paul Morel on the grounds of keen perceptions that become vignettes; they encapsulate the general mood or emotional connection in a literal, specific, immovable object like his father's neck, his mother's hands, the kitchen table, or the fireplace. Wordsworth refers to such perceptions as

> the ties
> That bind the perishable hours of life
> Each to the other, and the curious props
> By which the world of memory and thought
> Exists and is sustained.   (*Prelude*, 7:461–65)

Graham Greene describes this intensity of perception in his strange exploration of himself through West Africa in *Journey Without Maps*. "I had got somewhere new," he writes, "by way of memories I hadn't known I possessed. I had taken up the thread of life from very far back, from so far back as innocence."[12] And then, "one doesn't believe, of course, in 'the visionary gleam,' in the trailing glory, but there was something in that early terror and the bareness of one's needs. . . . The sense of taste was finer, the sense of pleasure keener, the sense of terror deeper and purer."[13]

Finally, and for the autobiographer, crucially, memory of

childhood also recaptures a time of significant creativity. Edith Cobb remarks on our "widespread intuitive awareness that certain aspects of childhood experience remain in memory as a psychophysical force—an élan that produces the pressure to perceive creatively and inventively, that is, imaginatively."[14] The child enjoys what Wordsworth calls "this infant sensibility, / Great birthright of our being" (*Prelude*, 2:270–71). The very memory of its existence serves as a stimulant. Dickens, for example, never managed to write a formal autobiography, but he places children at the center of his most important novels. He actually imbues his fictions with the nightmares of childhood to illustrate how truly the child is father of the man and to redeem his lost adults by a quality of imagination that brings their childhood close to them.

The autobiographer, then, uses this myth as a metaphor to explain important aspects of his own childhood and of ours, and he enhances many of these characteristic qualities by the very nature of the autobiographical enterprise. The activities of memory, perception, imagination, and creativity are exercised upon the time when those qualities were felt most keenly. The qualities that enhance Eden also enhance the written word. The autobiographer borrows the myth and contributes to it; the two feed each other, because the myth is not simply a convenience that has become a convention but, rather, has the force of necessity to it. Man inhabits it as part of his nature. Just as autobiography is an active recreation of the self, so this myth for childhood can be found both in the process of creation and in the product of the created self.

Like autobiography, childhood is relatively unimportant in literature until the turn of the nineteenth century. William Blake was among the earliest to hear a child calling from a cloud for him to pipe a song about a lamb. His "rural pen" and "happy songs" presuppose the innocence of childhood and establish it for his literary heirs. Rousseau had already insisted that man is born free but lives everywhere in chains. "How can the bird that is born for joy," Blake adds, "Sit in a cage and sing?"[15] Just over a decade later, Wordsworth complains of the sad transition from childhood to maturity:

> Heaven lies about us in our infancy!
> Shades of the prison-house begin to close
> Upon the growing Boy.[16]

Rousseau, Blake, and Wordsworth, in fact, launched the Romantic child "as a symbol of innocence and the life of the imagination."[17]

A study of the simultaneous emergence of the significance of the child in literature, of autobiography, and of the novel would almost certainly demonstrate a close link between the Romantic exploration of the self and the development of psychoanalysis. Peter Coveney points to the concern that Romantic and analyst share "to integrate the human personality by surmounting insensitivity to childhood."[18] Awareness of the significance of childhood, of course, allows the historically minded autobiographer to describe and explain himself in terms of his beginnings. Excavation of one's own childhood from the vantage point of maturity leads necessarily to the discovery of frequent causal connections. Such causal connections may describe simple character traits or serious problems. For the autobiographer who describes phases of his life in terms of mythic paradigms, causal connections extend from self-understanding to self-presentation. Even though the reader does not know the writer, for example, and does not know in detail "what happens next," use of the myth directs his expectations, limits the kind of thing that can happen next.

Rousseau in his *Confessions* and Wordsworth in *The Prelude* may be considered the "founding fathers" of childhood in autobiography, and both make elaborate use of such causal connections both for personal detail and in terms of childhood as Eden. At the personal level, for example, Rousseau describes how he read novels as a child and so became a man of feeling. He read Plutarch, and thence derives his pride and his hatred of servitude. His aunt was musical, so he loves music. He was tutored in the country, so he loves the country. Rousseau makes such a tidy list of factors affecting his development that he is able to summarize: "Such were the first affections of my dawning years; and thus there began to form in me, or to display itself for the first time, a heart at once proud and affectionate" (*Confessions*, p. 23).

Similarly, Wordsworth's analysis of his childhood aims to show the nurture and enforcement of his poetic spirit:

> For this, didst thou,
> O Derwent! winding among grassy holms
> Where I was looking on, a babe in arms,
> Make ceaseless music that composed my thoughts
> To more than infant softness, giving me
> Amid the fretful dwellings of mankind
> A foretaste, a dim earnest, of the calm
> That Nature breathes among the hills and groves.
> (*Prelude*, 1:274–81)

Not in vain, he feels, did the wisdom and spirit of the universe intertwine the passions that build up the human soul (*Prelude*, 1:406–7). Nor was it with vulgar aim that the very presence of nature, visions of the hills, souls of lonely places

> did make
> The surface of the universal earth
> With triumph and delight, with hope and fear,
> Work like a sea. (*Prelude*, 1:473–75)

The assumptions that both Rousseau and Wordsworth make about the Edenic paradigm are clear, extensively developed, and significant to later writers. Few other autobiographers, indeed, have given such lengthy attention to childhood; most often childhood fills only a chapter or two of a long life. We shall look first, therefore, at Rousseau and Wordsworth in order to see the myth at work as a metaphor that shapes each man's presentation and narration of his own past. For more examples of the function of this particular myth in autobiography, we can then turn briefly to the works of Moore, who describes the finite permanence that Eden and the memory of Eden enjoy in common. Then we will look at Aksakoff, Gorky, Hudson, and De Quincey, all of whom describe most poignantly the manner in which innocence is lost.

Rousseau and Wordsworth: Metaphors of Innocence

Rousseau's Eden lies at Bossey, where he and his young cousin lived and studied with a M. Lambercier. He enumerates the advantages of life at Bossey over his previous life in Geneva. Two years in the village "brought [him] back to the stage of childhood" (*Confessions*, p. 23). He learned to enjoy games as a relaxation from work. The country was a fresh experience for him. "Indeed the taste that I got for it was so strong that it has remained inextinguishable, and the memory of the happy days I spent there has made me long regretfully for a country life and its pleasures at every stage of my existence" (*Confessions*, p. 24).[19]

Intense nostalgia for paradise rattling the "mind-forg'd manacles" of later years is a common hallmark of childhood memories. Walter Pater, for example, refers to "that beautiful dwelling-place [that] lent the reality of concrete outline to a peculiar ideal of home, which throughout the rest of [Marius's] life he seemed, amid many distractions of the spirit, to be ever seeking to regain."[20]

Such was the harmony between Rousseau and his cousin, and such the gentleness of their guardians that if only the manner of their life at Bossey had lasted longer, "it could not have failed to fix [Rousseau's] character for ever" (*Confessions*, p. 25). He is wrong, of course. Maggie Tulliver promises to love Philip Wakem and kiss him as she kisses her brother. But when they meet again:

> The promise was void, like so many other sweet, illusory promises of our childhood; void as promises made in Eden before the seasons were divided, and when the starry blossoms grew side by side with the ripening

peach—impossible to be fulfilled when the golden gates had been passed.[21]

Like King Henry's old men who, when all shall be forgot, will yet remember with advantages those things that gave them pleasure, autobiographers frequently return to childhood in old age or from their sickbeds. Rousseau's *Julie* originates in such a memory, "which was the sweeter for the innocence associated with it. . . . Soon I saw all around me the persons I had felt emotion for in my youth. . . . My blood caught fire, my head turned despite its grey hairs" (*Confessions*, p. 397). Wordsworth's rejuvenating memories of childhood also arise out of the purposeless blank of his present moment. Rousseau has barely thought of Bossey for more than thirty years:

> But now [sick and in trouble] that I have passed my prime and am declining into old age, I find these memories reviving as others fade, and stamping themselves on my mind with a charm and vividness of outline that grows from day to day. It is as if, feeling my life escaping from me, I were trying to recapture it at its beginnings. (*Confessions*, p. 31)

The momentum of his memory moves his narrative into the present tense:

> I remember places and people and moments in all their detail. I can see the man- or maid-servant bustling about the room, a swallow flying in at the window, a fly alighting on my hand while I am saying my lesson. I can see the whole arrangement of the room in which we lived. (*Confessions*, p. 31)

Permanence of the memory both depends upon and conveys the stability of Eden. Gosse, for example, remembers with intense clarity the even flow of his life with his parents but cannot recall several unusual weeks that he spent with other children. The peripheral disappears. Only those aspects of childhood that are constant or important become permanent and abiding.

At the end of three long volumes of self-exploration, George Moore also finds his childhood quite amazingly intense and intact. His imagination preserves the physical realities of his surroundings, despite their evident change and decay with the passage of time. Moore's final visit in Ireland is to Moore Hall. "'You've a fine memory, God bless it, yer honour,'" says the groom. Here the old man confronts not only his own childhood but also its sacredness, its inability to alter, and its continuous presence. The Colonel, for instance, "threw open the door of the summer room . . . and in an instant the room returned to what it had been forty years before, my father sitting at the rosewood table in the evening, drinking a large cup of tea, telling me stories of Egypt and the Dead Sea, Baghdad, the Euphrates and the Ganges, stories of monkeys and alligators and hippopotami, stories that a boy loves" (*HF*, 3:224). This past, moreover, is already familiar to readers of Moore's book because he has earlier remembered his love of these stories and the way in which he embarrassed his father by insisting in company on all the exaggerations that made them exciting.

Moore Hall, endowed with Moore's memories of childhood, cannot be seen to have changed. He can barely see the garden because in its place stands the eighteenth-century garden of his memory. Certainly no change can be made in its future. The brothers stand together by the ruins of the greenhouse. They used to steal grapes even when the door was locked. Moore's father had once beaten him with a horsewhip for breaking the panes. Now they are two elderly men, and the Colonel has saved the bricks in case Moore should wish to rebuild that same greenhouse. But the ruins are the end. Once one has gone back to the beginning, any kind of change is impossible. Memory and narration can preserve Moore Hall intact even to the greenhouse with the grapes inside, and they will keep equally complete and infrangible the identity of the narrator through whom, in that joint past, all these things exist.

Eden is not subject to change, but it is necessarily lost. Rousseau loses his innocence in a dramatic fashion at the hands of Mlle Lambercier. He discovers an admixture of sensual pleasure with pain in the beating she administers. So keen is the pleasure that he provokes a second beating, at which Mlle Lambercier, clearly no fool, decides such punishment is not producing the desired effect and ejects the two boys from her bed and from her room. Henceforward, Rousseau laments, "I had the honour, willingly though I would have dispensed with it, of being treated as a big boy" (*Confessions*, p. 26).

For two further pages Rousseau elaborates this "first and most painful step in the dark and miry maze of [his] confessions" (*Confessions*, p. 28). He has eaten the forbidden fruit and knows himself to be naked. The price of such knowledge and shame must be ejection from the garden of innocence. Rousseau suffers a completely different punishment for a crime he has not committed. His outrage at such injustice alters his world absolutely:

> We lived as we are told the first man lived in the earthly paradise, but we no longer enjoyed it; in appearance our situation was unchanged, but in reality it was an entirely different kind of existence. No longer were we young people bound by ties of respect, intimacy, and confidence to our guardians; we no longer looked on them as gods who read our hearts; we were less ashamed of wrongdoing, and more afraid of being caught; we began to be secretive, to rebel, and to lie. All the vices of our years began to corrupt our innocence and to give an ugly turn to our amusements. Even the country no longer had for us those sweet and simple charms that touch the heart; it seemed to our eyes depressing and empty, as if it had been covered by a veil that cloaked its beauties. We gave up tending our little gardens, our herbs and flowers. We no longer went out to scratch the surface of the ground and shout with delight at finding

one of the seeds we had sown beginning to sprout.
(*Confessions*, pp. 30–31)

Rousseau, still a boy, returns to Geneva. He describes two
loves and two disastrous apprenticeships, and suggests that he
might have had the perfect life as a good workman, husband,
father, citizen, but his fate has been sealed in fiction more
firmly than in fact. Straying beyond the city limits one evening, he is shut outside the gates of Geneva. A casual incident
that befell many apprentices gives him the juncture he needs.
Book 2, like *Paradise Lost*, 12:646, like Wordsworth's *Prelude*, 1:14, and more immediately like Genesis 3:23–24, finds
Rousseau marching "confidently out into the world's wide
spaces" (*Confessions*, p. 54).[22]
One value of a familiar myth is that very slight verbal clues
like this one persuade the reader to make all the necessary
inferences. As we have seen with De Quincey's departure from
school, a slight mistake can be turned into a monstrous sin by
simple equation with the fall of man. Rousseau has explicitly
and painfully described his taste of the knowledge of good
and evil in terms of discovery of his own sexuality. Many
pages and many adventures later, he needs only to use this
phrase to remind us that he has fallen and that now, like the
closing of the door for De Quincey, the locking of the gates of
Geneva forces him to accept the inevitable consequences of his
loss of innocence and to leave Eden behind him forever.
Rousseau is too young and foolish to appreciate his loss at
the time, but he does spend the rest of his life reseeking his lost
Eden.[23] He recreates it briefly at Les Charmettes with
"mamma." "Here begins the short period of my life's happiness" (*Confessions*, p. 215), he writes about his time at Les
Charmettes, reminding us of the transience of Eden even before he reconstructs it. He prays for these times to pass slowly
through his memory, and his memory answers his prayer.
There is some confusion about this country place where Rousseau was so happy with "mamma." It may even have been
bought for Vintzenreid, who succeeded Rousseau in Mme de

Warens's affections. Certainly Rousseau was not there alone with Mme de Warens for the two summers that he details so lovingly. Yet "I recall that time in its entirety," he writes, "as if it existed still" (*Confessions*, p. 216). His routine is a happy one of study, followed by the tendance of bees and pigeons and garden. "Mamma" is his constant and loving companion. Return to Les Charmettes for a second summer is "like resurrection into Paradise" (*Confessions*, p. 222).

Rousseau leaves Les Charmettes because of a suspected polyp on his heart that can be treated at Montpellier. His affair with Mme de Larnage, his fun with the medical students at Montpellier (his polyp all but forgotten), and his conscious determination to return from pleasure to duty suggest a less than perfect Eden. Yet the considerable tension and foreboding built into his return prepare dramatically for another mythic fall. He finds Vintzenreid in his place at Les Charmettes, and suddenly his whole being is thrown completely upside down. He is alone. Life holds no further joy or hope:

> I, who even from childhood had never contemplated my existence apart from hers, found myself for the first time alone. It was a frightful moment; and those which followed it were just as dark. I was still young, but that pleasant feeling of joy and hope that enlivens youth left me forever. From that time, as a sensitive being, I was half-dead. I could see nothing before me but the sad remains of a savourless life; and if sometimes afterwards some thought of happiness awakened my desires, it was no longer a happiness that was really my own. I felt that if I obtained it I should not really be happy. (*Confessions*, p. 249)

Rousseau describes his last attempt to regain "mamma's" affections in terms of alienation and perpetual loss:

> I had returned to rediscover a past which no longer existed and which could not be reborn. I had scarcely been with her for half an hour when I felt that my old happiness was dead for ever. . . . [H]ow could I bear to be su-

perfluous beside her to whom I had once meant everything, and who could never cease to be everything to
me? . . . [T]he incessant return of so many sweet memories aggravated my sense of what I had lost. (*Confessions*, p. 256)

Once more he sets out into the world's wide spaces, this time
for Paris.

This first part of the *Confessions* was written at Wootton in
England in the autumn and winter of 1766. Rousseau apparently considered the work complete at the time, insisting that
he must stop here and only time, if his memory descended to
posterity, might lift the veil. This fall, in other words, is final.
However, in the second half of the *Confessions*, written in
Paris in 1775–76, he describes two more Edenic interludes
and two more expulsions into the wilderness. The first, at
Mme d'Epinay's Hermitage, fills the lengthy ninth book and is
colored throughout by regret for Les Charmettes. Mme Le
Vasseur, Thérèse's mother, is explicitly the serpent who manipulates his friends behind his back. His departure is sudden,
enforced, takes place in winter, and represents "the catastrophe which divided [his] life into two such different parts, and
which from a trivial cause produced such terrible effects"
(*Confessions*, p. 441). His final Eden is the island retreat of
Bienne, from which he is evicted, again in winter, at the end of
book 12.

Rousseau loses each surrogate Eden through his own folly,
one might say through the failings of character fixed by the
first fall, or through the cruelty or sinfulness of his fellow
men. The specific causes for each loss are irrelevant. Eden is
part of the past, an essentially irretrievable place of innocence
and joy. No reconstruction can survive. Men have dreamed of
reconstruction in terms of an earthly paradise, a utopia, a
New Jerusalem, maybe a revolution that will alter the bleak
world of maturity, maybe a surge of creative power that will
keep the adult world green and golden. (Christopher Milne
returns to *The Enchanted Places* only to realize that his father was reconstructing his own childhood with the Pooh

books.)[24] Essentially, each surrogate Eden, every attempted reconstruction, represents a desperate defiance of mortality. That original tree in the Garden of Eden was not merely the tree of knowledge but also the tree of death.

Wordsworth understands his fall in terms of failure of the imagination, of a discontinuity between his richest perceptions of life and those perceptions that are accepted in the duller world of men. He identifies the poetic spirit, furthermore, as the spirit of the child that does not commonly survive. Reconstruction of childhood, then, serves to resurrect this poetic spirit. Brief memories are adequate to stimulate his creative powers, revive his mind, and help him choose his theme. He quickly finds that his road lies plain before him because he narrows his direction to one purpose that combines both the deeds of his life and the doing of his poem, making the poem an enactment of its own purpose. In other words, like an honest steward, he chooses to render his account and show whence he fetches his poetic gift. *The Prelude* both analyzes and justifies the calling of an infant Samuel.

Unlike Rousseau, who states his desperate purpose and plunges with commendably unShandyan decisiveness into the facts of birth and parentage, Wordsworth's autobiography takes an epic form. He begins in medias res. He begins, therefore, not with paradise but with the invigorating memory of paradise striking a man who has already fallen. More explicitly and emphatically than Rousseau, Wordsworth demonstrates the interdependence between Eden and memory and the creative powers that they generate. His fall is implicit in his need to return to his youth in order to restore his creative powers. Taking a survey of a man's mind, *The Prelude* shows how Wordsworth, like Rousseau, falls again and again. Descent becomes a major structural image for the poem. At Cambridge, in London, in France after the Revolution, the poet suffers from a temporary alienation of the spirit that threatens poetic mortality. Wordsworth, however, combines in himself the qualities of Keats's Saturn and of his Hyperion. He is by turns the dying god and the god of the new day.

Saturn, for example, illustrates his devastating fall from

power with two significant examples. First, he has gone away from his own bosom; he has left his strong identity, his real self. Second, he cannot create, form, or fashion forth another universe. *The Prelude* opens on a calmer note, but the poet has "escaped / From the vast city," a notorious antithesis to Eden; his soul has shaken off the burden of its unnatural self. The gentle breeze that fans his cheek meets a correspondent breeze within to break up a long-continued frost. Although he, like Milton's Adam and Eve and like Rousseau, finds "the earth is all before me," he is not despairing; the virtue of beginning in medias res is that one travels not forward into that bleak world but back to

> Those recollected hours that have the charm
> Of visionary things, those lovely forms
> And sweet sensations that throw back our life,
> And almost make remotest infancy
> A visible scene, on which the sun is shining.
>
> (*Prelude*, 1:631–35)

Wordsworth redeems the time, fashions forth his universe, through memory. Hyperion demonstrates the significance of memory for a full realization of identity and creative powers. To Mnemosyne, visiting him in the morning twilight (the dawn, the spring, the beginning of his day) and finding him sad, he says:

> "For me, dark, dark,
> And painful vile oblivion seals my eyes:
> I strive to search wherefore I am so sad,
> Until a melancholy numbs my limbs;
> And then upon the grass I sit, and moan,
> Like one who once had wings."[25]

Hyperion is essentially voicing Mark Twain's complaint that youth is wasted on the young; the present moment, without memory and without context, is relatively meaningless.

Youth, of course, is wasted on the young specifically because it is not finished, it does not form a finite memory, and has accordingly no meaning, can be subjected to no explanation or definition. A significant value of the myth of Eden for the autobiographer, then, lies in its efficiency in recapturing the endless quality of childhood within the framework of the finite. The intense perfection that Eden defines and describes derives no small part of its intensity from the fact that it is finished. (Could Adam and Eve, one wonders, truly appreciate the garden before they were cast into the wilderness?) Once again the myth demonstrates its compatibility both with the commonest features of the individual psyche and with the narrative needs of the autobiographer.

Like Hyperion, who reads a wondrous lesson in Mnemosyne's face and finds that "Knowledge enormous" makes a god of him, Wordsworth hopes to renew his creative powers by exercising his memory on childhood, the time for him of purest harmony with nature and therefore of finest creativity. Fleeing from the city and the mature years that have deadened the flow of his internal life, the poet sees himself as "a Pilgrim resolute" on the "road that pointed toward the chosen Vale" (*Prelude*, 1:91 and 93). He shakes off the burden of his unnatural self and can breathe again, inhaling promise of another spring. The new spring is realized by the memory of childhood that restores his faith in his creative powers and in the basic harmony of his identity. These two he combines into the work that is at once a poem and a recreation of his original paradise.

Wordsworth's boyhood sounds rather healthier than many: out in all weathers, as the saying goes, in the river, on the hillsides, with friends, on his own. He recalls incidents not unlike those that appear in most autobiographies of childhood. One time he steals a boat—Saint Augustine steals some pears. On other occasions, he goes skating or riding or fishing, or he flies his kite or plays cards. Unlike many others, however, he sees these happy times as not entirely lost if he can still tap the strength of their gift. Wordsworth reconstructs the essence, therefore, not the mere event. He studies his spiritual growth and sees it as essentially organic, in tune with the natural world.

Wordsworth's choice of organic imagery is certainly appropriate given the growth of a young boy in the open countryside. It is worth noting, however, the common use and flexibility of such imagery among autobiographies of childhood. Rousseau not only yearns for the country; he specifically remembers planting small gardens and watching them sprout. When outcast from Eden, he loses, temporarily at least, all interest in gardening. Edmund Gosse refers to his soul as a little child, "planted, not as in an ordinary open flower-border or carefully tended social *parterre*, but as on a ledge, split in the granite of some mountain," with no hope of salvation for any rootlet that strayed beyond its inexorable limits.[26]

Wordsworth uses organic imagery less for narrative purpose than to convey the quality of his growth. "Fair seed-time had my soul," he writes, both in his native birthplace and "in that beloved Vale to which erelong / We were transplanted" (*Prelude*, 1:300–305). The "immortal spirit" grows like harmony in music. Like the biological analogy, musical harmony suggests a cyclical range of possibilities from which selections once made become inevitable, satisfying, and beautiful. In the natural world, in musical harmony, and in the human spirit, discordant elements are somehow reconciled to move or cling together in one society. All the ingredients of the poet's youth have borne a needful part in making up the calm existence that is his when he is worthy of himself. This natural or organic analogy is sustained to emphasize the harmony that is resought in recreation. The poet remembers himself as a small boy who held

> unconscious intercourse with beauty
> Old as creation, drinking in a pure
> Organic pleasure from the silver wreaths
> Of curling mist, or from the level plain
> Of waters coloured by impending clouds.
>
> (*Prelude*, 1:563–66)

Or who gathered

> Through every hair-breadth in that field of light,
> New pleasure like a bee among the flowers.
>
> (*Prelude*, 1:577–80)

Or who drank the visionary power and deemed

> not profitless the fleeting moods
> Of shadowy exultation.   (*Prelude*, 2:311–13)

Such harmony with the natural world describes an essential aspect of Eden. Man in this context is powerful because he is untrammeled, pure, and therefore keenly perceptive and aware. Both the original Eden, then, and this exercise of memory enable him to retain those truths that, once alive, will never perish. Wordsworth celebrates an Edenic childhood by means of the poetry that springs from it and which holds it forever still.

The events, too, that stand out in Wordsworth's memory do not relate him merely to other healthy children who run wild in the countryside. His soul, we recall, was fostered alike by beauty and by fear. Episodes of fear or suffering are seen as

> Severer interventions, ministry
> More palpable, as best might suit [Nature's] aim.
>
> (*Prelude*, 1:355–56)

When he steals a boat, he is admonished by the looming peak that strides after him as if it were alive. When he poaches animals from other hunters' snares, he hears low breathings coming after him. From the first dawn of childhood, his soul is built of all the human passions intertwined. Not in vain is the informing soul of the universe thus purifying

> The elements of feeling and of thought.
> And sanctifying, by such discipline,
> Both pain and fear, until we recognise
> A grandeur in the beatings of the heart.
>
> (*Prelude*, 1:410–14)

Recognition of divine purpose springs not from Eden but from Eden remembered. The gifts he has received must be acknowledged by the quality of his "perpetual benediction" on them. Through them he can create the perpetually present life of art that expulsion from Eden denies. Memory, in fact, comes as redeemer to fallen man.

Words like "purify" and "sanctify" derive from an early baptism in sun and water, from a sense of special selection more commonly enjoyed by fervent members of a fundamentalist faith. In spirit, Wordsworth is not unlike a born-again Christian. He finds in himself "that first great gift, the vital soul," and recognizes a constant and favorable intervention on his behalf by the creative powers of the universe. No adventure of the growing boy, no aspect of the natural world is wasted. Even in a group of children galloping "in uncouth race" through the ruined abbey at Furness, Wordsworth is affected by

> that single wren
> Which one day sang so sweetly in the nave
> Of the old church . . .
> So sweetly 'mid the gloom the invisible bird
> Sang to herself, that there I could have made
> My dwelling-place, and lived for ever there
> To hear such music.   (*Prelude*, 2:118–28)

If he goes bird's-nesting, a mean inglorious plunderer,

> yet the end
> Was not ignoble. Oh! When I have hung
> Above the raven's nest, by knots of grass
> And half-inch fissures in the slippery rock
> But ill-sustained, and almost (so it seemed)
> Suspended by the blast that blew amain,
> Shouldering the naked crag, oh, at that time
> While on the perilous ridge I hung alone,
> With what strange utterance did the loud dry wind

> Blow through my ear! the sky seemed not a sky
> Of earth—and with what motion moved the clouds!
> (Prelude, 1:330–39)

The child's landscape is informed with spiritual meaning, giving a rare strength to the growing youth when he is exposed to the cruder world of men:

> The props of my affections were removed,
> And yet the building stood, as if sustained
> By its own spirit. (Prelude, 2:279–81)

Or again:

> Thus while the days flew by, and years passed on,
> From Nature and her overflowing soul
> I had received so much, that all my thoughts
> Were steeped in feeling; I was only then
> Contented, when with bliss ineffable
> I felt the sentiment of Being spread
> O'er all that moves and all that seemeth still;
> O'er all that, lost beyond the reach of thought
> And human knowledge, to the human eye
> Invisible, yet liveth to the heart. (Prelude, 2:396–405)

If he seems to refer to the Holy Ghost, we must remember that he is a favored being. *The Prelude* is inspired from the very outset by the breath of life. Loss of this gift would mean death for the poet for whom the poem of his life is a form of life on its own. The poem celebrates its own lasting life, the perennial spring that it derives from the poet's sacred childhood.

Beside possible loss of such a gift, mere loss of life is relatively insignificant. Like Rousseau's discovery of his own sexuality, however, the discovery or realization of death destroys the innocence of childhood with alarming frequency. Death is less easily accommodated into life than sex. Its long shadow reaches into the earliest years and casts a blight on Eden. Wordsworth's most graphic experience of physical death is worth contrasting in this context with a similar experience that traumatized the young Serge Aksakoff.

Roving alone by the banks of Esthwaite, Wordsworth comes at twilight across a pile of clothes. Gradually a crowd gathers. A boat puts out with grappling hooks:

> At last, the dead man, 'mid that beauteous scene
> Of trees and hills and water, bolt upright
> Rose, with his ghastly face, a spectre shape
> Of terror; yet no soul-debasing fear,
> Young as I was, a child not nine years old,
> Possessed me, for my inner eye had seen
> Such sights before, among the shining streams
> Of faery land, the forest of romance,
> Their spirit hallowed the sad spectacle
> With decoration of ideal grace;
> A dignity, a smoothness, like the works
> Of Grecian art, and purest poesy. (*Prelude*, 5:448–59)

Wordsworth's scene here, as so often, is perceived as a still for the mind to contemplate. Aksakoff also presents his experience in terms of the basic contrast between the living world and the dead man. He actually witnesses the transition from life to death, however, and his reading does nothing to lessen his shock. His first spring in the country, with the ground flooded and swampy after the long winter snows, and then finally alive and negotiable, brings him to an ecstasy that culminates with the festivities of Easter Day. Then, very suddenly, with everyone watching, the drunken miller drowns in the flooded river. Aksakoff has read and heard, he tells us, that people do die. Indeed, he has recently endured the shock of his own grandfather's death:

> Yet, for all this, the death of the miller, who under my very eyes had walked and sung and talked and then instantly disappeared forever, produced on my mind a different and much more powerful impression. . . . I was seized with a blind fear that something similar might happen at any moment to my father or mother or all of us.[27]

Wordsworth's imagination is so allied with the immutable structures of nature and art that he does not suffer. He could not imagine the shock experienced by young Aksakoff at seeing a living man become suddenly dead. He would find such suffering soul-debasing. To admit Aksakoff's fear that such sudden death could happen to one's parents or oneself would be to limit the world not only to the mutable but to the distinctly fallible. Most men, however, do not belong to the happy Wordsworthian few. Aksakoff is distinctly vulnerable to these basic fears that all the safety one knows, the strongest and surest people on whom one relies, indeed one's own body that is so certainly alive, all shall certainly be broken in pieces like a potter's vessel.

Death, like sex, introduces change too extensive and disruptive for paradise to contain. It introduces insecurity and a sense of otherness to the child whose world becomes accordingly alien and uncontrollable. Gosse, we have seen, describes this shock in terms of his discovery that his father is distinctly fallible. Similarly, Rousseau loses respect for and intimacy with his guardians: "We no longer looked on them as gods who read our hearts" (*Confessions*, p. 30). Gosse and Rousseau describe a phase of maturation that, in one form or another, is inevitable.[28] That death provides the most forcible shock, however, and the most violent alienation may best be demonstrated by Samuel Johnson's subconscious response to the death of his mother. It is significant in this context that *Rasselas*, the novel that steamed out of him at high speed to pay the expenses of her funeral, should have been the story of a young man who discovers after very brief exposure to the illusions of the world that Eden, even as a prison, is the only good place to be. The subconscious power of Johnson's response to death, like the inevitability of Gosse's discovery of his father's human frailty, substantiates yet again the efficiency with which this myth contains and defines common psychological truths, making them portable and explicit for the autobiographer's convenience.

Aksakoff, Gorky, De Quincey, and Hudson:
Innocence Lost but Memory Regained

Aksakoff's first intimation of death is brought by a galloping horseman, who recalls the congregation to church after the Sunday service, announces the death of the Empress Catherine, and demands an oath of allegiance to the new czar. Soon after this discovery that even an empress can die, the small Seryozha is prepared for his grandfather's death. For days the family travels through the Russian winter to be present at the deathbed. The journey is strenuous and distracting, but the image of death controls Seryozha's imagination:

> My chief fear was, that grandfather would begin to say goodbye to me and would die with his arms around me; his arms would stiffen, so that I could not be released from their grasp; and it would be necessary to bury me in the earth with him. . . . The terror of this thought seemed to paralyse my heart.[29]

The sensitive child seems to enlarge on that capacity common in childhood for identifying with a situation or assuming an inevitable involvement. The servants casually tell him that the body is stiff and one eye is closed. He falls into disgrace with all his relations for his hysterical avoidance of the proprieties of visiting the corpse.

Despite his involvement with death and his fear of it, Aksakoff does not plot his autobiography so that any specific experience of death results in a sudden loss of innocence. Rather, having spent his early childhood under his mother's intense and neurotic surveillance, he learns to identify with and love his father and matures to the point at which he is sent away from home to school. This departure from childhood, as inevitable and yet as emphatic as Leigh Hunt's departure from school, follows the highly emotional death of his grandmother.[30]

Four significant deaths in one short childhood provide a major part of the emotional structure of Aksakoff's autobiography. Each death moves the story of the boy's development one stage further. Each death after the first involves a struggle with vast distances and with the elements of a Russian winter. Each provides a recognition and an involvement in the basic fears of extinction that mature into an ability to be independent of the fantasies of security, of what Pater calls "home as a place of tried security."[31] In other words, it becomes possible to leave childish things behind. Each such episode also demonstrates the close connection that subsists between the reality and the metaphor, between childhood and the myth of Eden that describes it. Had any journey caused by a death taken place in summer, Aksakoff would merely have found other details with which to convey the terrible knowledge that death brings, its disruption of security, peace, and harmony between the child and his world.

Gorky's childhood, altogether more traumatic than that of Aksakoff, also moves from death to significant death.[32] He opens his story with the image of his father's body on the floor. It is long and white. The toes are strangely splayed out. The fingers are distorted. Black discs of copper coins seal the once shining eyes. His kind face has darkened. His teeth are nastily, frighteningly bared. The burial day is wet. Frogs, trying to escape from the grave, are thrown back in by the clods of earth. The frogs' deaths are more vivid to the boy than his father's. Frogs are like Aksakoff's miller, one moment living and then very suddenly dead. The small boy is immediately concerned with the frogs.

Gorky, of course, is not adhering to the narrative sequences of the Edenic myth. He therefore provides an excellent example of the way in which slight verbal reminders of the myth can serve the autobiographer's needs. Verbal reminders tune us in to a common language more significant than the particularities of different experience. They serve to contrast the expectation that they arouse with the reality that Gorky describes. They also enable him to enrich many aspects of that reality with the full resonance that the myth bestows.

His father's death affects Gorky more gradually than that of the frogs in his father's grave; it throws him, an outcast, onto his mother's crazy and brutal relations. Years later, he begins to fictionalize his father into another outcast like himself but romanticized by vagueness, a kind of Oedipus:

> At nights, when I lay sleepless, gazing at the dark blue sky, and the trail of stars slowly sailing across the heavens, I used to invent sad stories, which centred on my father, who was always on the road alone, walking somewhere with a stick in his hand and a shaggy dog at his heels.[33]

Gorky's mother leaves him with her parents, returning to him occasionally and briefly to reinforce her central role in all his fairy tales and legends. He experiences much brutality, squalor, sickness, and a rich sense of his own past. His mother's marriage, however, ends one portion of his childhood. Her suitor will buy the boy some paints, which he does not want. The suitor's mother is dressed all in green, to the very hairs on her wart that creep over her clean, yellow, wrinkled skin. Her dead hand smells of carbolic soap and incense. His distrust and sense of betrayal bear comparison with those of Alyosha Karenin on his meeting with Vronsky or of David Copperfield on his introduction to the Murdstones. As he watches the wedding droshky bounce away around the corner, something within him, like De Quincey's door, like the gates of Geneva, bangs shut, closes up.

Yet he is not, even now, entirely alone. His crazy old grandmother sleeps outdoors with him through the magical summer nights. Together they enjoy a brief Eden. Woken by the sun, with the apple leaves shaking off the dew, vapor rising from the bright green grass, the sky turning a deeper and deeper lilac and one lark singing, the boy feels that "every flower and sound seeped like dew into my heart, filling me with a calm joy."[34] He shuns companions, wishing to protect the sanctuary that he has built and made beautiful out of the ugly pit where Uncle Peter committed suicide. "This was the most peaceful and impressionable period of my life, and in that summer a feeling of confidence in my own powers was born in me and strengthened from day to day."[35]

Young Gorky's Eden is destroyed by the return of his

mother, bitterly unhappy with her husband. She has two babies, both of whom die slowly in infancy. Her husband beats her. The grandparents' marriage is also disintegrating after decades of hostility. When his mother dies, there is no home for Gorky anywhere. His grandfather tells him to fend for himself and turns him out of the house. After his father's death, he travels by river to a new home. Many years older and tougher, his mother's death sends him out into the wilderness. "And so," he writes, in clear and conventional terms, "I went out into the world."[36]

Gorky's "world," like Rousseau's, is a wilderness. The phrasing is conventional. It describes the equally conventional fairy-tale youth, his red spotted handkerchief knotted around his worldly goods, setting off on a journey to seek his fortune. It describes the physical, financial, and emotional independence of the youth who no longer lives at home. Most importantly, in each case, it describes the sense each child achieves of separate identity, of the need to rely only on oneself, of the otherness of all other people. Pip, too, delighted to leave the marshlands of his guilt behind him, finds he cannot get off the coach to bid a decent farewell to Joe, "and it was now too late and too far to go back, and I went on. And the mists had all solemnly risen now, and the world lay spread before me."[37] His world is a wilderness too, damaged by loss and death, dominated by his increasing responsibility for the guilt that he thought he had left behind.

The mortality rate of infants and, indeed, their parents was much higher a hundred years ago than it is today. Yet these autobiographies do not treat death in any form as a commonplace. No autobiographer can pass it by without comment. Most either remember specific deaths as crucial to their childhood or at least make sure that these deaths take their appropriate place in the experience of the autobiography. None, perhaps, realizes this so effectively as De Quincey.

De Quincey never achieved the formal architecture of an autobiography, though he repeatedly told the story of his life in one form or another. Like Newman, he might be called "le plus autobiographique des hommes." He is constantly con-

cerned to reveal "his own secret springs of action and reserve," to explore not the activities but the emotions that create the unity of being. To do this, he returns constantly to
his childhood. The *Autobiographic Sketches* opens with a re-
printed section from *Suspiria de Profundis*, here called "The
Affliction of Childhood." Quite apart from the specific references to *Paradise Lost* in the opening pages, this essay illustrates once again the powers of the Edenic paradigm to contain and explain childhood experience.[38]

De Quincey begins with his sense of loss, which is as dramatically fictionalized as any account so far. "About the close
of my sixth year," he writes, "suddenly the first chapter of my
life came to a violent termination; that chapter which, even
within the gates of recovered paradise, might merit a remembrance. *'Life is finished.'* was the secret misgiving of my heart
. . . 'now is the blossoming of life withered forever.'"[39] With
the death of his sister Elizabeth, he loses the peace and central
security belonging to a love that is past all understanding. Her
death is an event that runs "after [his] steps far into life."[40]

In returning to his childhood after promising to relate his
dreams, De Quincey, like so many of his literary contemporaries, shows a remarkable anticipation of Freud. Despite his
clear perception of "angel infancy" and the holiness of love
among children, he is not merely indulging in the nostalgia
common to sick and elderly autobiographers. He is assuming
that in childhood lies the source of the complex emotions and
sensations of the man, of what Woolf calls the "anguish that
for ever falls and rises and casts its arms upwards in despair."[41] As early as the 1822 version of the *Confessions*, he
assumes, as we have seen, that details of his childhood will
create "some previous interest of a personal sort in the confessing subject, apart from the matter of the confessions,
which cannot fail to render the confessions themselves more
interesting" (*CEOE*, p. 349). His sister's death, for example,
clearly prepares him for the small servant in London (Dick
Swiveller's Marchioness), for Ann of Oxford Street and the
Daughters of Lebanon, for all his close kinships with lost and
waiflike women. For, when he leaves his sister's deathbed, he

knows that "the worm was at [his] heart . . . the worm that could not die."[42]

De Quincey's immediate experience of death, furthermore, is of a dreamlike nature. Standing in his sister's room, between an open window and a dead body on a summer's day, he hears a solemn wind begin to blow, the saddest he has ever heard. "It was a wind that might have swept the fields of mortality for a thousand centuries."[43] In spirit he rises as if on billows in pursuit of the throne of God that flees away forever on a shaft of light. The vision of stillness and eternity and loss rolls from image to image until it is complete. The vision ends, and he passes forever from his sister's room. The finality of the "forevers" of his losses haunts him. Solitude stretches out the scepter of fascination even to the infant of six years old.

Like many of these autobiographers of childhood, W. H. Hudson also returns to memories of his childhood in South America when he is an old, sick man. Perhaps better known as a naturalist than as an autobiographer, Hudson is clearly familiar with the common literary conventions. His narrative lacks the drama of De Quincey's or Gorky's but is comparable to that of Aksakoff in its rambling, sensitive appreciation of detail and its ability to convey the delicate emotions that are significant in a child's day-to-day existence. His clouds of glory, according to all accounts that he has received, ceased to be visibly trailed by the time he was three. He remembers himself only as "a little wild animal running about on its hind legs, amazingly interested in the world in which it found itself."[44]

The most important event of Hudson's childhood, "the first thing in a young life which brought the eternal note of sadness in,"[45] is the death of his old dog, Cassar. Hudson, like De Quincey, is only six at the time. His discovery of the reality of death and burial contrasts with his rapturous delight in nature and existence, a delight that he feels has only been adequately expressed by some religious mystics. The dog's death introduces a terrible new darkness, the fear of death.

For the most part, however, life is only beginning to open up for the small boy. He is given his own pony and allowed to go as far from home for as long as he likes. He feels like a young bird that suddenly becomes conscious of its power to fly when it first quits the nest. He constantly discovers and thrills to new delights in the natural world. Little yellow finches sing in great flocks amid the huge peach trees in pink bloom. As we have seen, his first sight of flamingos exceeds by many degrees of delight his experience on scores of later occasions. Like Aksakoff, he too thrills to the chase and feels a primitive lust for the kill.

Hudson's boyhood is comparable to Aksakoff's and also to Wordsworth's in its experience of nature and in the basically even tenor of its flow. Like Aksakoff rather than Wordsworth, Hudson feels no great calling. His Eden is truly innocent in its lack of all self-consciousness. His fifteenth year, however, "was a time of great events and serious changes, bodily and mental, which practically brought the happy time of [his] boyhood to an end."[46] Hudson contracts typhus in Buenos Aires and is struck dumb during the illness. He spends his fifteenth birthday as a convalescent, grappling for the first time with his identity, his destiny, and the likelihood of his having any control over either.

> It was as though I had only just become conscious; I doubt that I had ever been fully conscious before. I had lived till now in a paradise of vivid sense-impressions in which all thoughts came to me saturated with emotion, and in that mental state reflection is well-nigh impossible.[47]

Hudson's early horror has been death. This wound is partially healed when he learns of the immortality of the soul, but his understanding of death provides an analogy for the transition now facing him from boyhood to manhood:

> To pass from boyhood to manhood was not so bad as dying; nevertheless it was a change painful to contemplate. That everlasting delight and wonder, rising to rapture, which was in the child and boy would wither away and vanish, and in its place there would be that dull low

> kind of satisfaction which men have. . . . And now it
> seemed that I was about to lose it—this glad emotion
> which had made the world . . . an enchanted realm . . .
> it would be lost as effectually as if I had ceased to see
> and hear and palpitate, and my warm body had grown
> cold and stiff in death, and, like the dead and the living,
> I should be unconscious of my loss.[48]

Indeed, no other flamingo matches the beauty of the first he ever saw. The fever that strikes at so susceptible an age for contemplation is followed by rheumatic fever and heart trouble. The maturing youth learns to consider survival an adequate redemption. Yet his interpretation of his loss and its relation to death is among the most sensitive, the truest to the paradigm, and, in many ways, the most flexible. He speaks of boyhood not as lost with the banging of a gate but receding with suffering and thought. He retains the knowledge both of joy and of its sources in nature. But Eden, nevertheless, has faded, and this sick and elderly man, like all the others, is recalling a golden time that cannot come again. And if death and ending seem more significant than the joy once known, that is because joy, like death, is hard to record from *in the middest*. Loss of Eden is the only kind of death for which we have a retrospect. The only certainty about everyone's Eden is that it is lost.

Because it is lost, Eden belongs to memory and can be retrieved as a completed aspect of the past. As a completed aspect of the past, Eden is also perfect. Like childhood, it is untouchable, beyond the reach of any further transience or damage. Because it is permanent, Eden also belongs to the world of art where it can exist in a constant present tense looking as if it were alive, the result of a creativity deriving from its original existence. Because it is single and permanent, Eden stands in sharp contrast both to the multitudinous "otherness" of the world outside its gates and to the shocks and changes to which mortal, fallen man is constantly subjected.

Eden, then, encapsulates a mythic past for the human race,

represents psychological realities that we all tend to recognize, and, combining the general and the personal essences of what is felt on both counts to be true, becomes the most efficient myth, as form and content, for the autobiographer who hopes to convey some essential truths about himself for others to understand.

When paradise is lost, and when the tree of life is guarded by the angel with the flaming sword, Adam and Eve spit from their mouth the withered apple seed and set out into the wilderness. Hand in hand, two sexed, shamed beings, born to die, they are the first human adventurers to seek their fortune, their spotted handkerchiefs containing all their worldly goods. Adam and Eve journey to find a new home and make a new life in the wilderness. For the maturing child whose development their expulsion represents, this journey becomes a quest. Let us turn, then, to this quest for identity and purpose in the post-Edenic world.

3. Youth: The Heroic Journey and the Process of Art

The young man and woman who are metaphorically cast out of Eden undertake an inevitable journey. They are forced from their childhood garden into the wilderness, where they must earn their bread by the sweat of their brow, bring forth their children with pain, and behave in general like sensible grown-ups. Their journey represents a rite of passage, a particular metamorphosis, which is celebrated in archetypal myth, in religion, in literature, and in the everyday life of societies both primitive and sophisticated. It marks the process of coming of age.

Margaret Mead describes the strong and structured society in Samoa, which "ignores both boys and girls from birth until they are fifteen or sixteen years of age. Children under this age have no social standing. . . . But at a year or two beyond puberty . . . both boys and girls are . . . invested with definite obligations and privileges in the community life."[1] Such obligations and privileges are recognized in many Western societies by assumption of the rights to work, marry, vote, or be considered fully responsible for a crime. Maturity sufficient for such enterprises derives from the quality of experience that brought an end to Eden. The maturing individual no longer perceives the world as single and unalterable, as an extension of himself and his will. Rather, perceiving the world as mutable and essentially other than himself, the maturing youth accepts the obligations and privileges of coming of age by "making a life" for himself in some way or by altering his world; he engages in a struggle either for personal survival or the attainment of an ideal, or both. His struggle and survival, of course, are represented by Adam's sweating to till the wilderness in order to eat. Just as Adam's enjoyment of Eden represents a significant phase in the psychological development of the child, so his physical struggle for survival represents a psychologically significant phase for the maturing youth.

The adolescent can reason about the future and he is an idealist. He is capable of abstract thought and, as Piaget describes, frees himself from the concrete, "locating reality within a group of possible transformations." This is "the age of great ideals and of the beginning of theories, as well as the time of simple present adaptation to reality."[2] It is a time of transition, exploration, and testing of various possible roles in order to find the secure identity that makes sense both to the inner person and to the outer world. Secure identity is attained specifically by the sense that the adolescent can make of his role and his capabilities in the real world. S. N. Eisenstadt describes this stage as that at which "the individual's personality acquires the basic psychological mechanism of self-regulation and self-control, when his self-identity becomes crystallized."[3] Graduation from a protected to an autonomous state is inevitable. It incurs both stress and a sense of adventure. Crucially, during this period of tenuous identity and purpose,

> egocentrism is one of the most enduring features of
> adolescence. . . . [T]he adolescent not only tries to adapt
> his ego to the social environment but, just as emphatically, tries to adjust the environment to his ego. . . .
> [T]he adolescent goes through a phase in which he
> attributes an unlimited power to his own thoughts so
> that the dreams of a glorious future of transforming the
> world through ideas . . . seems to be not only fantasy
> but also an effective action which in itself modifies the
> empirical world.[4]

The journey metaphor, which derives from those rites of passage that transform the child into an adult, is particularly efficient at describing both this phase of exploration, stress, and attainment of identity and the way in which the individual explains himself within a social and historical context. It describes both the stage of life for the maturing individual and the place, or arrival, of that individual in his world. It is worth remembering, however, that journey is a metaphor of duration; it does not limit its usefulness to this phase of life. It suggests, indeed, a movement that lasts until death, and the adventures that occur may occur at any age. The journey, in other words, can be seen to derive its particular patterns from experiences that are especially important in adolescence or early youth, but the metaphor is useful in general for description of the whole of a recordable life.

Among the varying modes in which different societies recognize the transition from childhood to maturity, certain features recur again and again. If we look briefly at these common features, we can see how they accumulate into this significant metaphor that recurs in autobiography. Familiarity both with its sources and with the sense that it makes of individual experience can help us to see in the journey not simply a convention common to Western literature but also a metaphor crucial to autobiography by virtue of its descriptive and explanatory powers. Whether it shapes the whole narrative or merely provides internal allusions, the journey, like paradise, provides a significant and sensible metaphor with which the autobiographer can describe important features of his development and experience.

Bruno Bettelheim describes the complexity of rites that initiate boys and girls into the full life of their community. Seclusion plays an important part. The Carrier Indians of British Columbia apparently isolate a girl for several years at the onset of menstruation. For the Australian aborigine, initiation is a rebirth. Seclusion and rebirth commonly make use of long winding paths and all-but-inaccessible, womblike caves.[5] Mircea Eliade emphasizes the frequent cruelty of such rites, which, at the very least, entail separation from the mother, isolation (possibly under the supervision of a guide), and varying forms of the enactment of death and rebirth.[6] Clearly, the youth must put off childish things and his society makes sure that he is seen to do just that. Ritual transforms the *chronos* of many years' experience into the *kairos* wherein the child becomes a man.

Propp's *Morphology of the Folktale* supports the assumption that such a journey entailing separation, death or wounding, and rebirth or return is a common feature of the narrative imagination.[7] He describes the functions of the characters as stable, constant elements in a fairy tale, constituting the fundamental components of the tale. The sequence of these fundamental components is always identical. The main functions of the hero as Propp describes them bear close comparison with the rites of passage described by Bettelheim or Eliade. According to Propp, the hero leaves home, is tested, receives magical powers or help, meets an enemy in battle, is wounded but victorious, and returns home to recognition and power. This précis skips all the permutations, but it is worth mentioning that the hero's expedition begins with some villainy to be remedied or some lack to be filled and that the failure to receive recognition on return home may necessitate display of the hero's identifying wound or magic gift. To the common features of initiation described by Bettelheim and Eliade— seclusion or solitude, the presence of a guide, winding or tortuous paths, remote retreats, death and rebirth—Propp's list adds a struggle in which the hero is wounded but victorious and a magic power or redemptive gift that the hero brings back from his ordeal.

This wounding and the subsequent acquisition of power describe the central experience of the initiation, the descent into the underworld or the conversion, which will form the subject of chapter 4. Here it is simply worth remembering Campbell's description of the "standard path of the mythological adventure of the hero," which we examined in chapter 1 as a structural motif and which he describes as "a magnification of the formula represented in the rites of passage: *separation—initiation—return.*"[8] When the mythological hero sets out on his adventures, he too is separated from his family and his society and must struggle with the hardships of his way. Specifically, he encounters fabulous forces, is victorious over them, and returns with the power to bestow a boon on his fellow men. Henderson describes the psychological counterpart of the archetype as a significant rupture of continuity, an ordeal, a trial of strength on the road to "individuation," which is ultimate maturity.[9]

The process of individuation need not, of course, take place at maturity. Arnold Toynbee provides many pages of names of the heroes who have found a journey, an absence, crucial to their assumption of power. Indeed, only common knowledge of the complete paradigm could make sense of the death of the Messiah, Barbarossa, or King Arthur. Having withdrawn from their fellow men, they are bound to return with healing on their wings. One variant form of the journey describes the foundling who becomes king (Oedipus, Perseus, Romulus), prophet (Moses), or god (Zeus and Jesus). Another variant describes the perilous quest. (Underhill describes the mystic quest as an inevitable stage on the road to spiritual consciousness.)[10] The variants, like the original, insist on a formula that enjoins solitude, the confrontation of some force stronger than the hero, a taxing struggle, a victory, and a return to society with the hero now endowed with special knowledge or power to help his fellow men. "This is evidently," Toynbee concludes, "a *motif* of cosmic range."[11]

Certainly, autobiography has adopted this "motif" as an important metaphor. "The most comprehensive and central of all Romantic themes," Frye notes, "is a romance with the poet for hero."[12] His life, like all others, includes certain typical stages, such as the discovery of who one is and what one can do, that fall into typical forms. His autobiography accordingly will depend on shapes that oft were thought but ne'er, he hopes, so well expressed. After all, the "artist-hero, like the hero with a thousand faces, is always the same man and the conflicts he faces are essentially the same conflicts."[13] For the Romantic writer, however, the journey tends to describe alienation from society (Esau or Ishmael rate higher than Jacob and Isaac) and an inner search for the dark, hidden ground of identity between man and nature. He is, furthermore, self-conscious. For him, the journey describes the activity of his life as he has lived it, the activity of acquiring self-knowledge, and, perhaps closely related to this last as a form of active recognition, the activity of writing his life into a Life. The "process of creating," writes Anton Ehrenzweig, "is always reflected in the work of art and . . . represents its minimum content."[14]

Autobiography lends itself to being its own subject matter. Quite apart from the occasional sensation that one is looking into mirrors that show images of oneself looking into mirrors, there is also the practical fact that the author begins his story at its end; he must describe how he has reached the point from which he writes. That he is where he must be a foregone conclusion. No one turns to the end of an autobiography to find out what happens there. An autobiography, therefore, needs to accumulate meaning as distinct from action, and the journey metaphor is particularly useful for this purpose.

Todorov connects the activities of journey with narration for the acquisition or accumulation of knowledge. Odysseus, for example, tells the story of his life to seven different people on seven different occasions, the variants in that story being determined both by the interlocutor and by the time of telling. "Every one of Odysseus' narratives is determined by its end, by its point of arrival: it serves to justify the present situation. These narratives always concern something which has already been done, they link a past to a present: they must end by an 'I . . . here . . . now.'"[15] Todorov further describes two Odysseuses in the *Odyssey*:

> One has the adventures, the other tells them. It is diffi-
> cult to say which of the two is the main character. . . . If
> Odysseus takes so long to return home, it is because
> home is not his deepest desire. . . . Odysseus resists re-
> turning to Ithaca so that the story can continue. The
> theme of the *Odyssey* is not Odysseus' return to Ithaca;
> this return is, on the contrary, the death of the *Odyssey*,
> its end. The theme of the *Odyssey* is the narrative
> forming the *Odyssey*, it is the *Odyssey* itself.[16]

The applicability of this connection to autobiography has already been suggested in the discussion of the autobiographical narrator: his existence is necessitated by the translation of life into narrative; it can serve to free the original subject from inhibitions and to provide him with a voice and style, and it is essential in order to bridge the gap between the then of action and the now of narration. Odysseus resists an ending in his life because he is resisting an end to his narrative life. Clear identity and knowledge achieved through the narrative establish the struggle and the journey of life beyond the extinction of death.

Like the Odysseus who narrates the adventures, the narrator of *The Quest of the Holy Grail* constantly anticipates events and avoids surprises. "The reader's interest . . . does not come . . . from the question which habitually provokes such interest: what happens next? We know, from the beginning, what will happen, who will find the Grail, who will be punished and why. The interest is generated by a very different question: what is the Grail?"[17] Two kinds of interest derive from two kinds of narrative. The first is a narrative of the doing of events, what Todorov calls "a narrative of contiguity," the second is "a narrative of substitutions," which accords meaning to events. In this case, "we know from the start that Galahad will complete the quest victoriously; the narrative of contiguity is without interest. But we do not know precisely what the Grail is, so that there is occasion for an enthralling narrative of substitutions, in which we slowly arrive at comprehension of what was given from the beginning."[18] Gawain and Lancelot need adventures to relate but only the good knight Galahad succeeds in having them. As the sage explains, adventures are the signs and apparitions of the Holy Grail. The Grail, Todorov concludes, "is nothing but the possibility of narrative."[19] One is reminded of the etymological connection between narration and knowledge.

Like the narrators who find through narrative the meaning for a journey whose end is known, the autobiographer, who relates the process of self-discovery, tends to attribute more significance to meaning than to action. Moreover, by using the journey as his metaphor for both life and its narration, he ensures that his ending provides not surprise but connection with all the parts complete, a recognition of the starting place seen as if for the first time.

Art as the means of the discovering of the self becomes a Romantic quest in its own right. The blank page waits like a wilderness for the self-conscious "I" to begin its journey. When a quest is successful, moreover, words cover the barren space; victory brings fertility to the wasteland.[20] The autobiography becomes the gift described by Propp, the knowledge or power ascribed by Toynbee and Campbell as the achievement of the journey. The author-hero may be maimed in his struggle, but as Odin and Jacob know, crippling is often the price of knowledge. Indeed, he may disappear, subsumed into the written life. Just as the archetypal journey outlives its many travelers, so the written life remains infrangible long after the life of the man who writes it.

Four autobiographical works will exemplify some ways in which autobiographers commonly use the metaphor of the journey: Carlyle's *Sartor Resartus*, Wordsworth's *Prelude*, Rousseau's *Confessions*, and George Moore's *Hail and Farewell*. Together, they span a wide period of time. Over a hundred years lie between publication in France of Rousseau's *Confessions* and publication in England of Moore's *Hail and Farewell*. Rousseau introduces a solipsistic, introspective genre that George Moore needs to revitalize with a transfusion of objectivity, self-effacement, the assumption that the artist exists only for art's sake. Between these two, Carlyle writes a flamboyant treatise masked as an autobiography, or an autobiography masked as a novel, or a novel containing autobiography and treatise, or all three; and Wordsworth writes two drafts of a long poem designed as letters to a friend.

These writers and their life stories indeed form an odd combination. They have little in common except their wish to write about themselves, their conscious artistry, and their deliberate exploration of autobiography as an art form. Accordingly, it is significant for the generality and usefulness of the metaphor of the journey that all four writers should make it so central to their work. They do not merely cover distances. They do not simply allude to the river of life flowing into the sea of death. They demonstrate the connection they find between movement and imagination; they enact the tortuous journey of self-revelation, the process of autobiography. They all observe in varying degrees the pattern of separation, initiation, and return. Wordsworth and Carlyle trace this pattern in the rivers of their lives, Moore in his search for his Irish identity, Rousseau only in a dream that he cannot realize. Each insists on the virtue of his quest and the richness of the gift he brings. For each one, the process of autobiography transforms his life into a fiction that describes both the making of his story and the hero he chooses to be.

Carlyle: Fabrication of Self

Of these four travelers, Carlyle is the most generous to the analyst in that he adheres more fully than the others to the detailed possibilities of the metaphor. First he relates the adventures of Teufelsdröckh, a man who travels both in body and in thought; he takes his pilgrim staff and sets off around the world, and he evolves the amazing Philosophy of Clothes. Then he provides an editorial voice to narrate Teufelsdröckh's process of self-exploration, to trace the physical journey, and to unravel the meaning of his unusual philosophy. For Teufelsdröckh and his editor, the journey provides the shape and meaning of the work. Beginning in confusion of purpose and possibilities, they find by the end that they have "travelled some months of [their] Life-journey in partial sight of one another" (*SR*, 3:298), and conclude with a clear sense of arrival. The tailor or fabricator, in other words, makes the very process of patching his story together as important as the story itself. No sartor, after all, can survive except resartus. The progress of one and the process of the other amount to the same thing. As Frye writes: "Identity and self-recognition begin when . . . the great twins of divine creation and human recreation have merged into one, and we can see that the same shape is upon both."[21] In this case, life is once again transfigured into narrative life.

Teufelsdröckh establishes his solitude (important for any

significant journey) with the awful question: "'Who am *I*; the thing that can say "I"?'" He fears that the secret of man's being is still like the sphinx's secret, for ignorance of which he will suffer the worst death of all, a spiritual death. "'The world, with its loud trafficking, retires into the distance; and . . . the sight reaches forth into the void Deep, and you are alone with the Universe, and silently commune with it, as one mysterious Presence with another'" (*SR*, 1:53).

Teufelsdröckh is a natural solitary. No biography can be gathered from his home town of Weissnichtwo. He is a stranger there, merely wafted to the place by circumstance. Curiosity has indeed bestirred herself about him but has been satisfied with most indistinct replies. For himself, he is "a man so still and altogether unparticipating" (*SR*, 1:17) that questions demand unusual delicacy. He is able to divert intrusions. He is spoken of secretly as parentless, everlasting, a Wandering Jew. In his lonely tower, by the feeble rays of his single tallow-light, Teufelsdröckh broods through the vast void night, separate from the teeming varieties of life, "'alone with the Stars'" (*SR* 1:23). His self-seclusion is godlike, indifferent. "Here, perched-up in his high Wahngasse watch-tower, and often, in solitude, out-watching the Bear, it was that the indomitable Inquirer fought all his battles with Dulness and Darkness; here, in all probability, that he wrote this surprising Volume on *Clothes*" (*SR* 1:27). In what he calls the destitution of his wild desert, this Ishmael acquires the greatest of all possessions, self-help, but it is a desert, howling with savage monsters. He stresses the solitude with which he undertakes his world pilgrimage, unable to escape from his own shadow. Mephistopheles explains to the bewildered Faust that everywhere he goes is hell; for the uncondemned man it is important to remember that he carries his own soul with him, that there is no possible flight from oneself, that a physical journey can heal the soul only insofar as it is also a spiritual journey. For the autobiographer who undertakes essentially a journey in search of himself, the physical journey becomes, by contrast, a valuable analogy for his search.

Teufelsdröckh refers to himself as the Wanderer. He sees

himself leaving Weissnichtwo much as the Hebrews left their servitude in Egypt. More prosaically, with some irritation, the editor sees him as a little boat leaving the fleet to sail off by sextant and compass of its own. The editor's annoyance seems justified by the hero's instant catastrophe on Calypso's island, yet the ennobling of the wonderful spoof story of Blumine by such analogy with the *Odyssey* reinforces the importance of Teufelsdröckh's enterprise.

The story of Blumine deserves a moment's attention. In tone reminiscent of *The Rape of the Lock*, this episode parodies a main feature of heroic adventure, the hero's brave encounter with a fabulous enemy in order to win a beautiful lady. Notably, the story of Blumine derives entirely from editorial conjecture. It is the editor who imagines that Teufelsdröckh must have been ushered into the garden house, if not for Aesthetic Tea, then maybe for Musical Coffee. The Wanderer advances with foreboding and finds his Queen of Hearts, Blumine. He must go forth and meet his destiny. His intervening monster takes the form of "one 'Philistine'; who even now, to the general weariness, was dominantly pouring-forth Philistinism . . . little witting what hero was here entering to demolish him!" (*SR*, 2:140). A Philistine at Aesthetic Tea or Musical Coffee needs demolishing with "Socratic, or rather Diogenic utterances"; he also serves as a metaphor for his original, the Philistine from Gath who threatened the whole army of Saul. The equation likens Teufelsdröckh to the young David who left his father's flocks to save Israel, maybe even to God's other warrior, Samson, who destroyed the whole temple of the Philistine enemy. A tea-party bore, in other words, threatens not only the pleasure of the party but also the survival of civilized society, certainly the survival of the chosen hero.

The editor's wild surmise, taking this form of parody, alerts us to Teufelsdröckh's real encounter with a fabulous enemy, which is the main adventure of his journey. Whereas the mock-hero leaves the expedition to sail by his own compass, meets Calypso, overcomes an enemy to win her, is made immortal by a kiss, but is then rejected and surely destroyed, the true hero makes the distress that follows from his misplaced love a cause for his journey. "He quietly lifts his *Pilgerstab* (Pilgrim-Staff), 'old business being soon wound up'; and begins a perambulation and circumambulation of the terraqueous Globe!" (*SR*, 2:147).

Distraught by the final blow, however, the sight of Blumine married to Towgood, Teufelsdröckh meets an apparently insuperable monster in the form of despair. Just as the Philistine is Teufelsdröckh's enemy in the garden house, so despair, or the Everlasting No, confronts him midway on his journey. Like Dante and Bunyan before him, Carlyle endows his monster of the spirit with a specific character; Teufelsdröckh's battle is with the Time Prince or Devil himself. Life becomes "wholly a dark labyrinth" (*SR*, 2:152) along which the hero stumbles, flying from specters. Guiltless, he travels like Cain or the Wandering Jew, writing his *Sorrows of Teufelsdröckh* over the whole surface of the earth with his footprints. Like Goethe writing "his *Sorrows of Werter* before the spirit freed herself, and he could become a Man," so "Your Byron publishes his *Sorrows of Lord George*, in verse and in prose, and copiously otherwise: your Bonaparte represents his *Sorrows of Napoleon* Opera, in an all-too stupendous style. . . . Happier is he who . . . can write such matter, since it must be written, on the insensible Earth, with his shoe-soles only; and also survive the writing thereof!" (*SR*, 2:156–57).

Teufelsdröckh's soul drowns in a quagmire of disgust. He finds neither pillar of fire by night nor pillar of cloud by day to guide him. He trembles with an indefinite, pining fear. Heaven and earth become the boundless jaws of a monster waiting to devour him. He is saved by sudden conversion, which rushes over his soul like a stream of fire, releasing him from fear, enabling him to stand up in protest against the immeasurable, indifferent "Steam-Engine of non-existence" that has threatened to destroy him.

Teufelsdröckh's victory in this battle does not win him a lady. Rather more significantly, it achieves the answer to his original question; he knows now who he is. He dares to stand up and call himself a man. His encounter with his monster is worth quoting at length because it demonstrates an entirely conscious use of the paradigm, operating in this case within a Christian framework:

> Name it as we choose: with or without visible Devil, whether in the natural Desert of rocks and sands, or in the populous moral Desert of selfishness and base-ness,—to such Temptation are we all called. Unhappy if we are not! Unhappy if we are but Half-men, in whom that divine handwriting has never blazed forth, all-sub-duing, in true sun-splendour; but quivers dubiously amid meaner lights: or smoulders, in dull pain, in dark-ness, under earthly vapours!—Our Wilderness is the wide World in an Atheistic Century; our Forty Days are long years of suffering and fasting: nevertheless, to these also comes an end. Yes, to me also was given, if not Vic-tory, yet the consciousness of Battle, and the resolve to persevere therein while life or faculty is left. To me also, entangled in the enchanted forests, demon-peopled, doleful of sight and of sound, it was given, after weariest wanderings, to work out my way into the higher sunlit slopes—of that Mountain which has no summit, or whose summit is in Heaven only! (*SR*, 2:184)

Teufelsdröckh's victory over despair, or metaphorically death, is further signified by his name, "devil's dung," which sug-gests quite specifically that he has journeyed through hell or the body of the devil. Teufelsdröckh's journey, covering the terraqueous globe, overcoming monsters from outside and within, wins no less a prize than the Philosophy of Clothes. Like the Golden Fleece, the apples of the Hesperides, fire, or the promise of spring, this philosophy is the gift with which he returns to his fellow men.

His editor, on the other hand, must work backwards from the known to the unknown on a parallel journey of his own. He works from this amazing gift of the Philosophy of Clothes back to the mystery of the man who evolved it. His journey rings loud with complaints. His materials are given him in a state of confusion, obfuscated by absurd degrees of metaphor. "Towards these dim infinitely-expanded regions, close-bordering on the impalpable Inane, it is not without apprehension, and perpetual difficulties that the Editor sees himself journeying and struggling" (*SR*, 1:74). When it finally becomes clear that Teufelsdröckh imagines his temptation in the wilderness as the preface to his apostolic work, "the somewhat exasperated and indeed exhausted Editor" (*SR*, 2:204) complains: "Would thou hadst told thy singular story in plain words! . . . Nothing but innuendoes, figurative crotchets: a typical Shadow, fitfully wavering, prophetico-satiric; no clear logical Picture" (*SR*, 2:184–85).

Teufelsdröckh's journey of life begins in the verdant paradise of Entepfuhl; "'Sleep on, thou fair Child,'" he apostrophizes, "'for thy long rough journey is at hand!'" (*SR*, 2:90). It continues through the marshlands of school: "Green sunny tracts there are still; but intersected by bitter rivulets of tears, here and there stagnating into sour marshes of discontent" (*SR*, 2:103). Then the howling desert of university precedes his redemption of self and of mankind.

Similarly, the editor begins his task full of enthusiasm and hope but begins to lose his step with concern that this confusing pedant will prove unpalatable to the British reading public. He then flounders completely among the six paper bags, each marked with a sign of the zodiac, which contain shreds and snips of paper covered with Teufelsdröckh's scarcely legible cursive script. He finally triumphs over his despair with the realization that his desperate struggle has indeed recreated both the man and the work. This frustrating editorial task has been his journey, "a laborious, perhaps a thankless enterprise" from which his fellow men may derive "some morsel of spiritual nourishment" (*SR*, 3:292). His effort to sort and select his materials has ensured the reader's sense of composition as a constant, present activity. Like Dante's Vergil, he is the reader's guide (reading, too, is a process) over difficult country toward an important discovery. He forms a hell-gate bridge over Chaos. It cannot be his sober calculation but only his fond hope that many may travel by this means without accident, for it is a desperate bridge of rafts: "Alas, and the leaps from raft to raft were too often of a breakneck character; the darkness, the nature of the element, all was against us!" (*SR*, 3:268). Yet the river of Teufelsdröckh's history, traced from its tiniest fountains, is not lost even though it "dashes itself over that terrific Lover's Leap; and, as a mad-foaming cataract, flies wholly into tumultuous clouds of spray!" (*SR*, 2:153). From pools and plashes far below the cataract, the worthy editor finds once again, though with difficulty, the general stream, "nor, let us hope . . . will there be wanting . . . some twinkling of a steady Polar Star" (*SR*, 2:206).

Teufelsdröckh's editor is unlikely to lose his bearings, for he acts as Carlyle's autobiographical narrator and therefore knows the end of his story. He selects his facts from the Hofrath's bundle. The six bags sealed with the signs of the zodiac give him glimpses of the inner man. Selecting and interpreting as best he can from his knowledge of the man and the facts of his life, the editor transforms a past life into a present art form. Like the two main characters described by Todorov in the *Odyssey*, Teufelsdröckh suffers and the editor recounts and tries to explain that suffering. Carlyle expands the editorial role so that the editor's narrative in the present can express pity or contempt or provide a cynical check on Teufelsdröckh's moods of the past. He wishes, for instance, that "this farrago" would end because his voice is that of a later time easily distinguished from the then of the emotional despair. Notably, the dialogue in *Sartor* is established only in the work. The editor addresses Teufelsdröckh, but only on paper; not in the then of Teufelsdröckh's distress, but in the timeless now of the novel as artifact. Carlyle's several voices (Teufelsdröckh's, the editor's, even the Hofrath's) enable him to deal with that discontinuity of the personality so keenly felt between the now of editorial dispassion (or recollection in comparative tranquillity) and the then of passionate involvement when, crucially, the future was not known.

Wordsworth: Revelation of Poetic Spirit

Wordsworth, too, faces this disconnection:

> so wide appears
> The vacancy between me and those days
> Which yet have such self-presence in my mind,
> That, musing on them, often do I seem
> Two consciousnesses, conscious of myself
> And of some other Being.   (*Prelude*, 2:28–33)

Wordsworth is also explicitly concerned with the process of turning his life into a work of art. He, too, chooses the theme of a life journey based on and incorporating mythic journeys in order to convey the complexities of his development and the process of self-recreation. For journey essentially describes movement toward a clear or destined goal; it simplifies the landscape by prescribing a purpose.

> Who doth not love to follow with his eye
> The windings of a public way? the sight,
> Familiar object as it is, hath wrought
> On my imagination since the morn
> Of childhood, when a disappearing line,
> One daily present to my eyes, that crossed
> The naked summit of a far-off hill
> Beyond the limits that my feet had trod,
> Was like an invitation into space
> Boundless, or guide into eternity.
>
>   (*Prelude*, 13:142–51)

From the open school of such lonely roads the young man learns to study "men as they are men within themselves" (*Prelude*, 13:226), to dedicate himself to his theme, "No other than the very heart of man" (*Prelude*, 13:241).

Wordsworth claims at the end of *The Prelude* that he has traced the stream of his own life

> From the blind cavern whence is faintly heard
> Its natal murmur; followed it to light

And open day; accompanied its course
Among the ways of Nature, for a time
Lost sight of it bewildered and engulphed;
Then given it greeting as it rose once more
In strength, reflecting from its placid breast
The works of man and face of human life.

(Prelude, 14:194–202)

The course of Wordsworth's life as traced both in this
analogy for the autobiography and in the complete poem does
indeed run, in good autobiographical fashion, from birth
through childhood and youth to early manhood. It includes
the experiences of the city, of travel, of education and friendships, and, most crucially, both the hope and the disappoint-
ment he felt in the French Revolution. The contingent realities
of this process are linked with the poet's spiritual growth,
which is kindled and protected by the natural world around
him. His depression and failure of poetic spirit, blamed on the
less perfect world of men, are healed, so that the river can be
seen to rise once more in strength, reflecting from its placid
breast, like the earlier activity of poetic memory, the "works
of man and face of human life." The anticipation of poetic
gifts has been fulfilled.

Within the framework of this broad autobiographical journey, Wordsworth interpolates small journeys that describe
central experiences in his life, discoveries about his identity
and conviction of his poetic gift. The adventure of the gibbet
demonstrates one of Wordsworth's spots of time; this is no
mere happening but an event, *chronos* transformed into
kairos:

I remember well,
That once, while yet my inexperienced hand
Could scarcely hold a bridle, with proud hopes
I mounted, and we journeyed towards the hills.

(Prelude, 12:225-28)

The act of memory, the youth, the inexperience, the hope, and
the journey are all committed to four lines. An ancient servant

acts as guide, but some mischance separates the two. Frightened, the youth dismounts and stumbles down the rough and stony moor to the bottom, where a murderer had once been hung in chains. The gibbet, corpse, and chains have long since gone, but, like the works of Ozymandias, the name remains:

> still, from year to year . . .
> The grass is cleared away, and to this hour
> The characters are fresh and visible.
>
> (*Prelude*, 12:242–45)

Like the beggar's label, like *The Prelude* itself, these characters suffice to convey "his story, whence he came, and who he was" (*Prelude*, 7:642). Faltering and faint, the poet flees back up the stony road, looking for his guide but finding only the vision of the naked pool and the girl who bears a pitcher on her head and walks against the wind. Like the beggar's label, the murderer's name brings an absolute knowledge that overwhelms the finder.

Wordsworth loses his guide again at the Simplon Pass, and again he loses his way. In this case, however, he is actually directed to take the stony road downhill. Disappointed to realize that he has already crossed the Alps, that he has failed to notice the transition from one side to the other, he discovers that hope, effort, expectation and desire, "And something evermore about to be" (*Prelude*, 6:608) suffice the soul better than trophies. The soul is strong

> in beatitude
> That hides her, like the mighty flood of Nile
> Poured from his fount of Abyssinian clouds
> To fertilise the whole Egyptian plain.
>
> (*Prelude*, 6:613–16)

For Wordsworth, this beatitude is imagination. An awful power, it rises from the mind's abyss "like an unfathered vapour that enwraps / At once, some lonely traveller" (*Prelude*, 6:595–96). Imagination takes the form of fertilizing water, flooding the soul as the Nile floods otherwise barren land. Represented by water, imagination acts as guide and redeemer both to Wordsworth in life and to Wordsworth in the act of recreating his life into poetry. Still hoping to climb the Alps, he finds that his path in fact leads downward with the current of the stream. In dejection, his sister's vitalizing influence is felt like that of a brook that crosses and accompanies the road. Wordsworth links water quite specifically with the fertility of the creative spirit in his early address to the river Derwent, fairest of all rivers, and is afraid to find that the small brook in his garden represents a more plausible metaphor for his own life:

> The froward brook, who, soon as he was boxed
> Within our garden, found himself at once,
> As if by trick insidious and unkind,
> Stripped of his voice and left to dimple down
> (Without an effort and without a will)
> A channel paved by man's officious care.
>
> (*Prelude*, 4:51–56)

Such a possibility would be tantamount to poetic dearth.

It is a watery road, too, that leads Wordsworth to the top of a sharp rise where he finds the uncouth shape of the desolate soldier. In contrast to the crises of discovery that occur at the base of an unguided descent, this steep ascent leads the poet proudly to affirm his dedication. Furthermore, the soldier, though guided in fact by Wordsworth to a place of rest, represents the mythical guide so important to a successful journey. Reaching for the oaken staff that he had dropped, as if for the golden bough, which is also idle until needed, this "ghostly figure" moves by the poet's side and answers his questions with calm detachment. Like Aeneas with the sibyl, Wordsworth and the soldier journey "in silence through a wood gloomy and still" (*Prelude*, 4:447). The parallels with Aeneas's journey are explicit. Like Aeneas, Wordsworth discovers his destination only during the course of his journey.

At Snowdon, again after a steep ascent and again with "a trusty guide," the poet knows that he has reached the end of his journey and attained "that peace / Which passeth under-

standing" (*Prelude*, 14:126–27). So steep is the ascent this
time that,

> With forehead bent
> Earthward, as if in opposition set
> Against an enemy, [he] panted up
> With eager pace, and no less eager thoughts.
>
> (*Prelude*, 14:28–31)

Through the mist and dark, travelers' talk giving way to silence, Wordsworth and his companions breast the ascent to
see the sun rise from the top of Snowdon. Notably, however, it
is the moon that greets them, the reflected light, not, one
might say, the original life but the reflecting art. In concert
with the roar of waters, this "full-orbed Moon" lends a vision,
which appears to the poet

> the type
> Of a majestic intellect, its acts
> And its possessions, what it has and craves,
> What in itself it is, and would become.
> There I beheld the emblem of a mind
> That feeds upon infinity, that broods
> Over the dark abyss, intent to hear
> Its voices issuing forth to silent light
> In one continuous stream; a mind sustained
> By recognitions of transcendent power,
> In sense conducting to ideal form,
> In soul of more than mortal privilege.
>
> (*Prelude*, 14:66–77)

This final equilibrium, following the disruption of despair,
fulfills the original anticipation of creative genius with which
the narrative began. Coming full circle, the poet returns to his
beginnings in order to find his theme and prove his gift. His
initial journey has brought him, as such a journey should, the
highest bliss that flesh can know, the consciousness of who he
is (*Prelude*, 14:113–15). Because he is a poet, it has also made
him certain that he is one of the few who

> from their native selves can send abroad
> Kindred mutations; for themselves create
> A like existence. (*Prelude*, 14:93–95)

The initial journey is equivalent to the inner life of Teufels-dröckh. To transform his life into autobiography, the poet must take the second journey of composition, the editor's journey in quest of his subject and in creation of his work. Like Carlyle's editor, but in his own voice, Wordsworth sets out consciously and explicitly to discover and declare his theme.

His search for a theme is linked with his fear of a mortality that encompasses not only man but even the works of man:

> Things that aspire to unconquerable life;
> And yet we feel—we cannot choose but feel—
> That they must perish. Tremblings of the heart
> It gives, to think that our immortal being
> No more shall need such garments. (*Prelude*, 5:20–24)

It is also linked, of course, with his wish to leave some monument behind him that pure hearts should reverence (*Prelude*, 6:56–57). He identifies with the spirit of the Arab of his dream, who appears like a guide at his side, indeed, emphatically close at his side. Quixote-like he rides to rescue geometry and poetry, what Frye calls "the two great instruments that man has invented for transforming reality,"[22] from the wastes of time and the flood of extinction. Chiding himself for failure to use the talents he knows he has, the poet lapses inadvertently into the subject that perfectly satisfies all his needs: himself. The very guide he looks for, whether wandering cloud or floating object on the river, turns out to be his own self responding to the breeze, reflecting in the water, retreading familiar ground with a new purpose. Any further appearance of a guide, like the soldier, the guides on the Alps or on Mount Snowdon, or the spirit of Coleridge ever at his side (*Prelude*, 3:199), serves to support his spirits, to test or affirm his dedication, but never to question his main direction.

The narrator explains his task in terms of a journey over varied landscape. He himself is a pilgrim, or home-bound laborer, in search of a haven. Before the end of book 1, however, he recognizes in the act of memory a journey that refreshes his poetic spirit. The story of his life provides a theme "single and of determined bounds" (*Prelude*, 1:641). Having begun with the certainty that he could not miss his way, he now finds that his road lies plain before him. Explanatory interjections repeatedly fill in the details of this journey of memory and narrative. With the passing of early childhood, for example, the path becomes more difficult:

> and I fear
> That in its broken windings we shall need
> The chamois' sinews, and the eagle's wing.
> (*Prelude*, 2:273–75)

Solitude becomes as significant as the world of Nature for exploration of his inner self. His road runs through a countryside that is both around him and within:

> and what I saw
> Appeared like something in myself, a dream,
> A prospect in the mind.   (*Prelude*, 2:350–52)

Indeed, his state of mind determines the physical geography that shapes his path. He is, after all, a traveler whose tale is only of himself (*Prelude*, 3:195). Having retraced his life up to an eminence, he descends into a populous plain. Apathy at Cambridge is compared to a floating island, an amphibious spot,

> Unsound, of spongy texture, yet withal
> Not wanting a fair face of water-weeds
> And pleasant flowers.   (*Prelude*, 3:333–36)

Even this easy traveling with the shoal, however, is beneficial to a mind that has hitherto stood alone:

> Like a lone shepherd on a promontory
> Who lacking occupation looks far forth
> Into the boundless sea, and rather makes
> Than finds what he beholds.   (*Prelude*, 3:513–16)

In conclusion he likens his song to a lark that has surveyed
from great height the "Vast prospect of the world which I had
been / And was" (*Prelude*, 14:381–82).

Even Carlyle is not more explicit about this journey that the
narrator undertakes. His editor is not in top condition, perhaps; mostly he complains about the hardships of the journey.
Wordsworth's narrator, on the other hand, is perfectly fit. He
travels a road he has traveled before, but this time over the
landscape of his soul's history. His words form the journey,
rather like the "Mouse's Tale" in *Alice in Wonderland*. He
accuses himself of loitering (*Prelude*, 3:579). He finds a solitude on the public road at night that is more profound than
that of pathless wastes. He is forever walking within his narrative, in the Lake District, in the labyrinthine streets of London, on the continent. He is journeying over the smooth sands
of Leven's ample estuary when he receives news of Robes-
pierre's death. His narrative pauses at the end of book 6, but
then winter, on his accustomed journey from the north, brings
renewed vigor. The poet recalls his first attempts "to pitch a
vagrant tent among / The unfenced regions of society" (*Prelude*, 7:56–57). At the beginning of the ninth book, he pauses
again:

> Even as a river,—partly (it might seem)
> Yielding to old remembrances, and swayed
> In part by fear to shape a way direct,
> That would engulph him soon in the ravenous sea—
> Turns, and will measure back his course, far back,
> Seeking the very regions which he crossed
> In his first outset. . . .
> Or as a traveller, who has gained the brow
> Of some aerial Down, while there he halts
> For breathing-time, is tempted to review

The region left behind him. . . .
So have we lingered.   (*Prelude*, 9:1-17)

The significant value of retracing one's steps, of exploring familiar landscapes, lies in recognition. In this journey of narrative as in the original journey of life, acquiring the consciousness of who one is marks the success of the journey. The poem, or autobiography, both creates and is the place of arrival, a green landscape refertilized by the waters of the imagination.

Rousseau: A Maze of Self-Knowledge

Like Wordsworth and Carlyle, Rousseau also covers his inner landscape with journeys. Indeed, the first half of his *Confessions* bears close affinity with the picaresque novel. Unlike Wordsworth's narrator and Carlyle's editor, however, Rousseau finds narration more strenuous than living. Whereas Wordsworth's narrator and Carlyle's editor retread the ground of their biographied selves, Rousseau in confession travels a darker and rougher road than his earlier self. Carlyle's editor must make sense of his collected materials for his reading public; his journey parallels that of his hero. Wordsworth has grown up in the Lake District; his autobiographical act consists in retreading its familiar ways in order to regain the vigor that will enable him to reconstruct his life. For Rousseau, however, there is a harsh contrast between the sunlit journeys of his youth and the miry maze of his confessions.[23] In the former, as in the picaresque novel, revelation or development of the hero takes second place to continuous movement, random encounters and adventures, the pleasures of the road. In the autobiographical journey, on the other hand, revelation and awareness of the narrator count for more than the scenery through which he travels. He has, after all, acquired the luggage of life and must travel with all the responsibility of a social being.

The continuous traveling that Rousseau enjoys in his youth is confessedly irresponsible, undertaken entirely for pleasure and frequently to the detriment of a possible career. The aging autobiographer comments with some irony on the youth he had been who had managed to get himself dismissed from a good and promising position, "though indeed not without some difficulty," in order to pursue "the ineffable bliss of a journey" (*Confessions*, p. 100).

If the pleasures of the journey are of first importance, however, they also contribute to the development of the picaresque hero. Rousseau is quite clear about the value of such traveling to his talents and his character:

> In thinking over the details of my life which are lost to my memory, what I most regret is that I did not keep diaries of my travels. Never did I think so much, exist so vividly, and experience so much, never have I been so much myself—if I may use that expression—as in the journeys I have taken alone and on foot. There is something about walking which stimulates and enlivens my thoughts. When I stay in one place I can hardly think at all; my body has to be on the move to set my mind going.   (*Confessions*, pp. 157–58)

In every aspect of the life that he chooses to reveal, Rousseau clearly lacks discipline. He finds his imaginary worlds infinitely more attractive than the grind of subservience, which offers the only alternative of his youth, or the demands of society when he has made himself a name. It is as if his heart and his brain, as he puts it, did not belong to the same person (*Confessions*, p. 113). His finest work grows out of daydreams. He himself is free in his fantasy world from the inhibitions of shyness or the possibly worse frustration of being unable to match his appearance to others with the inner man known only to himself. Specifically, as he puts it, good health, independence, and pleasant country

> serve to free my spirit, to lend a greater boldness to my thinking, to throw me, so to speak, into the vastness of

things, so that I can combine them, select them, and make them mine as I will, without fear or restraint.

(*Confessions*, p. 158)

Even with freedom of movement, his methods of work are not unlike scene changing at the opera in Italy. Like the apparent destruction on the stage that gives way to a delightful spectacle, so his writing is "blotted, scratched, confused, illegible." "I have never been able to do anything with my pen in my hand," he concludes, "and my desk and my paper before me; it is on my walks, among the rocks and trees, it is at night in my bed when I lie awake, that I compose in my head" (*Confessions*, p. 113). On solitary walks along the lakeside at Geneva, he digests his plan for *Political Institutions*, contemplates a history of the Valais, and plans a prose tragedy on Lucrece. At the Hermitage, he sets aside his afternoons for walks and reckons that the forest of Montmorency is his study. His output is prolific. He trusts to the sheer weight of his papers and his publications to silence ill-wishers who deride his sincerity in loving solitude. But the world is too much with him. His *Confessions* respond, with frequent bitterness, to the society he has tried to avoid. His journey over his own past feels less like the open road than like a "dark and miry maze" (*Confessions*, p. 28). Well might he contrast "the vastness of things" with the confusion and instability of his own emotions, his inability to shape or color his life in any way that he would like.

Significantly, however, the shape that he forces onto intransigent events is essentially the shape of the journey paradigm of separation, initiation, and return. He considers himself an original, isolated man, totally individual. He craves rural solitude, which gives him freedom of spirit. His happiest memories lie in the country. With his literary and musical success in Paris, however, he achieves both fame and notoriety. He courts and is repulsed by the high society and the society of the men of letters among whom he is a genius both courted and despised. Bravely he attacks this monster of society with his pen. Wounded but fierce, society retaliates, and Rousseau is forced to flee. An old and sick man, he turns again to the country for retreat, to the pursuit of botany, to a desperate quest for the paradise he has lost. Needless to say, his early years are smirched with misdeeds and suffering and his middle years see recognition and prosperity. Yet Rousseau's attempt to enforce this narrative pattern describes in part the process of transforming contingent reality into a story for others to understand.

Despite his valiant pursuit of the paradigm, however, Rousseau never does manage to return to his starting place. After all the carefree, sunlit journeys, his *Confessions* lose their end in a miry maze for several important reasons. First, he is a pioneer in difficult country; he explores and reveals his own complex character, admitting to peculiarly shameful misdeeds. Memories embarrass him. He has taken a public stance, built his reputation on qualities that he himself has failed to maintain. His explorations are convincingly ruthless and original. Pursuit of such originality almost certainly must produce misshapen creation that will not conform to a shape that makes sense for others.

Second, Rousseau is lost in the political in-fighting of Parisian society. He makes fast friendships and loses them. He places absolute trust and finds his confidences become public knowledge. He feels at once innocent and guilty, aided and oppressed, and then, as the book progresses, increasingly persecuted, but by whom he is never sure. In contrast to the free journeys of his youth, he now endures the "wandering life" to which he sees he is "condemned." He considers himself "a fugitive upon the earth" (*Confessions*, p. 548). He begins book 12 as a work of darkness; he suspects a plot against him but loses himself "in the obscure and tortuous windings of the tunnels which lead to it" (*Confessions*, p. 544).

Then, too, despite the many journeys of the second half of his story, his early years of "vagabondage, follies, and hardships" (*Confessions*, p. 169) must contrast with the established career of a public figure. The journeys of the youth can be sunny precisely because they combine health and freedom and unknown possibilities. With age, ill-health, and disappointments, however, only the religious or the irrepressible remain buoyant. Again, the journeys of youth are told with happy memories. Time that approaches the present becomes more confused, lacks a clear sense of an ending. "Now," he writes, "my story can only proceed at haphazard, according as the ideas come back into my mind" (*Confessions*, p. 574).

Rousseau's maze leads him into increasing darkness. He does not accomplish the desired return, but he does achieve a gift for his fellow men. The gift consists not only of the written work but also of the thread he has unwound on his way through the maze in search of himself. His own character has developed paranoid insecurities and fears as well as original talents, so his search for himself becomes as much a justification as a confession. Indeed, he assumes pardon for confession and is accordingly strident at the assumed hostility of his readers. Self-pity, even petulance, irritate the reader with a constant sense of emotional blackmail. He even seems, worst of sins in an autobiographer, unreliable as a narrator, largely because other characters in the text respond to situations in ways that make more sense of them than Rousseau does himself. His world is solipsistic, his voice plangent. But that thread he unwinds on his way into the dark has proved a remarkable gift. He may be correct that his enterprise has no precedent, but hosts of autobiographers have followed his example.

Moore: Redemption of Self through Art

To be more clearly successful, however, the artist needs to stand out of his own light. This is a hard task for a man whose subject is himself, but it is achieved with such deliberate consciousness by George Moore that his contemporaries accused him of writing pure fiction in place of autobiography.[24] Like Rousseau, Moore was a public figure at the time of writing. (Seamus O'Sullivan enters a tobacconist's at Moore's heels "with the mad idea of buying two cigars of exactly the same brand which [he] had seen him select.")[25] Like Rousseau,

Moore is involved in the political and social life of his time. Like Rousseau, Moore has drifted through his youth aware of his talents but unable to discipline his energies, submitting to every influence that offers him a possible direction. Like Rousseau, too, Moore has enemies even among his friends. Moore would insist on a crucial difference between them, nonetheless. When Edward Martyn tells him that he has begun himself out of nothing, "developing from the mere sponge to the vertebrate and upward" (he might well have said the same of Rousseau), Moore concedes the validity of the description but would add to such natural development the unusual feature of complete and conscious artistry. He is, he would add, "at once the sculptor and the block of marble of [his] own destiny" (*HF*, 3:62).

Moore's book begins with a dream of a book as he wanders in the Temple in the early hours of the morning inspired by Edward Martyn's wish to write his plays in Irish. It ends with his bleak return from Ireland many years later, having been in process, like Moore's life, the whole while, and finally dictating not only its own end but also his live departure. For one of Moore's most remarkable achievements is this sense of autobiography and life as present and parallel process and journey.

Moore's method of narration reveals this activity by means of a continuous present tense, a stream of consciousness that moves back and forth in time and is interrupted by the present moment. "My garden is an enchantment in the spring," he writes, "and I sit bewitched by the sunlight and by my idea" (*HF*, 2:134). "My gardener's rake ceased suddenly, and, opening my eyes, I saw him snail-hunting among the long blades of the irises" (*HF*, 2:142). Himself as a picture of reverie is, moreover, nature's picture: "Myself, an elderly man, lying in an armchair listening to the fire, is a far better symbol of reverie than the young girl that a painter would place on a stone bench under sunlit trees" (*HF*, 3:21). His memories rise and fall with the fire. He stirs them with the coals. He is interrupted by a visitor. His dreams, moreover, come as a direct result of his inability to read, an inability that disturbs him because reading is such a worthwhile occupation for a man of letters. In this case, however, he is a man of life-into-letters. He visits the past, "and drowsing in my armchair, unable to read, the sadness that I had experienced returned to me, and I felt and saw as I had done thirty years before" (*HF*, 3:9). He casts a net that "is woven of fine silk for the capture of dreams, memories, hopes, aspirations, sorrows, with here and there a secret shame" (*HF*, 2:17). Such a process, like the process of life, is self-explanatory and self-revealing. A sudden thought, for instance, darting across his mind, leaves a sentence unfinished, and he wonders what sort of man he is. "That day, sitting under my apple-tree, it seemed to me that I had suddenly come upon the secret lair in which the soul hides itself" (*HF*, 2:23). The process of finding his own identity involves the cracking of his English mold, the overthrow of the Englishman who wrote *Esther Waters* by the Irishman always latent in him. The full realization of this Irishman, furthermore, can only be achieved by a return to Ireland and a persistent return to his own Irish past.

Just as memory and narration provide continuous action through three volumes, so also is the hero of the autobiography in frequent physical movement. He walks the streets of London, climbs stairs to visit friends, and travels by train to Bayreuth for the Wagner season; he travels down to Sussex, back and forth to Ireland, by bicycle with Æ in search of Druid gods, by train to the west coast, and finally back to London. Moore is aware that repetition of any journey necessarily alters the memory that now receives a second impression. He wishes, for instance, to alter his happy memories of a springtime ride to a gypsy fair in the Sussex downs, so he takes the same ride again in foul February weather. By just analogy, his narrative journey alters the journey of his life; he makes sense of his experience as part of the Irish literary movement by converting that experience into the mythic journey of the hero.

Moore is called to Ireland's service. He comes as her hero in an hour of need, to resurrect her art, to inaugurate a new era of culture. Yet Ireland is also the monster that stands in his way. She fades into a speck on the horizon of his life but then returns suddenly in tremendous bulk to frighten him. She is an ugly hag extorting youth and promises from her heroes. She is a god demanding human sacrifice. She is a human, not merely a geographical entity. Will she meet him, he wonders, as a friend or as an enemy? Will she appear from the boat as small as a pig's back or, rather, as a land of extraordinary enchantment? On arrival in Dublin, Moore finds that Edward Martyn is submitting his dramas to the church for approval. The *Countess Cathleen* plays to hoots and hisses. Between the stranglehold of the church and the ignorance of the people, Ireland meets Moore as an enemy.

Moore separates himself from the comfort and culture of Europe in the first volume of his autobiography, initiates himself as an Irishman in the second, but must return, *atque in perpetuum*, in the third to tell his story. His physical travels take him essentially from England to Ireland and back again to England. His narrative journey begins with the aging author in search of himself: "Bad Art is bad because it is anonymous. The work of the great artist is himself" (*HF*, 3:102). It ends with rediscovery of Moore Hall, his early childhood, and his realization that he can only fulfil his mission by leaving all this behind him. "Art is a personal rethinking of life from end to end," he writes, "and for this reason the artist is always eccentric" (*HF*, 3:103). He comes to Ireland in a springtime of hope and leaves on a cold, bleak February morning, uninspired, humble, but ready now to complete the work of liberation because his eyes have seen and his heart has felt the story that he has to tell.

Autobiography is a strange form for a sacred book that is meant to redeem the Irish people. However, by transforming life into art in the process of recognizing youth change to age and the heroic past become the complex present, Moore overcomes the monster that he finds in Ireland's intractability and chronicles at the same time his own heroic self-sacrifice. (There is no use for brave deeds unless there be chroniclers to relate them.)

Memory and narration, furthermore, remove the process

from life in which Moore Hall decays and the young boy grows old, the loved beauty becomes the worn hag, the young lover an impotent, elderly man, the heroic venture a bubble bursting into thin air. For the process becomes entirely that of art, a constant present after all the dreams. The life writing succeeds where the life itself could not in bringing literature to Ireland, or, to use the terms of his Wagnerian allusions, in reforging the sword that lay broken in "Mimi's" cave.

Identification of this elderly aesthete with Siegfried, the warrior-hero, demonstrates a significant value of such metaphor for autobiography. It allows Moore, in this instance, to make his point very clearly without the solipsistic blur that confuses Rousseau. Both men's autobiographies end in apparent public failure, but metaphor enables Moore to establish the successful realization of the true purpose of his journey, which is the realization of his own identity. He is not Siegfried, of course, but the heroic analogy describes Moore's security in his roles as Irishman and artist; just as Siegfried can repair the broken sword and fight, so Moore can combine these two main features of his identity and achieve specifically his autobiography.

The heroic metaphor in general describes more than the wishful thinking in which every adolescent indulges; it describes the main achievement of every mature adult: securing an identity that is of value to himself and to his society. Just as the journey describes the quest for identity, so the hero defines the fullest possible security that such an identity has been achieved. Rousseau's failure to control the last part of his *Confessions* is a literary failure to resolve the metaphor with which he has begun, to bring it to its necessary conclusion. He finds, in effect, no sensible metaphor for his life other than the anxiety that its journey return to Eden. Given the affinity between the literary metaphor and the psychological state that it describes, it is fair to assume that Rousseau's literary failure stems from a personal failure, which he in fact describes, though not in these terms; unlike Carlyle, Wordsworth, and Moore, Rousseau never matured beyond the adolescent phase. He has no clear sense of identity to describe. He can reach no end to his journey, no sensible place of return.

The mythic journey based on initiation rites, which are external manifestations of and directives for internal developments, is of particular value to autobiography because it combines personal and public truths with the means for expressing those truths. The case of Rousseau would suggest, however, that the metaphor cannot function any further than its description of the man it represents. It is not an autonomous entity to which the narrative life may be made to conform. Rather, it springs from the original life, makes sense of that life, and cannot function beyond the sense that it makes.

4. Maturity: Conversion or Descent into the Underworld

Despite its apparently religious context, conversion, like the journey or lost innocence, can be traced back to the time of pagan literature and early mythology, where it describes descent into the underworld. As part of the heroic journey, it explores identity and purpose. Like the myth of Eden, it enriches the meanings of birth and death. Like the metaphors of Eden and the heroic journey, furthermore, conversion derives from a specific psychological condition that is not as inevitable as childhood or adolescence but is, nonetheless, very common. This is a condition of identity crisis, self-doubt, and despair, followed by a dramatic sense of resurrection to a clear self and a clear purpose. Whereas the journey, however, describes the process of self-discovery, conversion describes recognition of the self in terms that frequently suggest discovery of an apparently objective meaning in life, a meaning that is in some fundamental sense different from what had been assumed to be the case. It represents a reversal whereby Teufelsdröckh, for example, discovers that he is born not of the devil but of God, that he is not alien but part of the world. Equally, it represents a reversal simply in the psychological condition it describes; Wordsworth makes no new discovery about who he is, but he regains the equilibrium that allows him to be a poet. By replacing identity crisis with a sense of self and of purpose, conversion centers on the realization of that crucial aspect of the maturing process noted earlier in discussion of the journey, the satisfactory harmony between the individual and his environment. Neither the meaning ascribed to life nor the process of the conversion need have any grounding in religion beyond the contribution made by religion to the metaphor.

Just as the language of religion can provide an analogue

for secular experience, so Christianity borrows from classical sources the metaphors that most effectively describe common experiences. Christian pilgrims, seeking "ferne halwes, kowthe in sondry londes," represent a rephrasing of the ancient story of man's inevitable journey. For pagan and Christian alike, that journey takes him through the Valley of the Shadow of Death. For many knights pricking on the plain, hell or the underworld is the central place of initiation. Death is the monster confronting the hero. Victory is not experienced as survival but as a second birth. "It was like an abnormal birth," writes Saint Paul, "and the last enemy to be abolished is death."[1]

Writing about themes of descent as a common feature of the poetic imagination, Frye describes a "night world, often a dark and labyrinthine world of caves and shadows where the forest has turned subterranean. . . . If the meander-and-descent patterns of paleolithic caves, along with the paintings on their walls, have anything like the same kind of significance, we are here retracing what are, so far as we know, the oldest imaginative steps of humanity."[2] Frye enlarges the scope for this imaginative journey with his reminder that the dark and labyrinthine world is "either the bowels and belly of an earth-monster, or the womb of an earth-mother, or both."[3] He cites Tiamat of Mesopotamian myth, the primeval creature whose body formed the created world. We have seen how Maui, hero of Polynesian legend, failed in his attempt to travel through the body of death and return with the gift of life. Frye calls this "disappearance of the hero, a theme which often takes the form of *sparagmos* or tearing to pieces."[4] Whether the hero is destroyed, in which case his achievement becomes a posthumous bequest, or simply wounded before returning to the world above, this encounter with some form of death is central to initiation. This central trial of heroic strength and the reward of such heroic effort with special power or knowledge may be described as the main features of conversion.

In ancient times, this trial is made of Orpheus for love, of Herakles as an act of heroism, of Odysseus and Aeneas for understanding sufficient to save both themselves and their people. When Odysseus learns that he can only reach home after consulting Teiresias in the underworld, he throws himself down on Circe's bed to weep. "This news broke my heart," he tells Alcinous. "I sat down on the bed and wept. I had no further use for life, no wish to see the sunshine any more."[5] His sailors hear the news with equal despondency. Yet as Odysseus tells his mother's shade, he has no choice but to meet the dead. He learns about his future from Teiresias. He receives intelligent advice from his friends among the dead. They are sources of finite experience that is easy to understand because it is complete. For Odysseus and Aeneas, the knowledge they gain from the underworld determines the conclusion of their stories.

Christ, too, the redemptive hero of a new era, descends into hell, rises again on the third day, and ascends into heaven to live in power and glory for ever more. His role in this context is directly comparable to that of Yama in the Hindu myth of creation or Maui in the Polynesian myth. He conquers death to save his fellow men from dying. Later Christians have tended to internalize heaven and hell; it forms part of the landscape of human nature. Milton, with all his careful geography, presents hell as an inescapable state of mind. For Mephistopheles, even Faust's study is hell and he cannot escape. Fallen man contains both good and evil within himself, and conversion to a higher state involves the harrowing of a very private hell—private, and yet, as the longevity of the metaphor would suggest, universal.

Though conversion was not a common religious phenomenon in the days when gods were lenient and traveled in herds, it was, as A. D. Nock points out, a frequent aspect of philosophical training.[6] The schools of philosophy were competitive and claimed the loyalty of their adherents; they also offered answers to the troubled inquirer. Conversion, representing a dramatic, exclusive, or speeded-up version of man's journey through hell to the achievement of some invaluable perception is not exclusively a by-product of Christianity. The names used by Christians for what they find simply differ from those of the early philosophers or, later, from the terminology of the secular experience in which revelation leads to knowledge.

William James, exploring the psychology of conversion, calls it "a normal adolescent phenomenon, incidental to the passage from the child's small universe to the wider intellectual and spiritual life of maturity."[7] Carl Jung, for example, describes a momentous experience on his way home from school one day:

> Suddenly for a single moment I had the overwhelming impression of having just emerged from a dense cloud. I knew all at once: now I am *myself*! It was as if a wall of mist were at my back, and behind that wall there was not yet an "I." But at this moment *I came upon myself.* Previously I had existed too, but everything had merely happened to me. Now I happened to myself. Now I knew: I am myself now, now I exist. Previously I had been willed to do this and that; now *I* willed.[8]

As a manifestation of "an active subliminal self,"[9] such conversion frequently occurs in older people too. Dante specifies middle age for his dark night of the soul:

> Midway this way of life we're bound upon,
> I woke to find myself in a dark wood,
> Where the right road was wholly lost and gone.[10]

William James describes such loss of direction, confusion, lack of hope or purpose, and sense of divided will as virtually commonplace:

> Now in all of us, however constituted . . . does the normal evolution of character chiefly consist in the straightening out and unifying of the inner self. The higher and the lower feelings, the useful and the erring impulses, begin by being a comparative chaos within us—they must end by forming a stable system of functions in right subordination.[11]

The more intense, sensitive, or psychopathic the character, the more likely is extreme turmoil at this stage, bringing conviction of sin, self-loathing, or despair. "Were we writing the story of the mind from the purely natural history point of view, with no religious interest whatever," he continues, "we should still have to write down man's liability to sudden and complete conversion as one of his most curious peculiarities."[12]

Conversion, in other words, is a psychological phenomenon common in all ages, exclusive to no creed or even, indeed, to religion. It is commonly experienced as a state of despair or total apathy, followed by disgust, trial, or crisis, and then by a new illumination, James's "sense of higher control," a positive ecstasy. It finds a biological parallel in fever, where the term crisis is also used and where closeness to death is superseded by recovery into life. It is also common for the religious convert to speak of his crisis as an illness and his completed conversion as a return to health. Still struggling with doubts, for example, Saint Augustine refers to "those whose healthful affections I heard of, that they had resigned themselves wholly to thee to be cured."[13] Dickens frequently passes his characters through a serious illness before they can see the world and their part in it clearly.[14]

Whether represented by fever, an arduous descent into the depths of the world or the depths of oneself, or merely a sense of confusion and despair, the process of conversion entails finding the appropriate answer. Dante explores the depths of hell, interpreting the universe, as Dorothy Sayers puts it, in terms of his own self-exploring, and finds both Beatrice and God. Odysseus rediscovers Ithaca. Aeneas ensures the foundation of Rome. Saint Augustine is shown the absolute simplicity of the choice he has to make. Conversion, in other words, entails the journey through hell, but it also ensures a way out again. Conversion hinges upon a crucial discovery about oneself, or the purpose of life, or the meaning of the universe, that entirely alters the convert.

Saint Paul, of course, is the arch-convert of the Christian era; he establishes a clear model for others to copy. Rousseau, who is "converted" to Catholicism in book 2 of his *Confessions* and converts back to Protestantism in book 8, makes little of either incident. His truly important conversion is to the philosophy of life for which he became distinguished, and, in describing this, he follows the stereotype for religious conversion established by Saint Paul. To this conversion, Rousseau ascribes a Pauline passion and detail.

Walking to Vincennes on a hot day, he reads the topic title for the Dijon essay prize: "Has the progress of the sciences and arts done more to corrupt morals or improve them?" "The moment I read this," he writes, "I beheld another universe and became another man" (*Confessions*, p. 327). He reaches Vincennes in a state bordering on delirium. From that moment, all is lost. He has become too hot on his walk and this leads to the recurrence of his old kidney problems. He suffers fever. He then renounces his post as cashier to the receiver-general of finance. His reform leads him to break the fetters of prejudice with no fear of public opinion. He gives up gold lace, white stockings, his sword, his watch, even his fine linen. He now consciously rationalizes the surliness for which he became noted to harmonize not with his inability to handle social graces but with his new program of independence and indifference to opinion.

Rousseau describes "this intoxication" with virtue as bringing such exhilaration that "there was nothing great or beautiful that can enter into the heart of man, between earth and heaven, of which I was not capable. . . . I was truly transformed" (*Confessions*, p. 388). Unfortunately for Rousseau, however, this state of euphoric confidence lasts for only six years; when it leaves him, he falls below his former level of self-assurance, suffering thereafter continuous oscillations of soul, a permanent state of disturbance.

Apart from such relatively idiosyncratic personal experiences recorded in literature, whole sects of Christians receive adherents only after an avowedly Pauline conversion. Edmund Gosse describes how the Plymouth Brethren wait until the path of salvation has been revealed

in such an aspect that [the converts] would be enabled instantaneously to accept it. They would take it consciously, as one takes a gift from the hand that offers it. This act of taking was the process of conversion, and the person who so accepted was a child of God now, although a single minute ago he had been a child of wrath. The very root of human nature had to be changed, and in the majority of cases, this change was sudden, patent, palpable.[15]

William Hale White is rather more cynical than Gosse about such routine conversion:

> Before I went to college I had to be "admitted." In most Dissenting communities there is a singular ceremony called "admission." . . . It is a declaration that a certain change called conversion has taken place in the soul. . . . As may be expected, it is very often inaccurately picturesque, and is framed after the model of the journey to Damascus. A sinner, for example, who swears at his pious wife, and threatens to beat her, is suddenly smitten with giddiness and awful pains.[16] He throws himself on his knees before her, and thenceforward he is a "changed character." (*EL*, pp. 56–58)

In *The Autobiography of Mark Rutherford*, written some thirty years earlier than *The Early Life*, Hale White sharply contrasts this mockery of conversion so common in dissenting chapels with the reality that he and many like him experience, as if beyond the call of duty, as an unexpected movement of the soul toward salvation: "Nothing particular happened to me," he writes, "till I was about fourteen, when I was told it was time I became converted" (*Ab.*, p. 11). From this cynical beginning, he elaborates the real meaning of conversion, the fact that conversion, even based on the Pauline model, can be entirely true:

> There may have been prompt release of unsuspected powers, and as prompt an imprisonment for ever of meaner weaknesses and tendencies; the result being literally a putting off of the old, and a putting on of the new man. (*Ab.*, p. 12)

Not only does Rutherford believe this, but he also illustrates it in human terms:

> The exact counterpart of conversion, as it was understood by the apostles, may be seen whenever a man is redeemed from vice by attachment to some woman whom he worships, or when a girl is reclaimed from idleness and vanity by becoming a mother.
>
> (*Ab.*, pp. 12–13)

Having given real meaning to the term conversion, Rutherford's cynicism about his own conversion is acidic; comparison with the emotional reality is used to convict him personally of meanness of spirit and the community at large of gross hypocrisy:

> I knew that I had to be "a child of God," and after a time professed myself to be one. . . . I was obliged to declare myself convinced of sin; convinced of the efficacy of the atonement; convinced that I was forgiven; convinced that the Holy Ghost was shed abroad in my heart; and convinced of a great many other things which were the merest phrases.   (*Ab.*, p. 13)

Such confession of sin and conversion, Rutherford notes, was never vivid or valuable. Admission essentially meant clanship, not enlightenment. After all, if Brother Holderness, the traveling draper who reveled in the humility of finding his soul a mass of putrefying sores, had actually had one indiscretion brought home to him, he would have been visited with suspension or expulsion.

Rutherford describes his formal conversion in terms that contrast its finest possibilities and the aridity of the particular that is endorsed by the whole community. It is also effectively contrasted with his truly serious conversion, which, like Rousseau's, is nonreligious but refers to the Pauline model. On one day in his third year at theological college,

> a day I remember as well as Paul must have remembered afterwards the day on which he went to Damascus, I happened to find amongst a parcel of books a volume of

> poems in paper boards. It was called "Lyrical Ballads,"
> and I read first one and then the whole book. It con-
> veyed to me no new doctrine, and yet the change it
> wrought in me could only be compared with that which
> is said to have been wrought on Paul himself by the Di-
> vine apparition. (*Ab.*, p. 23)

It brings to birth in Rutherford a habit of inner reference, a
dislike for business that does not touch the soul, a recreation
of the supreme divinity.

It is this kind of experience of conversion that is rooted in
human psychology. It takes many forms, but the variations
tend to merge into a pattern that remains recognizable whatever the occasion. Nock discusses the way in which different
accounts of conversion do not represent "the literal truth—
at least not the whole truth, for a process of conversion as
looked at afterwards by the man himself commonly assumes a
new colour. Few of us are capable of entirely faithful autobiography. Yet the main lines are clear and significant."[17] Or,
as Sallust puts it: "All this did not happen at any one time but
always is: the mind sees the whole process at once, words tell
of part first, part second."[18]

Even in the mind, before the act of writing, a private experience of conversion must be made to conform to a recognizable generality. Jonathan Edwards knew this:

> A rule received and established by common consent has
> a very great, though to many persons an insensible in-
> fluence in forming their notions of the process of their
> own experience. . . . Very often their experience at first
> appears like a confused chaos, but then those parts are
> selected which bear the nearest resemblance to such par-
> ticular steps as are insisted on; and these are dwelt upon
> in their thoughts, and spoken of from time to time,[19] till
> they grow more and more conspicuous in their view,
> and other parts which are neglected grow more and
> more obscure. Thus what they have experienced is in-
> sensibly strained, so as to bring it to an exact confor-
> mity to the scheme already established in their minds.[20]

Just as the journey can lead to Ithaca or Rome or the Celestial City or the center of self, so conversion can be to a philosophy or a religious faith, a secular perception of self and the world, a calling, or the meaning of life. Whatever the specific content, the form remains much the same.

Furthermore, conversion fulfills prophecy by making evident what was always there. Like a prophet, the convert writes from the vantage point of his converted state; like the narrators of the *Odyssey* or *The Quest of the Holy Grail*, like every autobiographer, he knows as he tells his story what has happened at its end. Having reached the high-water mark of his spiritual capacity, the convert orders his experience so that it is meaningful for all men and he himself is merely representative or exemplary. Having found the answers, he must proclaim them to all who have ears to hear. If these men, like Lazarus come back from the dead, cannot tell us all, they do at least relate their death and rebirth in a manner that all can recognize.

At the center of the journey described by Wordsworth and Carlyle, each autobiographer places his own descent into the underworld. We have seen the successful conclusion of their journeys, the authority with which each autobiography concludes its exploration of identity and purpose. Here we shall look at the crisis that is central to each journey. For Wordsworth and Carlyle, as for Aeneas and Odysseus, this episode is central to the journey but functions also as a distinct episode in its own right. Its possible separation from the journey metaphor may be seen in its use by John Stuart Mill. Of all the autobiographies studied here, Mill's is the most prosaic, the least imaginative, the least likely to be influenced by literary conventions or the attractions of poetic license. Mill certainly does not see his childhood as Edenic or his life as a journey. However, he does describe what was most probably a nervous breakdown as a crisis of identity, as a conversion. Whereas Wordsworth and Carlyle use all the resources of the narrative pattern for the journey and include a central crisis of conversion as a descent into the underworld, Mill uses only that element that matches his descriptive needs. The only mythic metaphor in Mill's autobiography is that of his conversion.[21] Just as it seems fair to assume that Rousseau's narrative journey was prevented from reaching its necessary conclusion by its essential adherence to his psychological condition, so it seems plausible that Mill was driven by the urgency of his need to describe his mental crisis to use the particular pattern that could describe it most efficiently. Whereas Rousseau's inner life impeded his metaphor, Mill's inner life created one.

Mill, Wordsworth, and Carlyle were all exceptional men who received the hearing that prophets claim, who both led and represented their time, who wrote under the shadow of Goethe and were affected by Romantic self-consciousness and self-analysis. For all three, the objectified worship of *deus de deo* was transfigured into their individual selves holding the lamp and knocking at the door as "Ecce homo." All three men experienced some significant change of heart. All three write with a purpose and from a special point of view. In different styles and with different voices, all three present two selves and would be capable of saying that the early self had seen through a glass darkly, whereas the twice-born self saw clearly face to face. It is not, therefore, surprising to find the three of them listed in Thomas Hardy's notebook as authors to be turned to in times of despair.[22]

Commemorating the one hundredth anniversary of Mill's birth in 1906, Thomas Hardy recalls going as a young man to hear Mill speak. He and his friends knew Mill's *Liberty* by heart, and he was moved to hear the "religious sincerity of his speech" and to see the prophet who "stood bareheaded, and his vast pale brow, so thin-skinned as to show the blue veins, sloped back like a stretching upland, and conveyed to the observer a curious sense of perilous exposure."[23]

Mill: A Crisis of Identity

Mill was justified in assuming that the development of his mind would provide a useful record for his fellow men. He wrote it, accordingly, with great care, with many revisions over a wide span of time:

> It is in this way that all my books have been composed. They were always written at least twice over; a first draft of the entire work was completed to the very end of the subject, then the whole begun again *de novo*; but incorporating, in the second writing, all sentences and parts of sentences of the old draft which appeared as suitable to my purpose as anything which I could write in lieu of them. I have found great advantages in this system of double redaction. It combines, better than any other mode of composition, the freshness and vigour of the first conception with the superior precision and completeness resulting from prolonged thought.
>
> (*JSM*, p. 162)

As the autobiography of the development of a mind, this book receives much the same treatment as a system of logic and is quite as deliberate as an essay on liberty. Jack Stillinger's edition of the early draft, with annotations that give yet earlier readings of words, phrases, and even whole passages, indicates the rigor with which emotional biases were corrected to leave as clearly as possible a picture only of the mind, as well as the adjustments, either from discretion or from altered vision, that were made to the emphases.

Summarizing the quality of Mill's revisions in his introduction, Stillinger points to the increased detachment of style. Writing about the crisis in his mental history, for instance, Mill refers originally to onetime pleasures as now "indifferent or disgusting." He revised this phrase to read "insipid and indifferent," and finally added the comparison between his dejection and "the state . . . in which converts to Methodism usually are, when smitten by their first 'conviction of sin.'"[24] He begins, in other words, by defusing the quality of his own emotion and ends by detaching that emotion altogether from the specifically personal and objectifying the whole experience onto a pattern that contains and defines it. "In all probability," he also adds, "my case was by no means so peculiar as

I fancied it, and I doubt not that many others have passed through a similar state" (*JSM*, p. 111).

With revision, Mill shows increased awareness of an audience. He controls outbursts of egotism, omitting entirely or altering the terms in which he mentions his work and his part in discussions and debates. He substitutes generalities for experiences first given as specifically personal and omits many details. Stillinger comments that "it is a fuller and more varied life that he presents in the early draft."[25] More significantly, he tones down descriptions of his father, his family, and the more unfortunate aspects of his education. With an "access of charity" toward his father and his father's friends, Mill omits to mention his father's temper or the mocking caricatures with which he would correct his son's reading. Whereas Mill originally felt that the severity of his education, which made it an education of fear rather than of love, acted as an unfavorable moral agency on his boyhood, he later hesitates to pronounce whether he lost or gained by such severity.[26] By adding comparisons between his father and Bentham, Mill softens the final account into a virtual eulogy.

Similarly, the considerable handicaps that he originally attributes to his education receive less emphasis in the final version. He omits whole pages describing himself as totally unfit for everyday life and incapable of action or decision. Indeed, his dependence upon his father is revised within the text that remains. His "taught opinions," for example, become his "adopted opinions," suggesting some autonomy with which he can enlarge the basis of his intellectual creed.

The whole direction of each revision contributes to "the more formal and generalized character of the later version," the successive revisions within the early draft also showing "the same kind of progress from private to public, and from public to more public voice."[27] Mill himself might have felt this autobiography to be his closest approximation to a work of creative art, "for it is the artist alone in whose hands Truth becomes impressive and a living principle of action."[28] Action and usefulness were Mill's constant sources of purpose. Clearly, the objectivity he arrived at here, in writing of the personal and traumatic, becomes an artistic achievement. Mill never attains the quality of artistry that he learned to admire in Wordsworth and Carlyle, but he does achieve the wide accessibility that cannot be found in personal particulars but that exists in embodying archetypes.

Mill states the purpose of his autobiography at the very outset: it is to be a useful record of an unusual education; it may be of "interest and benefit" to note the successive stages of a mind that is always pressing forward; it fulfills his wish to acknowledge "the debts which [his] intellectual and moral development owes to other persons." His rigorous adherence to these three purposes is apparent in the very phrasing and never wavers at any point throughout the whole.[29] John Morley contrasts Mill's analysis of his mental history with the more frequent Sturm und Drang of the period and with conversions to transcendentalism. The *Autobiography* is not "a work of imagination or art, but . . . the practical record of the formation of an eminent thinker's mental habits and the succession of his mental attitudes; and the formation of such mental habits is not romance but the most arduous of real concerns."[30] Mill certainly never loses sight of the way in which his problems may also be problems for other people. Part of his purpose consists in making specific problems very clear. In the midst of his mental crisis, accordingly, he asserts that "the destiny of mankind in general was ever in my thoughts, and could not be separated from my own. I felt that the flaw in my life must be a flaw in life itself" (*JSM*, p. 114). Or, in other words, "if Bentham's theory of life can do so little for the individual, what can it do for society?"[31]

It is not surprising, then, to find his mental crisis presented very largely in terms of questions that arise and answers that are painfully found. He had been happy in his old purposes and methods until he awakened from such enjoyment as from a dream. The waking reality is described as stemming from an entirely rational question: if all the objects in his life were fulfilled, would he be happy? The distinct answer that he would not comes, notably, from an "irrepressible self-consciousness." This vague generality, however, is not allowed to take over in the description of events. His hopelessness leads to two eminently rational decisions: not to ask such questions that confuse means with ends and to cultivate the inner man. The first "now became the basis of my philosophy of life," and the second "became one of the cardinal points in my ethical and philosophical creed" (*JSM*, p. 113). After exposing himself to new influences, social and literary, he adds:

> If I am asked, what system of political philosophy I substituted for that which, as a philosophy, I had abandoned, I answer, no system: only a conviction that the true system was something much more complex and many-sided than I had previously had any idea of.
>
> (*JSM*, p. 123)

The explosive word "conviction" is toned down by the very reasonableness of its context.

Similarly, Mill's description of Saint-Simonian thinking about history provides a reasonable metaphor for his personal experience:

> During the organic periods (they said) mankind accept with firm conviction some positive creed, claiming jurisdiction over all their actions, and containing more or less of truth and adaptation to the needs of humanity. Under its influence they make all the progress compatible with the creed, and finally outgrow it; when a period follows of criticism and negation, in which mankind lose their old convictions without acquiring any new ones of a general or authoritative character, except the conviction that the old are false.   (*JSM*, p. 215)

Discussing Comte's "natural succession of three stages in every department of human knowledge," from theological to metaphysical to positive, Mill acknowledges the relevance of these theories on academic subjects to his own emotional unbalance. "This doctrine," he writes, "harmonized well with my existing notions, to which it seemed to give a scientific shape" (*JSM*, p. 126).

Given that Mill's explicit concerns are so emphatically

theoretical, it is a relief to find in his subsequent anxiety over philosophical necessity, which weighs on his existence like an incubus, an echo of Saint Augustine's equally intellectual but more intensely emotional concern with free will:

> Myself when I was deliberating upon serving the Lord my God now, as I had long purposed, it was I who willed, I who nilled, I, I myself. I neither willed entirely, nor nilled entirely. Therefore was I at strife with myself, and rent asunder by myself.[32]

Mill, however, despite the incubus, completes the episode with his usual restraint:

> The train of thought which had extricated me from this dilemma seemed to me, in after years, fitted to render a similar service to others; and it now forms the chapter on "Liberty and Necessity" in the concluding book of my *System of Logic*.[33]   (*JSM*, p. 129)

As we have seen, the form of Mill's crisis, as well as a number of the remedies that he finds for it, are more conventional and less intellectual than the main drift of this chapter in his autobiography would suggest. Though it is triggered by a simple question, it is a question asked at a time of exhaustion, when he "was in a dull state of nerves. . . . the state, I should think, in which converts to Methodism usually are, when smitten by their first 'conviction of sin'" (*JSM*, p. 107). The detachment that enables him to make such a quiet comparison only veils the quality of the allusion borne out by words like "converts" and "smitten," though he feels bound to place "conviction of sin" within quotation marks. He describes the "dry heavy dejection of the winter of 1826–1827," during which he did all things mechanically and from which he remembers "next to nothing." His tolerance of hopelessness was exhausted, he could not imagine living in such a state beyond the year, and then came his first relief.

In Mill's case, the exhaustion and apathy common in accounts of conversion take the form of an inability to feel any

emotion. He is quite clear that the lack arises from his education, that the "habit of analysis has the tendency to wear away
the feelings" (*JSM*, p. 109). For the first time he confronts
what he describes Bentham as totally ignoring, about half of
the "mental feelings" that human beings are capable of, "including all those of which the direct objects are states of their
own mind."[34] Like Louisa Gradgrind, he might cry to his
father: "'What have you done, O father, what have you done,
with the garden that should have bloomed once, in this great
wilderness here!'"[35] And he would also have had to add:
"'You have brought me to this. Save me by some other
means!'"[36] His problem, however, is even more serious, for
not only does he feel that his father is the last person to whom
he can turn but he also suffers from an inability to confide in
anyone at all. He thinks frequently of Macbeth's appeal to the
doctor, but "there was no one on whom I could build the
faintest hope of such assistance" (*JSM*, p. 108). Notably, the
doctor's reply to Macbeth is that the patient must minister to
himself, and this Mill does, involuntarily or, as he puts it,
accidentally:

> I was reading, accidentally, Marmontel's *Memoires*, and
> came to the passage which relates his father's death, the
> distressed position of the family, and the sudden inspira-
> tion by which he, then a mere boy, felt and made them
> feel that he would be everything to them—would supply
> the place of all that they had lost. A vivid conception of
> the scene and its feelings came over me, and I was
> moved to tears. From this moment my burden grew
> lighter.   (*JSM*, p. 111)

Emotional release through a reading with which he could
obviously identify very powerfully gives evidence of what William James has called the "active subliminal life" and explains
the suddenness of the transition from apathy and despair to
revitalized feeling. Notably, Marmontel's inspiration is also
sudden. This passage about replacing a dead father is as appropriate for Mill as that about putting away concupiscence is

for Saint Augustine. The reaction, too, is comparable. Saint Augustine's conversion is immediate: "Instantly at the end of this sentence, by a light as it were of serenity infused into my heart, all the darkness of doubt vanished away."[37] For Mill there is also "a small ray of light" and his burden grows lighter from "this moment." Like Christian, he weeps on losing his "burden." More like Christian than like Saint Augustine, however, Mill's conversion is only partial and needs further nourishment.

The whole conception of Mill's *Autobiography* assumes the development of character through association and education. So fully did he learn about life from his father that his crisis stems precisely from the causes for which one might expect his father to despair. True to the careful planning of the book, Mill creates a sense of causal necessity by describing his father, some fifty pages before his own conversion, in these terms:

> He had . . . scarcely any belief in pleasure. . . . The greater number of miscarriages in life he considered to be attributable to the overvaluing of pleasures. . . . He thought human life a poor thing at best, after the freshness of youth and of unsatisfied curiosity had gone by. . . . He would sometimes say that if life were made what it might be, by good government and good education, it would be worth having; but he never spoke with anything like enthusiasm even of that possibility.
>
> (*JSM*, p. 54)

Not only, then, is the crisis comparable to classic examples of religious conversion but Mill also creates a sense of causal necessity by the very ordering of his account. These structural factors, combined with a stylistic detachment and restraint comparable to John Hersey's account of the bombing of Hiroshima, create an account that is strangely moving. (Both Mill and Hersey write like dispassionate reporters about appalling human suffering. In both cases the discrepancy between the experience and the style of the narration shocks the reader.)

Carlyle's reference to the *Autobiography* as that of a machine is only superficially true. He was ignoring the lack of authority that pervades Mill's account of his crisis, the recurring qualifications that he saw or thought he saw and so on. Twice he admits to embarrassment at his "in no way honourable distress." And his quotations from Coleridge, like his discussions of Carlyle and Wordsworth, derive explicitly from later experiences than those that they help to describe. Certainly rigor and concentration of purpose are apparent in Mill's writing. There is no irony or humor. Nevertheless, construction and style together work to invalidate Carlyle's conclusion and to support Morley's description of "the pale flame of strenuous self-possession."[38]

Wordsworth: Nurture of the Creative Soul

Mill writes of Wordsworth's poetry as a medicine for his state of mind, partly because it "seemed to be the very culture of the feelings, which I was in quest of," and partly because "I found that he too had had similar experience to mine; that he also had felt that the first freshness of youthful enjoyment of life was not lasting; but that he had sought for compensation, and found it, in the way in which he was now teaching me to find it" (*JSM*, p. 116). Like Mill, too, Wordsworth writes an autobiography of his own mind, "turning the mind in upon herself" (*Prelude*, 3:113). He also has a distinct purpose; he wishes to examine how far nature and education have qualified him to write a "literary work that might live" (*Prelude*, Advertisement). Like Mill's *Autobiography*, *The Prelude* was heavily revised, with many of the same results: a tendency to generalize where earlier the text had been personal; a tendency to use the passive voice and so achieve less intimacy with a wider audience; a general toning down of states of feeling and youthful opinions so that, like Mill's revised presentation of his father, the later version of *The Prelude* reads as an implicit criticism of the writer's first impressions.

Wordsworth is quite as rigorous as Mill in excluding or adapting and rearranging materials in order to achieve his entirely single-minded purpose. Written in part to test his recovery from deep depression, *The Prelude* aims to test and prove the survival of Wordsworth's poetic gift. It feeds on its theme. It deals with the rites of passage of the poet, covering the birth, growth, baptism, and confirmation of the poet's mind. It must accordingly include the most serious trial of all, the bleak depression that calls the quality of life in doubt. For Mill, such depression suggests that life is meaningless; for Wordsworth, it threatens his source of life, his creative soul.

Conscious of his literary sources, Wordsworth presents his valley of the shadow of death in two different ways; he introduces an equivalent to the mythic underworld and, quite separately, a recurring theme of personal conversion. The first is represented by the city of London. It is shaped by the mind but retains, nonetheless, an objective character of fact and place. The second is represented by moments of unusual insight that alter his life, his "spots of time," but most extendedly by the poet's mental crisis during the French Revolution. The Revolution was certainly an objective fact and certainly an apt objective correlative for turmoil of the inner man. Yet this second experience, compared with the visit to London, is essentially internalized, a matter for the private soul and psyche. Of his strength while in London, Wordsworth writes:

> Lo! everything that was indeed divine
> Retained its purity inviolate,
> Nay brighter shone, by this portentous gloom
> Set off.   (*Prelude*, 8:655–58)

Indeed,

> Neither vice nor guilt,
> Debasement undergone by body or mind,
> Nor all the misery forced upon my sight,
> Misery not lightly passed, but sometimes scanned
> Most feelingly, could overthrow my trust
> In what we *may* become.   (*Prelude*, 8:645–50)

In London, like Aeneas in the underworld, Odysseus encountering the dead, or Dante in hell, Wordsworth is an affected but inviolate observer. Charon's bark would sink with him because his person is heavier than the shades he sees around him. In France, on the other hand, his experience of the turmoil around him is internalized to such an extent that it escapes from his conscious control; it takes the form of nightmare:

> Then suddenly the scene
> Changed, and the unbroken dream entangled me
> In long orations, which I strove to plead
> Before unjust tribunals,—with a voice
> Labouring, a brain confounded, and a sense,
> Death-like, of treacherous desertion, felt
> In the last place of refuge—my own soul.
>
> (*Prelude*, 10:409–15)

Wordsworth comes to London, as all travelers come to their underworld, in the middle of his journey. He summarizes the experience at the end of book 8, describing himself as a "curious traveller, who, from open day, / Hath passed with torches into some huge cave" (*Prelude*, 8:560–61). Like Aeneas and Odysseus, he is "seeking knowledge at that time" (*Prelude*, 8:599). As for Odysseus, Aeneas, and Dante, moreover, the underworld commingles substance and shadow, light and dark, specters and ghostly semblances. It consists both of fact and of vision, or of fact transformed into vision as the poet "sees, or thinks he sees" (*Prelude*, 8:565) that shifting panorama in which he himself remains the only solid point of reference.

In book 7, too, where Wordsworth details his residence in London, he describes himself as pleased "to pitch a vagrant tent" (*Prelude*, 7:56). London as hell is not part of his condition, merely part of his experience. Its labyrinths and hubbub provide a context for the streams of humanity,

> The comers and the goers face to face,
> Face after face.   (*Prelude*, 7:156–57)

Noting among the crowd "all specimens of man" (*Prelude*, 7:221), the poet feels that

> 'The face of every one
> That passes by me is a mystery!'   (*Prelude*, 7:628–29)

Like Eliot, whose

> crowd flowed over London Bridge, so many
> I had not thought death had undone so many,[39]

Wordsworth watches

> Until the shapes before my eyes became
> A second-sight procession, such as glides
> Over still mountains, or appears in dreams.
> (*Prelude*, 7:632–34)

Part of the knowledge derived from such rich but passive experience entails the transformation of external reality into poetic vision:

> Though reared upon the base of outward things,
> Structures like these the excited spirit mainly
> Builds for herself.   (*Prelude*, 7:650–52)

Indeed, he fears that the places, people, and events

> Are falsely catalogued; things that are, are not
> As the mind answers to them, or the heart
> Is prompt, or slow, to feel.   (*Prelude*, 7:669–71)

He turns, accordingly, to Saint Bartholomew's Fair as an epitome of the "blank confusion,"

> Of what the mighty City is herself,
> To thousands upon thousands of her sons,
> Living amid the same perpetual whirl
> Of trivial objects, melted and reduced
> To one identity, by differences
> That have no law, no meaning, and no end—

> Oppression, under which even highest minds
> Must labour, whence the strongest are not free.
> > (*Prelude*, 7:722–30)

Though the picture weary the eye, however, and prove "an unmanageable sight," it can be controlled by the poetic vision, by him who sees the parts with a feeling for the whole, who has, in other words, a context that makes sense of bewildering variety.

Wordsworth's context derives in part from the rural setting of his childhood; he makes sense of confusion by contrasting it with organic health and harmony. In general, he never loses sight in his mind's eye of the natural world from which he comes into this world of the dead. Specifically, he juxtaposes Saint Bartholomew's Fair, representing the senseless confusion of city life, with the happy rustic fair at Helvellyn. Wordsworth derives his clearest context, however, from the mythic descent of the hero into the underworld; with this he transforms chaotic experience into an episode that is coherent, useful, and readily understood. Use of a clear paradigm helps also to maintain Wordsworth's detachment from London. He is profoundly affected by isolated incidents like that of the blind beggar propped against a wall, but even this episode works for his strength; it confirms his sense of what it is that constitutes identity. London strengthens the poet; it does not weaken or negate the creative soul.

Wordsworth's shock during the French Revolution, however, is essentially destructive. Just as Mill discovers with sudden clarity that Benthamite doctrines will not make people happy, so Wordsworth discovers, through violence done to every hope and expectation, that no Godwinian rule of reason is going to redeem mankind.

> O pleasant exercise of hope and joy!
> For mighty were the auxiliars which then stood
> Upon our side, us who were strong in love.
> Bliss was it in that dawn to be alive,
> But to be young was very Heaven! O times,

> In which the meagre, stale, forbidding ways
> Of custom, law, and statute, took at once
> The attraction of a country in romance!
> When Reason seemed the most to assert her rights
> When most intent on making of herself
> A prime enchantress—to assist the work,
> Which then was going forward in her name!
> Not favoured spots alone, but the whole Earth,
> The beauty wore of promise—. (*Prelude*, 11:105–18)

In face of such aspirations and such assumptions of common rejoicing, England's hostility to the Republic comes as a blow to Wordsworth's moral nature. Then the perversion of the Revolution itself into an irrational carnage shatters his faith in any possible rule of reason:

> A veil had been
> Uplifted; why deceive ourselves? in sooth,
> 'Twas even so. . . . (*Prelude*, 11:266–68)

Isolated and disillusioned, Wordsworth, like Mill, explores all possible means of making sense of his life:

> So I fared,
> Dragging all precepts, judgments, maxims, creeds,
> Like culprits to the bar; calling the mind,
> Suspiciously, to establish in plain day
> Her titles and her honours . . .
> . . . till, demanding formal *proof*,
> And seeking it in everything, I lost
> All feeling of conviction, and, in fine,
> Sick, wearied out with contrarieties,
> Yielded up moral questions in despair.
> (*Prelude*, 11:293–305)

For Wordsworth, as for Mill, violent loss of the intellectual convictions by which he lives leads to an emotional crisis and despair:

> This was the crisis of that strong disease,
> This the soul's last and lowest ebb; I drooped,

Deeming our blessed reason of least use
Where wanted most.   (*Prelude*, 11:306–9)

Mill's recovery begins with an imaginative and emotional response to the idea of replacing a dead father and is then nurtured by Wordsworth's culture of the feelings. Depressed, bewildered, refusing to accept the options of gay diversion or of idleness, Wordsworth turns to abstract science as an area in which the powers of reason cannot be disturbed. However, Dorothy saves him from the aridity of this direction, crossing his mind as a brook crosses a road or, as we have seen, like fertilizing water in a wasteland. She nurtures his creative soul by maintaining his intercourse with his true self:

                    for, though bedimmed and changed
Much, as it seemed, I was no further changed
Than as a clouded and a waning moon:
She whispered still that brightness would return,
She, in the midst of all, preserved me still
A Poet, made me seek beneath that name,
And that alone, my office upon earth.
                                        (*Prelude*, 11:342–48)

Wordsworth's conversion comes as a gradual return to his former equanimity. Nature, too, his original nurse, leads him

                    back through opening day
To those sweet counsels between head and heart
Whence grew that genuine knowledge, fraught with
          peace.   (*Prelude*, 11:352–54)

Saving intercourse with his true self, like "sweet counsels between head and heart," brings peace essentially because it restores the imagination and returns the poet to his former strength until he stands again in nature's presence, "a sensitive being, a *creative* soul" (*Prelude*, 12:207, Wordsworth's italics).

Wordsworth defines "creative soul" by describing the renovating virtue inherent in isolated experiences of conversion, or "spots of time." Every "spot of time," like Saint Augustine's "trembling glance," is a form of conversion bringing its own sudden discovery. Each experience, as one would expect, has to do with the making of a poet, just as each "trembling glance" for Saint Augustine is part of the process of making a Christian. In each case, the introduction is prosaic, the style incorporating the vacancy or apathy that precedes revelation. The restraint apparent in this literary technique acts, as it does in Mill, to balance and at the same time intensify the quality of emotion so that the natural and the apocalyptic are one and the same.

Such spots of time, the poet finds, are likely to occur

> Among those passages of life that give
> Profoundest knowledge to what point, and how,
> The mind is lord and master—outward sense
> The obedient servant of her will.   (*Prelude*, 12:219–23)

What the mind can create from a scene or an incident, whether it is a blind beggar, a deserted gibbet, or a sheep and a blasted hawthorn bush, is more significant than such scenes or incidents can be by themselves. Through such creative perception at crucial moments, Wordsworth discovers a replacement for Godwinian enlightenment, a conviction that feeling and emotion give importance to the situation, that no situation is significant unless it is made so by the poet's perception. The world he creates in poetry, like the bright moonlight breaking through the dripping fog on Snowdon, reveals higher truths than reason alone can command. Imagination, in truth,

> Is but another name for absolute power
> And clearest insight, amplitude of mind,
> And Reason in her most exalted mood.
>
> (*Prelude*, 14:190–92)

Endowed with this important understanding, he attains prophetic power. As a prophet of nature, he will teach men, as Mill puts it, to find compensation in the way in which he found it, or, in his own words:

> what we have loved,
> Others will love, and we will teach them how;
> Instruct them how the mind of man becomes
> A thousand times more beautiful than the earth
> On which he dwells, above this frame of things
> (Which, 'mid all revolution in the hopes
> And fears of men, doth still remain unchanged)
> In beauty exalted, as it is itself
> Of quality and fabric more divine.

(*Prelude*, 14:446–54)

Carlyle: From Crisis to Rebirth

The unfathered vapor of Wordsworth's imagination (*Prelude*, 6:595–640) becomes the dripping fog at the base of Mount Snowdon that precedes his final vision. It is like the vapor rising from the bowels of the earth in which the Delphic oracle saw truths invisible to common men, and it is absorbed by Carlyle into the very quality of his prose. The timeless and apocalyptic quality of Wordsworth's experience in the Simplon Pass ("Of first, and last, and midst, and without end") is paralleled by Teufelsdröckh's Everlasting No and Yea. Like Wordsworth and Mill, Carlyle writes from the basis of a personal experience in which he had to "bear [his] pain as Christian did his pack in *Pilgrim's Progress*, strapped on too tightly for throwing off."[40] Like Wordsworth and Mill, he also reworked his account, in his case from a series of articles into a novel, though indeed "properly *like* nothing yet extant."[41] It is a work of conscious artistry and deliberate, though factually based, fiction.

Teufelsdröckh's crisis of despair and conversion to action is central to his journey. Like Wordsworth's London, it falls in the middle of the book, the traditional location for the underworld. Like Mill, Teufelsdröckh is in a state of crisis, not under a cloud but under a "strange nebulous envelopment." His doubt darkens into unbelief, and loss of faith is loss of everything. Like Mill, Teufelsdröckh cries, "'Only this I know,

If what thou namest Happiness be our true aim, then are we all astray'" (*SR*, 2:160). Teufelsdröckh's problem is a "certain inarticulate self-consciousness"; in Mill's case, this is "irrepressible." For Teufelsdröckh, as for Mill and Louisa Gradgrind, there is not, in the wide world, any true bosom he can press trustfully to his, and he must keep a lock upon his lips. Like Mill, Teufelsdröckh records:

> To me the Universe was all void of Life, of Purpose, of Volition, even of Hostility: it was one huge, dead, immeasurable Steam-engine, rolling on, in its dead indifference, to grind me limb from limb.   (*SR*, 2:164)

Only a "certain aftershine" of Christianity, coupled perhaps with indolence, saves him from suicide. He is obsessed with fear.

For Teufelsdröckh, as for Mill, the actual crisis occurs in one paragraph:

> Full of such humour, and perhaps the miserablest man in the whole French Capital or Suburbs, was I, one Sultry Dog-day, after much perambulation, toiling along the dirty little *Rue Saint-Thomas de l'Enfer*,[42] among civic rubbish enough, in a close atmosphere, and over pavements hot as Nebuchadnezzar's Furnace; whereby doubtless my spirits were little cheered; when, all at once, there rose a Thought in me, and I asked myself: "What *art* thou afraid of?"[43]   (*SR*, 2:166–67)

His courage rises at the question and at the answers that he gives himself until, as he continues, "there rushed like a stream of fire over my whole soul; and I shook base Fear away from me forever." The irrepressible, inarticulate self-consciousness finds strength and voice so that "my whole ME stood up, in native God-created majesty, and with emphasis recorded its Protest." Whereas the Devil had called him a fatherless outcast, he is now able to reply that he is free, and his "Baphometic Fire-Baptism" enables him to begin to be a man directly.

The phoenix rising from the ashes of his former self is made a metaphor for the twice-born man. As with both Mill and Wordsworth, however, the conversion is not complete, and Teufelsdröckh must pass through the Centre of Indifference before reaching the Everlasting Yea. He continues his pilgrimage, taking note of politics, books, and war. Internally, he is evolving a course in practical philosophy. Externally, he is acquiring incredible knowledge of all knowable things. The editor comments on the value of Teufelsdröckh's "lucid intervals" and notes later that "the symptoms continue promising":

> We should rather say that Legion, or the Satanic School, was now pretty well extirpated and cast out, but next to nothing introduced in its room; whereby the heart remains, for the while, in a quiet but no comfortable state. (*SR*, 2:181)

Like Mill and Saint Augustine, Teufelsdröckh struggles next with the problem of necessity and freedom. Yet the image is consciously Christlike. Forty days in the wilderness present a barely endurable temptation. He is cast, however, into a healing sleep, evocative of that sleep from which the fever patient, having suffered his crisis, wakes into health. Notably, "the heavy dreams rolled gradually away, and [he] awoke to a new Heaven and a new Earth" (*SR*, 2:186). "'The Universe,'" he discovers, "'is not dead and demoniacal, a charnel-house with spectres;[44] but godlike, and my Father's!'" (*SR*, 2:188).

Just as the fatherless outcast feels he has a father, so he who yearns for a true bosom to press to his own calls now to his fellow men: "'O my Brother, my Brother, why cannot I shelter thee in my bosom, and wipe away all tears from thy eyes!'" (*SR*, 2:188). Like Mill, he is now concerned not with happiness as an aim but with the means by which a shoeblack can be made happy, and he feels, like Mill, an urgency to "'work while it is called Today; for the Night cometh, wherein no man can work'" (*SR*, 2:197).

Mill made little of the manuscript of *Sartor Resartus* but read it later in *Fraser's Magazine* "with enthusiastic admiration and the keenest delight" (*JSM*, p. 132). Yet he says of

Carlyle's early works: "What truths they contained, though of the very kind which I was already receiving from other quarters, were presented in a form and vesture less suited than any other to give them access to a mind trained as mine had been" (*JSM*, pp. 131–32). Carlyle's training, in total contrast to Mill's, results in "a haze of poetry and German metaphysics." Yet when their attitudes are traced through their two accounts of conversion, the parallels are striking, and there can be no doubt that they arrived at many of the same conclusions from radically different beginnings. Carlyle introduced himself to Mill as to "another Mystic," and Mill, humbly denying his own power, felt in Carlyle not a philosophy to instruct but a poetry to animate:

> I did not . . . deem myself a competent judge of Carlyle. I felt that he was a poet, and that I was not; that he was a man of intuition, which I was not; and that as such, he not only saw many things long before me, which I could only when they were pointed out to me, hobble after and prove, but that it was highly probable he could see many things which were not visible to me even after they were pointed out.   (*JSM*, pp. 132–33)

The things that Carlyle points out in the conversion of Teufelsdröckh, however, are different essentially only in manner of presentation. The philosophical concerns are largely the same, and the movement from despair to crisis, both immediate and protracted, and then to final illumination is common to both their works.

Although *Sartor Resartus* appeared in 1834, nearly thirty years after Wordsworth first drafted *The Prelude* and eight years after the beginning of Mill's crisis, it was the first of these accounts to be published. Together, they span the center of the nineteenth century, with the revised *Prelude* appearing in 1850 and Mill's *Autobiography* in 1873. Whereas it is possible that these men influenced each other's accounts, it seems more important to recognize the metaphor that all three used. It claims wide recognition because it contains a psychological truth and therefore becomes the available form in which three very different writers can present that truth. The conventional elements apparent even in so restrained a work as Mill's serve to verify that truth for narrator and reader alike.

All three men notably confine themselves to the development of a mind. For all three, that mind endures a crisis that each writer places at the center of his book. And all three assume prophetic roles. Each man reacted in his own way to the French Revolution and undertook the restoration of faith in God, nature, or the mind of man for a generation whose God had fled and for whom the ideals of the secular world had been found wanting.

The relation in each case of contingent reality to the created fiction, or indeed of the general psychological truth to the paradigm, may be explained by Vaihinger's "law of ideational shifts." According to this law, ideas develop in two directions: from fiction (*as if*) to hypothesis (*if*) to dogma (*because*), and the other way around, from dogma to hypothesis to fiction. Vaihinger's examples consist of the existence of God and Plato's Idea; they begin as fiction, move to dogma, and then move back again to fiction. The difference between finding an idea or form useful and believing it does not affect the idea or the form but only the author's attitude. The form, in other words, can be seen as absolutely true in itself (conversion in actual life), or it can provide a useful analogy for an actual truth, a means for abstracting from reality. Of the three writers considered here, Mill comes closest to believing in the actual truth of his conversion, to presenting it in a *because* style of narrative. Yet even he finds it necessary to use the occasional *as if*. On the other hand, Wordsworth and Carlyle, using the same form, present the same story as deliberate fiction. Vaihinger concludes: "To maintain a fiction as a fiction implies a highly developed logical mind, one that does not surrender too precipitately to the equilibratory impulse but carefully distinguishes between means and ends."[45]

Fiction as means provides the illusions that make life bearable and the myths that explain it. Fiction as process, as in *Sartor Resartus* and *The Prelude*, provides the metaphor of the journey or the creative act and insists that means are more important than the end. It is not necessary to know, in other words, *to what* a man is converted but only to be given the shape of his experience. Or, as a modern Greek poet writes in interpretation of every man's odyssey:

> Ask that your way be long.
> At many a summer dawn to enter
> —with what gratitude, what joy—
> ports seen for the first time. . . .
> Have Ithaka always in your mind.
> Your arrival there is what you are destined for.
> But do not in the least hurry the journey.
> Better that it last for years,
> so that when you reach the island you are old,
> rich with all you have gained on the way,
> not expecting Ithaka to give you wealth.
> Ithaka gave you the splendid journey.
> Without her you would not have set out. . . .
> So wise have you become, of such experience,
> that already you will have understood what these
>   Ithakas mean.[46]

The hero who approaches the end of his journey, rich with all he has gained on the way, will surely be asked at the courts of princes to entertain men with his story.

5. Confession: The Hero Tells His Story

We have been working until this point with three mythic paradigms that are very frequently found in nineteenth-century autobiographies. I have called them mythic because each provides the form and, in varying degrees, the content that the autobiographer wishes to use. I have called them metaphors because I claim that each acts as a valuable comparison for the experience it is intended to describe. I have tried to show in each case how the metaphor describes precisely those aspects of human experience that are least subject to cultural or even personal variation. And for these reasons, I have claimed, individual use of such metaphors to describe profoundly subjective experience has facilitated adequate expression for the writer and ready comprehension for the reader.

Having stressed the unchanging, universal aspects of these metaphors, having linked the metaphors, indeed, with the impressively general psychological conditions from which the myths themselves presumably derive, I need perhaps to acknowledge the relentless passage of centuries and the changes, subtle and profound, cultural and intellectual, that take place. I do not presume to sit Aeneas and Odysseus down side by side with Rousseau or George Moore. It would be as absurd to claim that the *Aeneid* was Vergil's autobiography as to suggest that Vergil and George Moore would have felt they were engaged in the same literary task. Indeed, if each were asked to identify what he was doing, he would do so in markedly different terms. Far from creating a timeless and universal brotherhood of man that enforces anachronistic behavior on almost everyone involved, I see the use of each myth in widely different periods of time as analogous, not identical. Surely there are ways in which Aeneas's descent into hell is equivalent to that of Teufelsdröckh or Mill, and surely such an equivalence is illuminating. What we are concerned with here, in other words, is not to collapse all significant distinctions but rather to draw attention to certain persistently common features that transcend such distinctions. Whether our culture be Samoan, Carrier Indian, ancient Mediterranean, or nineteenth-century European, whether our narratives take the form of folktales or epics or explorations of the individual psyche, the same forms persist and describe some enduring aspects of the human condition.

Such restatement of my initial assumptions seems particularly important before a discussion of confession, which is essentially a form of storytelling. We cannot pretend that Odysseus, Bunyan, Rousseau, and George Moore would have listened to each other with patience or necessarily understood what they heard. We can say of confession, however, as of the myths of Eden and the heroic journey, that it derives from situations common to the human psyche and from the universalizing metaphor for such situations in myth, and we can also describe equivalences and analogues that explain the usefulness of this form to the nineteenth-century autobiographer who has an entirely personal story to tell. Like conversion, confession receives its most immediate definition from Christianity, specifically from Catholicism. As with conversion, the process of confession need have no connection with religion beyond the contribution of religion to the metaphor. As Propp, Todorov, Campbell, Jung, or Frye would undoubtedly agree, the manner, not the matter, is at issue.

"It seems to be agreed," writes Georg Misch, "that men must reveal their souls, and the only question is how to do it."[1] For the Ancient Mariner who stoppeth one of three, revealing or confessing his soul consists simply in catching his audience, however busy that audience may otherwise be, and telling his story. So urgent is the story to be told that the anxious wedding guest sits down on a stone to listen; he cannot choose but hear. Rousseau appends a paragraph to his *Confessions* describing the occasion on which he read his *Confessions* to an illustrious assembly and then challenged anyone present to find him a dishonorable man. Notably, everyone "was silent. Mme d'Egmont was the only person who seemed moved. She trembled visibly but quickly controlled herself, and remained quiet, as did the rest of the company" (*Confessions*, p. 606).

In terms of the epic, confession of soul comes when the tired warrior justifies himself by a recitation of his deeds. Just as the underworld of classical mythology contrasts with the private internalized hell of the Christian, so the very personal story told by Rousseau or the Ancient Mariner contrasts with the essentially familiar story told by Aeneas or Odysseus. We have seen how Odysseus's narratives allow for no surprises and are determined by the present moment. Similarly, each telling seems to be not the first but simply the best, the most authoritative account.

The hero, who sits down in the halls of Alcinous or Dido, tells his story on request and tells it to people who know a great deal about it already. Almost by definition, the hero tells a representative story that contains recognitions and explanations and only such surprises as will gratify the hearer with the impression that he has been carried that much closer to reality. Homer presents this situation with delightful irony.

> "Odysseus," said Alcinous, "we are far from regarding you as one of those impostors and humbugs whom this dark world brings forth in such profusion to spin their lying yarns which nobody can test. On the contrary, not only is your speech a delight but you have sound judgement too, and you have told us the stories of your compatriots and your own grievous misadventures with all the artistry that a ballad-singer might display. . . ."
>
> In response to this the resourceful Odysseus went on with his story. "Lord Alcinous, my most worshipful prince, . . . far be it from me to deny you an even more tragic tale than you have heard already."[2]

Like Odysseus and Rousseau, the Ancient Mariner tells a story about a long journey in which he begins with energy and hope but then endures storm, suffering, guilt, and confrontation with death before homecoming. They all, in one way or another, enact the heroic journey as Campbell describes it, through separation, initiation, and return.

The three kinds of sacraments of the Catholic church suggest a pattern equivalent to that described by Campbell. The first kind are rites of passage; these are baptism and extreme unction. The second are rites of initiation; these are confirmation and Holy Orders. Confirmation and Holy Orders are also inner rites of passage, however, providing in this dual role a parallel with descent into the underworld and conversion, which are simultaneously part of the journey and descriptive of its central, initiatory experience. Finally, rites of participation are confession-and-penance, Eucharist, and marriage. Even the descriptive terms used for these rites by the church suggest a sense of transition, central crisis, and return equivalent to that in myth. Just as the psychological journey describes search for a mature identity that makes sense in and of its world, and the mythic journey tests the quality of its hero before returning him to his people with some boon, so the religious journey describes man's attempt to return to oneness or "participation" with God. In each instance, a successful journey results in harmony, safe homecoming, maturing of person and purpose, a sense of who and why and how one is.

When asked to shrieve the Mariner, the "Hermit good" asks, as Alcinous does of Odysseus, one very relevant question of the stranger who returns from the dead:

> "Say quick," quoth he, "I bid thee say—
> What manner of man art thou?"

The Mariner explains:

> Forthwith this frame of mine was wrench'd
> With a woful agony,
> Which forced me to begin my tale;
> And then it left me free.

> Since then, at an uncertain hour,
> That agony returns:

And till my ghastly tale is told,
This heart within me burns.[3]

The Mariner is burdened with terrible guilt after killing the albatross. His story is a form of confession; its narration acts as catharsis equivalent to absolution. Rousseau, too, is burdened with many specific instances of private guilt and with imputations by society of guilt where he feels himself to be innocent; he, too, derives considerable satisfaction from making his story known. Goethe recognizes the parallel between the relief enjoyed by the absolved Catholic and the relief that can be found in literary confession; in a letter to Göttling dated Weimar, 4 March 1826, he suggests that Protestants may be more prone to autobiography than Catholics who can turn to a confessor.[4]

Whereas the Catholic repents his sin and seeks absolution to relieve him of its burden, literary confession simply eliminates the burden of sin or guilt, or translates it into the burden of neuroses. Literary confession may express regret. It may demonstrate the painful acquisition of maturity, which in terms of character formation may be equated with amendment, but it does not need to share the assumption that what is found in the soul is sinful. Literary confession, in other words, shares with religious confession the pursuit of truth about the self through rigorous self-examination, but it does not need to share the contrition or penance.

The psyche needs salving as urgently as the soul needs saving, and the story that one tells follows essentially the same pattern, whether it is told to the priest, or the analyst, or as literary confession before many witnesses.[5] Odysseus and Aeneas, telling the story of their wanderings, are classical prototypes for literary confession; they externalize elements of their psyche onto the giants and monsters of their journey. Like their friends in the confessional, on the couch, or at their desks, they describe profoundly significant experiences that need to be described. All of them are compelled to tell their story.

Forcibly detained by the skinny hand and the glittering eye, the listener hears a story that borrows many specific ingredients from the religious confessional.[6] Literary confession shares with religious confession a central emphasis on the (guilty) self. Literary and religious confession alike travel from sin to redemption and enact their own penance and thanksgiving.[7] ("The sacrifices of God," sings the contrite King David, "are a broken spirit: a broken and a contrite heart, O God, thou wilt not despise.")[8] Like conversion, literary and religious confession describe places and states of mind that are radically different from the present. Their perspective on the past helps to shape the narrative.

Saint Augustine has established the model for examination of conscience, for rigorous pursuit of thoughts and feelings back to their source in the depths of his psyche. Examination of conscience and confession of what is found there distinguishes confessional literature, like confessional speech, from the general run of communication between people; it says that which is not normally said, shares that which is usually hidden. William Hale White describes both the urgency and the intimacy that are appropriate: "Direct appeal to God," he writes, "can only be justified when it is passionate. To come maundering into His presence when we have nothing particular to say is an insult, upon which we should never presume if we had a petition to offer to any earthly personage (*Ab.*, p. 8). Confession recognizes appropriate times for saying certain things about oneself that one would not normally say. The occasion is filled with awe, the account is in some way prodigious. "For behold," Saint Augustine tells God, "Thou lovest the truth, and he that doth it, cometh to the light. This would I do in my heart before Thee in confession: and in my writing, before many witnesses."[9]

It becomes necessary at this point to establish that confession represents more than a statement of past sin. The fact of its existence presupposes a faith. Confession can mean simply a profession of faith: "Every tongue shall confess that Jesus Christ is Lord, to the glory of God the Father,"[10] or, "I will confess his name before my Father, and before his angels."[11]

Confession, then, merges with testimony, which is a motivating force for works as different as those by Saint Augustine, Bunyan, and Rousseau. Persecution of early Christians and of seventeenth-century sectarians provides a common cause for such a testament, so that confession can also imply a righteous defense of oneself in the light of the faith one wishes to promulgate and glorify. Rousseau, for example, aims to exonerate a man condemned by society for being apparently irreligious, yet he is aware of the religious context for such confession. "J'envie la gloire des martyrs," he writes to M. de Saint-Germain in 1770. "Si je n'ai pas en tout la même foi qu'eux, j'ai la même innocence et le même zèle, et mon coeur se sent digne du même prix."[12] Faith, after all, need not be in church dogma but can be in oneself.

Literary confession, both of sins and as testimony, is above all not private. It therefore tends to assume the hieratic role reserved for the Christian witness rather than the Christian sinner. The sinner, of course, has arrived at a position of experience from which his witness counts:

> "Farewell, farewell! [cries the Mariner] but this I tell
> To thee, thou Wedding-Guest!
> He prayeth well, who loveth well
> Both man and bird and beast.
>
> He prayeth best, who loveth best
> All things both great and small;
> For the dear God who loveth us,
> He made and loveth all."[13]

De Quincey, for example, hopes that his *Confessions* "will prove, not merely an interesting record, but, in considerable degree, useful and instructive. In *that* hope it is, that I have drawn it up: and *that* must be my apology for breaking through that delicate and honourable reserve, which, for the most part, restrains us from the public exposure of our own errors and infirmities" (*CEOE*, p. 345).[14] But then, propagation of the faith and invitation to conversion have always been essential to believers for their own redemption. Having confessed his sins, King David promises: "Then will I teach transgressors thy ways; and sinners shall be converted unto thee."[15] Confession is an apt mode for reaching another's soul. As Saint Augustine writes: "Thou hast appointed that man should from others guess much as to himself."[16] Petrarch also finds this true and comments on Saint Augustine's *Confessions*, "I seem to be hearing the story of my own self, the story not of another's wandering, but of my own."[17]

We have seen how literary and religious confessions share the emotional need to unburden the self by exploring states of mind. (In general, as Saint Augustine realizes, "men go abroad to admire the heights of mountains, the mighty billows of the sea, the broad tides of rivers, the compass of the ocean, and the circuits of the stars, and pass themselves by.")[18] Unburdening, however, is not effective without an audience, and the audience needs to be clearly established by or within the text. Confession is necessarily a dialogue: the Catholic penitent talks to God through the priest; Saint Augustine speaks to God with a human audience as witness; Petrarch turns to Saint Augustine and the silent witness of the Lady Truth; Rousseau turns to society; and George Moore, in his *Confessions of a Young Man*, positively attacks his "hypocrite lecteur."

One final, important connection between religious and literary confession may be described as dramatic conflict or tension. This can take the form of dramatic confrontation: between Saint Augustine and God, Bunyan and the devil, Petrarch and Saint Augustine. Such conflict is an aspect of the dialogue form and of that perspective on the past that enables a known result to be juxtaposed with the difficulties preventing its achievement. It is seen at its most direct in *The Confessions of Saint Augustine* and in Bunyan's *Grace Abounding*, where past sins and present graces are most directly perceived. Rousseau and De Quincey exercise a subtler form of tension that is woven less visibly into the narrative in the form of fate or "echo-augury" controlling their lives. Tension is also an aspect of the need to unburden oneself of sin. De Quincey, rating his own *Confessions* in this respect above those of Saint

Augustine and Rousseau, believes that the very idea of breathing a record of human passion into the confessional suggests an impassioned theme.[19]

Despite the forms established by the church, for which analogues can be found in myth and ritual, folktale and epic, this impassioned theme is essentially personal and therefore the least clearly defined of the metaphors we have been studying. It is more affected by context, more culture-bound. Saint Augustine begins book 2 by calling to mind "my past foulness, and the carnal corruptions of my soul; not because I love them, but that I may love Thee, O my God."[20] Petrarch is notably less God-centered, but he is still concerned with the state of his soul. His dialogue ends with the wish that "I may raise up no cloud of dust before my eyes; and with my mind calmed down and at peace, I may hear the world grow still and silent, and the winds of adversity die away."[21] Bunyan's purpose, like Saint Paul's, is specifically hieratic: "Indeed I have been as one sent to them from the dead; I went my self in chains to preach to them in chains, and carried that fire in my own conscience that I perswaded them to beware of."[22] His *Grace Abounding* represents the spoils of his battle with the devil now dedicated to "maintain the house of God."[23]

These three stand in marked contrast to Rousseau, who is entirely concerned with himself in a social rather than a divine context. Rousseau exonerates personal guilt by displaying himself as he has been:

> as vile and despicable when my behaviour was such, as good, generous, and noble when I was so. . . . So let the numberless legion of my fellow men gather round me, and hear my confessions. Let them groan at my depravities, and blush for my misdeeds. But let each one of them reveal his heart at the foot of Thy throne with equal sincerity, and may any man who dares, say "I was a better man than he."   (*Confessions*, p. 17)

Moore may not have read Rousseau, but he virtually echoes him: "You, hypocritical reader, who are now turning up your eyes and murmuring 'horrid young man'—examine your weakly heart, and see what divides us."[24] In his 1917 preface, Moore claims that he had not known of Rousseau at the time of first writing his *Confessions* and so wrote without a model, but he pays direct homage to De Quincey and writes in the 1889 preface: "St. Augustine wrote the story of a god-tortured soul; would it not be interesting to write the story of an art-tortured soul?"[25]

These more modern confessions are secular, even antireligious, and essentially self-centered. Addressed to the public rather than to God, they move closer to the novel in tone and emphasis. Petrarch, for instance, resorts to metaphor to portray self-examination, internal debate, a state of mental anguish that resolves itself in calm. Bunyan expresses his lengthy crisis in such graphic, physical terms that abstractions like sin and the devil virtually become allegorical figures, and he turns to allegory in *Pilgrim's Progress*, which might be called the revision of *Grace Abounding*. In contrast, Rousseau uses the confessional for its contribution of a form rich with connotations in order to write the forerunner of the conventional bildungsroman of nineteenth-century literature. He stresses childhood, influences on his development, important features in his character, significant relationships. And these changes in reasons for and methods of writing are paralleled by changes in audience. The modern novel reader replaces the bishop, priest, or fellow Christian seeking enlightenment. God is replaced by the muses or one's fellow man. Yet confession, as a metaphor descriptive of self-analysis and the expression of private experience remains recognizably, deliberately, the same.

Saint Augustine, Petrarch, Bunyan

Saint Augustine's *Confessions* (c. 400), Petrarch's *Secret* (c. 1342), and Bunyan's *Grace Abounding* (1666) provide three useful examples of confession that is both religious and literary. Each serves to illustrate subjectivity or a central emphasis on self, penance and thanks, the need to unburden oneself, dialogue, assumption of faith or deliberate testimony or justification, a hieratic purpose, and dramatic conflict. Changes in context and expression over the wide time span covered by these three authors demonstrate, furthermore, how confession so easily converges in the nineteenth-century with autobiography and the novel. More immediately, these three penitents serve for our present purposes to establish those conventions of literary confession that less devout successors can use for nonreligious purposes.

Saint Paul probably gives the earliest Christian example of spiritual autobiography; the Acts of the Apostles contains at least three accounts of his conversion as told by himself. He sinned in persecuting God's people. He was smitten blind by a dazzling light and heard the voice of God reproving him. His sight was restored and he spent the rest of his life testifying to his new faith, gaining strength from repeated references to his early sins, which identified him with those he wished to convert. On the rock of Saint Paul, Saint Augustine then built the church of literary confession.

Saint Augustine's work, following the *res gestae* autobiographies of classical literature (note Caesar's use of the third person), is original for its central concern with subjective, emotional experience. Factual autobiography is the vehicle for this experience, so the stage is set in early childhood with emphasis on the tension between his sinful nature and his mother's prayers. Book 4, with the conversion and death of a close friend, provides a turning point, a sense of spiritual anguish replacing comfort in sin. Bunyan is foreshadowed in lines like this: "I bore about a shattered and bleeding soul, impatient of being borne by me, yet where to repose it, I found not."[26] Like Bunyan, Saint Augustine conveys a sense of the soul as a physical entity capable of exhaustion, bruising, and pain. Unlike Bunyan, he attributes the delay in his conversion to God's purpose: "I pressed towards Thee, and was thrust from Thee, that I might taste of death."[27]

The autobiographical narrative continues to build in spiritual anguish toward the climax of conversion in book 8. With the death of his mother and his own return to Africa in book

9, he feels no further need to refer to his personal life. Just as the whole book is essentially a form of praise and thanksgiving, so the human life at the center serves no purpose beyond exemplifying the ways of God to man.

Yet self-examination remains important even for the soul that God has saved. Near the end of book 10, before his lengthy discussion on time and his exegesis of the book of Genesis, Saint Augustine pauses to note his three-fold concupiscence: lust of the flesh and the eyes, and ambition in the world. He finds himself divided by sensual pleasures, even that of being hungry and then satisfied. He fears greed but is not disturbed by smells. He writes in summary:

> So I seem to myself; perchance I am deceived. For that is also a mournful darkness whereby my abilities within me are hidden from me; so that my mind making enquiry into herself of her own powers, ventures not readily to believe herself.[28]

Like Bunyan, Saint Augustine feels the need for vigilance.

> It is then our affections which we lay open unto Thee, confessing our own miseries, and Thy mercies upon us, that Thou mayest free us wholly, since Thou hast begun, that we may cease to be wretched in ourselves, and be blessed in Thee.[29]

Saint Augustine provides a model for subjective writing, especially about early childhood, for establishing an emotional conflict (between his mother and himself) as a thematic device, for the drama of conversion, for self-examination, for the form of dialogue with God, and for the justification of his faith (later shared for such different purposes by Rousseau and Moore). He is also important for the images he establishes. His dominant images are as physical as the state they describe is abstract. The fever of indecision and anxiety, for instance, results from the childhood sickness that first raises the question of sin and baptism and from the "scourge of bodily sickness" that threatens to bear him down to hell in book 5. In each case, Augustine's mother suffers not merely anxiety born of affection but, especially in the second instance, "a much more vehement anguish . . . in labour of me in the spirit, than at her childbearing in the flesh."[30]

Just as the biblical sources for confession refer to healing and cleansing, so Saint Augustine is washed from the mire, healed of disease, given food and drink when he is hungry and thirsty. These are hardly original metaphors for the believer in Christ who healed the sick and offered His body and blood as redemption, yet they cross the boundary here between biblical doctrine and the establishment through fiction of a spiritual reality.[31] Similarly, Saint Augustine is buffeted by storm (De Quincey uses storm with deliberate effect). He struggles in darkness so that even when his face is toward the light, the light is not yet on it. Significantly, he is oppressed by the clanking chains of mortality, by the chains of his human will that burden him and prevent him from acceding to God's will. Notably, all who confess make clear that they are free from the burdens and chains that once oppressed and hampered them, even, indeed, when they do not use these precise terms.

Saint Augustine also introduces a Madonna figure in the person of his mother Monnica. His real father being God, he barely mentions his earthly, non-Christian father. Nor does the brother Navigius appear until Monnica's deathbed. The Madonna intercedes for her chosen son to such effect that a bishop assures her "it is not possible that the son of these tears should perish."[32] She receives a vision of his salvation, rejoices at his conversion, and dies at the end of book 9, in the thirty-third year of his age, thus effectively ending his earthly life. (Similarly, Dante's journey ends with Beatrice and God in heaven.)

The interceding, redemptive Madonna appears in later confessions. She is muted into the Lady Truth, who bears silent witness to Petrarch's conflict, but is only vestigial in Bunyan's wife, who comes from a godly family, introduces him to spiritual matters, and comforts him in his anguish; however, she emerges again as spiritual mother beyond earthly contamination in Rousseau's "mamma" and in De Quincey's grand amalgam of his two dead sisters and Ann of Oxford Street.

Like the concrete images of pain and healing, hunger and feeding, bondage and freedom, the Madonna provides an important fictive analogue for love and hope, and represents that virginal, motherly bosom on which the grown man can weep without sin or shame.

Saint Augustine addresses God but is conscious of the human audience before whom his confessions become a testament of faith. Petrarch, however, turns to Saint Augustine as to a priest and confesses, or is forced to confess, with Truth for a witness. His *Secret* is important in the present context for its deliberate fictionalizing of subjective experience. The two main protagonists, confessor and penitent, are prototypes for the doppelgänger of later fiction. It seems unlikely that James Hogg, for instance, should have known Petrarch's *Secret*, yet his *Confessions of a Justified Sinner* (1824), "a bold theme for an allegory,"[33] presents a Jekyll-and-Hyde schizophrenia in terms of just such a debate.[34] Influence here is less important than the repeated discovery that Petrarch was self-conscious to a degree remarkable for his time and that he here anticipates a representation of inner conflict that became standard in the nineteenth-century novel. He anticipates it, moreover, in the form of confession, dialogue, self-examination, and emotional unburdening. The formal third-person dialogue also provides the distance not provided here by retrospect or redemption (the work seems current with the situation), the distance so necessary for artistic achievement.

Petrarch's spiritual crisis, like that of his confessor, turns on his inability to face the transience of worldly pleasures and fame, a difficulty of will in the face of knowledge, a wish that the prayers for what is known to be right may not be granted for awhile. An interesting development on Saint Augustine's *Confessions*, parallel with the device of the divided self, is the realization through the dialogue (nowhere through direct statement) that such dialogue is therapeutic. Petrarch, for example, frequently resists confession. Only torture or the block would get him to admit a certain point. But the examination of his conscience through dialogue (and Saint Augustine is an aggressive confessor) invariably alters his stance and provides a remedy for the sin. Petrarch is able, for instance, to avoid his main sin, *accidie*, by remembering that he stands comparatively high in the list of those whom fortune has blessed.

Petrarch, in other words, with his divided self, his therapy through dialogue, and his final freedom from worldly concerns, adds a new dimension to literary confession. Yet there are traces of the biblical language that Saint Augustine adopted: "Though I be not yet wholly set free from my burdens," he writes near the end of the third dialogue, "yet, nevertheless, from great part of them I do feel in truth a blessed release."[35] This influence also appears in an expression of gratitude: "for you have cleansed my darkened sight and scattered the thick clouds of error in which I was involved."[36]

Just as Saint Augustine is important for his concern with subjective experience and Petrarch for his formalizing of such experience into deliberate fiction, so Bunyan's confession is remarkable for the weight given to his conversion by the lengthy and painful account of his temptation and despair. It is possibly this distinguishing subjectivity that separates Bunyan as an artist from the mainstream of seventeenth-century confession. *Grace Abounding to the Chief of Sinners* was written while Bunyan was serving a twelve-year prison term for preaching. It is itself a form of preaching, offering as an example and a comfort Bunyan's own spiritual conflict and salvation. (Mark Rutherford modestly suggests that "it is not impossible that some few whose experience has been like mine may, by my example, be freed from that sense of solitude which they find so depressing" [*Ab.*, p. 3]). Later, in *Pilgrim's Progress*, Bunyan deliberately fictionalized his own experience, replacing analysis of subjective experience with allegory and the physical image with the pictorial. Ironically, however, *Grace Abounding* comes closer to that important link with autobiography and novel, the creation of character. Like *The Confessions of Saint Augustine*, *Grace Abounding* uses the events of a life merely as a vehicle for conveying spiritual experience;[37] Bunyan's soul is the main character, rather than his body. Indeed, his soul becomes a physical entity with weight and motion, capable of intense energy and intense pain, a character in its own right.

Bunyan is particularly effective at conveying moods, an important contribution to the creation of character. At one moment, inspired by a sermon, he could preach to the very crows on the ploughed lands before him. At another, he needs to lean with his spirit against temptation, knocks his fist against his chin to prevent his mouth from speaking, feels that only by jumping head first into a bog will he prevent himself from shouting blasphemy. "My peace would be in and out sometimes twenty times a day: Comfort now and Trouble presently; Peace now, and before I could go a furlong, as full of Fear and Guilt as ever heart could hold."[38]

It is worth commenting (this being the first of this group of texts not to suffer from translation) with what literary effect Bunyan swings his rhythm to the sense of his words. Much of *Grace Abounding* turns on biblical texts. Much also turns on immediate and personal situations like walking down a muddy lane, sitting by the fire, lying by his wife in bed. Monitoring between the external Word and the private life, Bunyan's peculiar prose rhythm creates a drama of its own. For example, he strives with the devil for the interpretation of a passage of Scripture, describing an event as physical as a tug-of-war, and yet it is not allegory but vividly sensed experience for which he has found a vigorous language. "Oh, what work did we make!" he writes, ". . . he pull'd and I pull'd; but, God be praised, I got the better of him, I got some sweetness from it."[39]

Sweetness from strength may be reminiscent of Samson. Final realization of God's grace brings peace, like raindrops after storm, in terms by now an accepted part of confessional vocabulary. However, Bunyan is unusually literal in his use of these conventional terms and extends this literalness into his objective, solid rendering of his soul and its physical conflict. His weary soul has now found the Word to lean upon, so that it may not sink forever, and it all but wipes its brow.

Like Saint Augustine, Bunyan accounts for his wicked

childhood. In place of the conflict provided by a saintly mother, Bunyan himself endures dreams and visions that struggle with his sinfulness. Further tension is then provided by his acceptance of the moral teachings of Christianity without realization of spiritual redemption. Like Saint Augustine and like Petrarch, who want to be saved but not yet, Bunyan finds his "unbelief to set as it were the shoulder to the door to keep . . . [the Lord] out, and that too," he says plaintively, "even then when I have with many a bitter sigh cried, Good Lord, break it open."[40]

This outpouring of subjective experience from the redeemed sinner to his flock is, like Saint Augustine's, hieratic and essentially a statement of faith. But with such emphasis laid on structural tension and with such vivid realization of mood and situation, enhancing both characters and relationships, confession moves closer, once again, to autobiography and the novel. Bunyan is more dramatic than Saint Augustine, more personal than Petrarch. He uses even the conventions in harness with carefully constructed prose to tell an urgent story. And with this novelistic talent, confession moves from the confessional out to the reading public.

Rousseau and the Nineteenth-Century Confessional Novel

Rousseau offers his public knowledge of himself through the book that he will present to God at the last trumpet. He begins by gathering his fellow men around him and ends with an epilogue to a live audience: "I have told the truth. If anyone knows anything contrary to what I have here recorded, though he prove it a thousand times, his knowledge is a lie and an imposture" (*Confessions*, p. 605). Constant internal incidents reaffirm the significance of man rather than God as the audience; Rousseau lies to the Holy Ghost, for example, in pretending to be converted to Catholicism and feels that for this he deserves the contempt of mankind. Yet Rousseau is ambivalent about the nature of confession. His later work,

Rousseau Juge de Jean-Jacques: Dialogue, admits neither God nor his fellow men as judge but only, as the title suggests, his public over his private self. He intended to deposit this manuscript on the altar of Notre Dame on 24 February 1776. Prevented by a new grill from fulfilling this intention, he looks for "un dépositaire discret et fidelle [*sic*]," and asks, "Est-il un plus digne instrument de l'oeuvre de la Providence que la main d'un homme vertueux?"[41] If his fellow men are the appropriate recipients of his confessions, then his decision to hand out his pamphlet to all passersby is more appropriate than laying it on the altar.

Rousseau's uncertainty about the nature of his faults, whether social or spiritual, and the appropriate ear for confession, divine or human, represents the trend that enables *The New English Bible* to substitute "guilt" for "sin." The significance of the event is internalized and made relative. Rousseau and *The New English Bible* both appear to deny what Saint Augustine and Bunyan understood as virtually physical facts, yet both recognize the psychological importance of a man's sense of his own failing. The transition in interpretation, however, is an important one. Sin is an objective fact for which God alone can grant pardon, whereas guilt depends on personal and social assessment of inadequacy in any given situation. For sin and its forgiveness, there are absolute rules. For guilt and its dispersal, there is the more variable quality of therapy. In a secular society in which guilt or neuroses and therapy have largely displaced sin and confession, confession acts as its own accuser and its own absolver. "When we blame ourselves," says Wilde, "we feel that no one else has a right to blame us. It is the confession, not the priest, that gives us absolution."[42] Or, as De Quincey puts it, "The dread book of account, which the Scriptures speak of, is, in fact, the mind itself of each individual" (*CEOE*, p. 315). Just as Saint Augustine models the transition from purely religious to religious-and-literary confession, so Rousseau models the modern trend from sacred to profane, from religious to secular.[43] He demonstrates the psychologizing process of confession.

Confession is a necessary part of Rousseau's social character. It represents his compulsive need to apologize for and justify his compulsive lying. Posing as a musician in Lausanne, he confesses his real identity to Lutold, a member of the orchestra, because he is overcome by "the impossibility of keeping my heart closed in my great distress" (*Confessions*, p. 146). Posing as interpreter to the Archimandrite of Jerusalem, he confesses his real identity once more to the French ambassador at Soleure. "I should not have said less even if I had made no promise, for a continuous need to pour myself out brings my heart at every moment to my lips" (*Confessions*, p. 152). Amusingly enough, the ambassador is "pleased with [his] little story" and asks Rousseau to write out a shorter version of it for his wife to read. Urgent confessions like these pervade the work. They are self-indulgent; they lack self-awareness and tend therefore to create a credibility gap in which the reader trusts any alternative perception of a situation above Rousseau's. These confessions are also frequently insensitive to their audience, and yet they are not unlike that more attractive confession made at the Café de Procope, that he was the author of the play that everyone had found so boring. They are disarmingly open to praise or blame.

Less pleasing than the impulse to unburden himself are the serious and painful specific confessions that punctuate the book with the proud, hieratic purpose of showing his fellow men the true picture of a man. Rousseau's complaint that Montaigne only shows himself in profile is not resolved by his own exposure of blemishes. W. A. Gill describes the problem well. What is usually hidden through interest or shame he calls "the nude." The problem of the nude is that it "has a peculiar and perhaps incalculable faculty of destroying proportion. . . . It 'thumps,' as painters say of a too glaring light."[44] From childhood peccadilloes (like peeing in Mme Clot's cooking pot!), Rousseau moves on doggedly: he enjoys being beaten by Mlle Lambercier but has never dared to ask another woman to give him the same pleasure; he accuses the servant-girl, Marion, of a theft of which he is guilty; he abandons his good friend, M. Le Maître, when he is having a fit in the street in Lyons; he dallies with courtesans in Venice; he sends his five children to the Foundling Hospital; in the arrogance of his independence, he refuses a present of game from the Prince de Conti.

The varying quality of these confessions reveals more of Rousseau's need to confess than it does of his character. His sexual pleasure in being beaten seems the hardest confession for him to make, yet he does not even count as a confession the story of his exposing himself to a group of servant-girls, maybe because he meets the threat of instant retribution in this latter case: he is in fact saved from the women, who turn on him in fury, by a big man with a big hat, and a big moustache, and a big sword, who (*mirabile dictu*) believes the story that he quickly invents! Rousseau's contemporaries were more indignant at his abandonment of his children. Apart from demonstrating an antisocial lack of paternal feeling, such abandonment also made a mockery of his theories of society and education. Rousseau therefore makes this confession but also hastens, as in no other case, to palliate the offense with high-flown theory.[45]

Gill is surely right in saying that the nude must thump at the author quite as much as at the reader. The nude destroys the proportions of the character it means to reveal. It destroys the proportions, too, of the work of art. Where it fails to work artistically, neither demonstrating the author's probity nor enlisting the reader's sympathy, this thumping nude is insensitive and importunate and therefore an embarrassment. As with his failure to recognize important distinctions between praiseworthy honesty and the kind of confession that is compulsive and self-gratifying, however, Rousseau's artistic fault is once again a matter not of commission but merely of degree. Navigating between the Scylla of the Catholic confessional and the Charybdis of the analyst's couch, Rousseau charts a new course that takes into account all the variables of confessional geography. He shouts his faults from the rooftops, thus exploring his own past, unburdening his psyche and his soul, and engaging the attention of everyone passing by. He is arrogant in his assumption that even failings like his may be counted in his favor if he sets each one up to be counted. In his arrogance he assumes the hieratic role reserved for the convert who can look on his sins as past. He travels, as we have seen, from sin (his repeated loss of Eden) toward a redemption that is never realized. He undergoes conversion and sets himself up as a prophet.

To some of the conventional religious images Rousseau adds new and vivid images that liken him to the narrator of the heroic journey. He sees himself as a wanderer on the face of the earth. His confessions are frequently likened to a labyrinth. He is several times caught up in a whirlpool. Not least, as we have seen, he tells his story to several people in the course of the story itself and then ends with the end of the complete telling to an assembly of nobles. For them, as for the courts of Dido and Alcinous, the story they were hearing must have been a well-worn tale. For his central emotional experience, however, Rousseau still turns to religion and borrows the Madonna.

All Rousseau's relationships seem like an incestuous search for parents (Thérèse is his aunt, Lord George Keith is his father), but none more so than his love of Mme de Warens, who was older than he and whom he called "mamma." His tendency to confess becomes an inability to keep anything secret from her. His "heart was open before her as before God" (*Confessions*, p. 185). This is not merely intimacy, it is a form of redemption. When he realizes that he will inherit the clothes of Claude Anet, her previous lover, her tears wash from his heart every trace of that low and contemptible thought so effectively that he has never since had a similar thought.

Rousseau's religious "conversions" lack any weight, but each one is connected with "mamma." She sends him to the hospice at Turin, and he accepts Catholicism for her sake. This is immediately after meeting her on Palm Sunday and becoming her young proselyte. "For in a moment I was hers, and certain that a faith preached by such missionaries would not fail to lead to paradise" (*Confessions*, p. 55). It does lead to paradise at Les Charmettes.[46] Their time at Les Charmettes is preceded by Rousseau's being (appropriately) blinded in a chemical experiment in "mamma's" service. He is then seriously ill with fever, and he is sustained and healed by "mamma." Notably, their sexual partnership is not happy and is entered on both sides in order to protect the young man from lascivious admirers! However, it does represent a privileged intimacy on which Vintzenreid intrudes.

As late as the tenth promenade of his *Rêveries du promeneur solitaire*, written just before his death in 1778, Rousseau remembers his first meeting with Mme de Warens and still sees it producing an instant and absolute effect on his life: "Ce premier moment décida de moi pour toute ma vie, et produisit, par un enchaînement inévitable, le destin du reste de mes jours."[47] This moment, like Saint Augustine's "thrust of a trembling glance," borrows from mystical experience the transformation of time from *chronos* to *kairos*. The bondage that is inevitable is reminiscent of courtly love whose conventions are largely inspired by the Virgin Mary.

Rousseau meets Mme de Warens for the last time when he returns to Geneva and formally reassumes his Protestant faith (book 8). His "reconversion" is an assertion of independence. It is paralleled by a meeting that he describes as a remorseful renunciation:

> Ah, that was the moment in which I should have paid my debt. I should have abandoned everything to follow her, to attach myself to her till her last hour, and share her fate, whatever it might be. I did nothing of the kind. Taken up with another attachment, I felt the tie which bound me to her loosening. . . . I sighed over her but did not follow her. Of all the remorse I have suffered in my life this was the bitterest and the most enduring. By my conduct I earned all the terrible punishments which have never since ceased to fall on my head. I hope they may have atoned for my ingratitude. (*Confessions*, p. 365)

To think of Mme de Warens at this meeting as a fat and dissipated woman of fifty is to realize both the strength of Rousseau's filial attachment and the idealized nature of his

love. As late as 1778, he is sighing, "Ah! si j'avois suffi à son
coeur comme elle suffisoit au mien!"[48] But the Madonna does
not smile on a Protestant philosopher, and the young man
must leave his mother and cleave unto his wife. Furthermore,
the Madonna, as De Quincey knows, is assumed into heaven
and remains only an aching, inspiring memory to her wor-
shipper below.

Introduced into confessional literature by Saint Augustine,
the Madonna figure becomes a major fictional character in
autobiographical novels. One need only think of Agnes Wick-
field in *David Copperfield*, Marmee in *Little Women*, or
Hardy's Idea in his late novel, *The Well-Beloved*, to name a
few. For Werther, the ideal takes the form of an unobtainable
woman who is worthy of heroic pursuit, like the Grail. That
the Madonna should become an ideal but earthly love is a
significant feature of the general development of religious
confession into the secular but still very personal story. Just as
the romance gives way to the novel, so the Madonna gives
way to a human love who can be a main protagonist in the
novel's essentially modern themes. Such development, natural
enough in a time of declining faith, is of practical importance
and technical value in the general transformation of religious
confession into secular autobiographical writings. It describes
the movement from the spiritual to the emotional and psychological history. It helps to explain why confession merges with
the novel.

In his study of the artist as hero, Maurice Beebe refers to
Werther and the *Confessions* of Rousseau as "these novels
[that] are similar enough to be recognised collectively as a
special genre of fiction."[49] Goethe himself describes how an
experience in his own life not unlike Rousseau's relationship
with "mamma" emerged as a confessional novel. Finding himself unable to commit suicide, he decides to live:

> But, to be able to do this with cheerfulness, I was
> obliged to solve a poetical problem, by which all that I
> had felt, thought, and fancied upon this important point
> should be reduced to words. For this purpose I collected

the elements which had been at work in me for a few
years, I rendered present to my mind the cases which
had most afflicted and tormented me, but nothing
would come to a definite form: I lacked an event, a fa-
ble, in which they could be overlooked.[50]

Into this dilemma comes the brief news of Jerusalem's suicide,
followed by a detailed description, "and at this moment the
plan of 'Werther' was formed, and the whole shot together
from all sides, and became a solid mass, just as water in a
vessel, which stands upon the point of freezing, is converted
into hard ice by the most gentle shake." Goethe describes writing *Werther* almost like a somnambulist, breathing into it all
the warmth that leaves no distinction between the poetical
and the actual. "I felt," he writes, "as if after a general confession, once more happy and free, and justified in beginning a
new life."[51]

Clearly Goethe is describing the catharsis that confessional
literature provides for its author. Werther stands to Goethe as
Mark Rutherford stands to William Hale White. We have seen
with Hale White and have no reason to doubt with Goethe
that the quality, the subjectivity, the detail and pattern of the
confessions are actually intensified by the adoption of an alter
ego. Goethe, like Hale White, has simply broken what Lejeune calls "le pacte autobiographique." He insists on bursting the limits repeatedly set by critics of autobiography who
would like to stop the spilling of so much blood. He demonstrates what Frye has called the merging of autobiography
with the novel "by a series of insensible gradations." As Frye
remarks, "After Rousseau—in fact in Rousseau—the confession flows into the novel, and the mixture produces the fictional autobiography, the *Künstler-roman*, and kindred
types."[52]

Wayne Shumaker describes the "total number of confessional autobiographies" as "not large, for the English mind,
when impelled to confess, has usually preferred the safer medium of the novel."[53] Shumaker's explanation apparently ap-
plies to Goethe too. "All . . . that has been confessed by me,"

he writes in his *Autobiography*, "consists of fragments of a great confession; and this little book is an attempt which I have ventured on to render it complete."[54] It is interesting, in the light of such a comment, to consider the regularity with which major novelists write autobiographical novels. Trollope, Dickens, George Eliot, Thackeray, Butler, Proust, Woolf, Lawrence, Joyce, to name only a few, all wrote at least one work of fiction with strong elements of autobiography clearly apparent in it. In terms of the patterns and metaphors described in this study, the distinctions that can be made between the autobiography and the novel matter less than the fact that autobiography provides no distinguishing features that the novelist cannot imitate. The novel has all the necessary means to express and describe the inner man and to tell his story. The confessional novel is a sensible extension of the fictive enterprise begun by the autobiographer who finds metaphor more satisfactory than direct narration to describe himself and the meaning he attributes to the events in his life. Literary confession came into its own when the Romantics discovered their urgent need to explore and express both the unique and the universal qualities of individual human nature, when the church began to lose ground, and before psychoanalysis gained any acceptance. Confession became, accordingly, a crucial feature in nineteenth-century literature, in the autobiography, in the novel, and in the extended lyric.

It has seemed most appropriate here to discuss confession in terms of its evolution precisely because it has evolved, consciously and deliberately, in tandem with the verbal forms that each age finds most readily available, constantly accumulating meanings and outlets but never shedding any that are significant. The perpetual quality of the metaphor is most specifically evidenced by its lineage from the confessional, through literature, and onto the analyst's couch. Clearly, however, the need to confess is so basic to man's character that sources of evolution can multiply without damaging each other's trade. Priest and doctor persist, both under oaths of secrecy. One's fellow man, whether Alcinous, Dido, Mme d'Egmont, or the reluctant wedding guest, is likely to enjoy the tale, admire the teller, and be struck by the resemblance between the confessions he is hearing and those that he himself could tell. It seems important to stress the necessity, the comprehensiveness, and the resilience of a metaphor that may fetch its immediate form from the confessional but that clearly derives its impulse, its meaning, and many of its ingredients from psychological needs and explanations as old as articulate man.

Despite its absorption into the body of nineteenth-century fiction and poetry, literary confession, like the myths of Eden, the heroic journey, and conversion or descent into the underworld, retains certain specific qualities that distinguish it from other forms of expression. We have noted the urgency of the narratives whose essential purpose is to describe their narrator. It is the hidden man, Jung's manikin, that is revealed, the man who would not be known about except for his story. His self-exploration through narrative acts as a catharsis equivalent to absolution; it redeems him as it redeems time and restores an equilibrium in the face of ignorance and death. As testimony, furthermore, such confession expresses assurance that the resolution that has been reached is a good one, that the self and the purpose that has been realized for life are equally necessary and in accord with one another.

It terms of its psychological origins, such analysis and resolution suggest the maturity of the narrator. He has been through the stages of development that are inevitable and maybe also through phases like conversion that describe intensely dramatic recognition of identity and purpose. Most important, he describes, and therefore must know, who he is and what his purpose is in life. He has made realistic sense of his inner life and of the world around him. He has matured to the point at which he can function sensibly as a complex individual in a complex society. This is not to say, of course, that such maturation is the sine qua non of confessional autobiography but simply that such maturity represents the psychological stage on which the confessing narrator models himself.

In mythic terms, the hero's narrative suggests arrival or return. In this sense, confession becomes the final metaphor for autobiography as a whole. It describes the entire journey of a life that does not continue beyond the final point of narration. It represents the closing of the cycle that is now complete. To continue would be to return to the beginning, or to run into Shandy's problem of the different speeds at which one lives and writes about living, or to perpetrate some ultimate confusion between the living and written identity. Marquez describes the last of a line of hero-victims reading the text that describes all their lives:

> Aureliano . . . began to decipher the instant that he was living, deciphering it as he lived it, prophesying himself in the act of deciphering the last page of the parchments, as if he were looking into a speaking mirror. Then he skipped again to anticipate the predictions and ascertain the date and circumstances of his death. Before reaching the final line, however, he had already understood that he would never leave that room, for it was foreseen that the city of mirrors (or mirages) would be wiped out . . . and exiled from the memory of men at the precise moment when Aureliano Babilonia would finish deciphering the parchments.[55]

Aureliano's reading himself out of existence provides an absurd contrast to the autobiographer who writes himself into existence. It suggests also why Odysseus's obsession with the process of narrative must not prevent the conclusion of his journey. Confession is the ultimate metaphor for autobiography not because all autobiography is confession but because, just as Eden represents the single and complete world of the child and the journey describes the process of life, so confession stands for the narration of that process. Confession implies redemption through the narrative that concludes at the present moment when the journey is complete.

Conclusion

I began this study by asking how and why four particular narrative patterns functioned as they did in autobiography. How and why do they extract meaning about one man and demonstrate it to many others? I have described the four patterns as mythic metaphors that condense and clarify complex experiences into comprehensible narrative, and I have tried to show how they derive not simply from the literary conventions available to the nineteenth-century autobiographer but more essentially from myth, which provides the archetypes for recurrent experience, and from those common psychological conditions that gave rise to the myths in the first place. These four metaphors, in short, have emerged in myth and become literary conventions because they derive from and explain crucial features of human development that in broad outline are always and everywhere the same.

I am very conscious that every period of time and every pocket of culture faces these stages of life "with a difference." Given the bewildering variety of personality, background, and public experience among the few writers we have looked at in this relatively limited time and culture span of nineteenth-century Europe, the differences are all too evident. When all of these writers, then, persist in using the same metaphors, I can draw one of two conclusions: either the Romantic discovery of the importance of subjective experience instantly took cover behind the communal barricades of literary convention, or, as I have tried to show, each writer reached for the most effective comparison he could find for the private experience that he alone could tell. The importance, then, of the metaphors to autobiography is explained by the fact that they describe what every autobiographer needs to describe, not simply because everyone understands the meaning they carry as conventions but crucially because they really do carry that meaning. The sense these myths make of one life to others is made not simply at the level of literary exegesis but profoundly at the subliminal level where understanding is both rich and immediate.

Attempting to demonstrate the nature of each metaphor and the way in which it has been used in a limited number of autobiographies, I have made the metaphors rather than the texts the focal point of my study. I have taken cross-sections, as it were, of the basic exemplary material in order to see the myth of Eden here, conversion there, and so on. It remains now to assemble the texts again and ask some more general, retrospective questions. Why do some authors use many of these narrative metaphors and others only one or two? What does the presence or absence of these metaphors do to an autobiographical text? Why, in other words, do some autobiographies become basic exemplary material for a study on this subject and others just random samples?

Answers begin, I believe, with the emotional content of any given work. Rousseau, for example, has contributed parts of his autobiographical body to each anatomical survey, Mill only one. Rousseau cultivated the feelings both in himself and in the society for which he wrote. By contrast, Mill cultivated the intellect; only after his mental crisis did he find it necessary to cultivate the inner man. It seems sensible, accordingly, that Rousseau should find the fullest and most evocative resonances for his story and that Mill should find only that one that described a time of intense emotional upheaval. I say *find* rather than *use* because I suspect but obviously cannot prove a subliminal activity of choice rather than an artistic decision.

Liam Hudson makes an interesting point that connects with this possibility. Writing about the distinction between waking a subject during REM sleep and waking him between phases of REM sleep, he says:

> If you wake someone while his eyes are actually flickering, he reports dreams that sound like irruptions into consciousness of images that are arbitrary, disconnected. Inasmuch as they make sense, they sound like jumbled, compacted metaphors; snatches of private poetry. If, on

the other hand, you awaken someone during one of the brief pauses between bouts of eye movement, the dream he reports will have a different character altogether: that of a story. The one sort of dream is known technically as 'primary visual experience,' the other as 'secondary cognitive elaboration.' . . . [T]he propensity to tell ourselves stories while asleep is universal. The easy, reflex-like part of our thinking we do without thinking about it, consists in the translation of our experience to narrative, irrespective of whether our experience fits the narrative form or not.[1]

Narrative embeds the images that seem bizarre in a fabric that seems more reasonable, and it does this at the subconscious level. He makes the further interesting point that "those who are sternly rational while awake have a greater need than others to dream. They pass more quickly into REM sleep." The images are necessary to mental health. The narratives of sleep that order experience, however disordered that experience may seem, are essential to the preservation of sanity.

Writing about the psychology of artistic imagination, Ehrenzweig describes a process of the waking, creative mind that is not unlike Hudson's description of the dream process.[2] The unconscious vision, he writes, proves capable of scanning wider surfaces and gathering more information than conscious scrutiny lasting one hundred times longer. By analogy, he suggests, any creative search involves holding before the inner eye a multitude of possible choices that would totally defeat conscious comprehension. Decisions must be left to the unconscious because only the unconscious can handle such open structures. He refers to the "vacant stare" of the artist who is allowing the unconscious to correct the conscious, like the syncretistic vision of the child that is more flexible than the analytic, adult view and must result from unconscious scanning. The rules of the work become clear only at the end.

What I am suggesting, in other words, goes back to the coherence of these narrative forms with the psychological conditions from which they derive and which they represent. It is supported by the possibility that Rousseau does not complete his journey because he cannot or, conversely, that Mill's use of metaphor describes most urgent need. In short, these metaphors do not sit on the shelf waiting for the academic autobiographer to browse through them at his leisure but erupt onto the page, with varying degrees of artistic success, as servants of the emotions they are intended to describe.

This is not to suggest, of course, that the autobiographer is the helpless victim of a few metaphors. He may choose to employ them as a deliberate part of a conscious scheme. This is surely what Wordsworth does when he locates London as the underworld at the center of his epic journey. We have seen that he remains sound and substantial among the instructive shades around him. By contrast, his crisis in France fills no particular requirement of the epic form but does describe an experience that threatens to destroy him. If we conclude that the first descent into hell fulfills a requirement of Wordsworth's carefully chosen poetic form and that the second expresses a deeply felt personal crisis, it by no means follows that such distinction leads to qualitative judgment. It would be hard to support the notion in this instance that the metaphor representing intense emotion becomes better poetry, for example, than the metaphor that satisfies convention. The artist essentially remains in control of his materials; they will only fail if they do not or cannot cohere with the condition of the inner man they are intended to describe.

The myth can function effectively in a text whether the autobiographer has spawned it from his subconscious or chosen it with conscious care, but it is crucial to recognize that the subjective condition that the autobiographer wants to describe cannot go anywhere on its own; it requires some vehicle for expression and comprehension, and of course translates into better poetry if that vehicle is the appropriate narrative metaphor.

Newman and De Quincey, as we have seen, both created their myths out of many experiences over a wide time span. Whether they did so with deliberation and foreknowledge is hard to say, but the coherence of each myth with the emotions it describes is indisputable. Whether imposed by the conscious artist or generated by intense emotion, these metaphors only make sense of particular kinds of emotions. Incoherence between the emotion and the metaphor found to describe it leads to artistic failure, whereas coherence facilitates the lucid expression of subjective meaning.

It follows that frequent use of narrative metaphor is found in a subjective text. Moore's *Hail and Farewell*, for example, for all its first-person reverie, is not subjective. The narrator establishes a delightful and entertaining intimacy that maintains polite limitations on the ensuing dialogue. It does not bare Moore's soul. More clearly than for Wordsworth or Rousseau, with more single-mindedness than Carlyle, Moore's mythic journey describes the creation of his book rather than the evolution of his life. The man is displaced onto the artist, the life onto the work of art. Furthermore, the irony of tone and the proximity to memoir prevent this autobiography from being a confession.

The contrast in subjectivity between Moore's autobiography and that of Wordsworth, Rousseau, or even Carlyle (who confuses the issue) is supported by the relative use of narrative metaphors in each text; Wordsworth and Rousseau write what becomes basic exemplary material for this study and Moore, although he provides considerable interest, does not. Like the distinction between Wordsworth's descriptions of London and of France, the judgment is one of kind, not quality. In this instance, indeed, it is fair to say that Moore's work gains from the distance established by the narrative stance what Rousseau's loses through solipsistic plangency.

The metaphors we have encountered, then, are of particular use to the autobiographer because they describe at a profound level those things that he needs to describe. They provide comparisons with his life that work in his text. He may organize his material, like De Quincey, in such a way that his narrative is clarified and improved by the introduction of the mythic metaphor. Or the matter may be beyond his control, as possibly with both Rousseau and Mill, in which case the metaphor that describes the psychological condition of the man is more efficient than he is himself at conveying that condition. In either case, however, the myth will not function in the text if it finds no original for which it can serve as metaphor. It is absent from autobiography either when the text is not particularly subjective or when the author has found some other comparison that also works, as with much of *The Autobiography of Mark Rutherford*. On the other hand, its presence, as in *Sartor Resartus*, helps to signal the essentially subjective nature of the work, despite Carlyle's deliberate obfuscation of the point.

Providing a positive reading of subjective content, such use of myth as metaphor becomes particularly appropriate for the nineteenth-century autobiographer. We can recall Shapcott's comment on Mark Rutherford as "a type of many excellent persons whom this century troubles with ceaseless speculations, yielding no conclusions and no peace."[3] Harriet Martineau describes the spirit of her time as self-analysis.[4] It is hardly surprising that men so given to introspection should produce autobiographies in unprecedented numbers. Spengemann, who published *The Forms of Autobiography* in 1980, describes the generic evolution of autobiography as "complete a century ago."[5] In other words, a whole genre, closely related to and dependent upon other literary genres, completed its evolution to a highly sophisticated stage because of the numerous individuals who needed at that time to tell their stories.

Taking the point even further, David DeLaura has examined what he calls "the autobiographical impulse in Victorian prose."[6] He suggests that Arnold's collected prose in particular forms a bildungsroman and that whole collections of prose will be found, under scrutiny, to be as impassioned and autobiographical as any poetry or novel, despite their cover of talking about something else. Gusdorf quotes Nietzsche's amazing suggestion that "'every great philosophy has been the confession of its maker, as it were his involuntary and unconscious autobiography.'"[7] He himself accepts the notion that "the artist's entire work" may well be described as one version of autobiography.[8]

This recognition of the constant excavation, both deliberate and subconscious, of personal experience for artistic expression is the result of many decades of entirely deliberate autobiography. The period of personal exploration that stretches from the Romantic poets to the late novels of Thomas Hardy, from Byron's lonely heroics to Jude's lonely death, explores in a great variety of ways the purpose, value, and meaning of the individual human life. We have been looking at several kinds of autobiography, both that which states its purpose and that which borrows the feathers of apparent "fiction." In poems, in novels, and in avowed autobiographies, we have seen four narrative metaphors recur to control and facilitate the autobiographical impulse and to signal the subjective, autobiographical nature of the work.

Recognition of these forms and of their common value introduces a new relationship between the autobiographer and his reader that emphasizes once again the community of human nature. It is interesting that Edwin Muir, who clearly sees his life in the form of loss, journey, and "reconciliation," moves from faith in the Nietzschean Superman through psychoanalysis to a deeply moving recognition of the shared characteristics of the human condition.

> I saw that my lot was the human lot, that when I faced my own unvarnished likeness I was one among all men and women, all of whom had the same desires and thoughts, the same failures and frustrations, the same unacknowledged hatred of themselves and others, the same hidden shames and griefs, and that if they confronted these things they could win a certain liberation from them.[9]

Everyone, he says elsewhere, "should live his life twice, for the first attempt is always blind."[10]

Notes

Introduction

1. Kermode, *The Sense of an Ending*, p. 133.

2. T. S. Eliot, *Four Quartets*, "Little Gidding" V, in *Collected Poems, 1909–1962* (London: Faber and Faber, 1963), p. 222.

3. *The Confessions of Saint Augustine*, bk. 7, p. 125.

4. Dudek, *The First Person in Literature*, p. 48.

5. Spengemann, *The Forms of Autobiography*, p. 32.

6. Louis A. Renza, "A Theory of Autobiography," in *Autobiography*, ed. Olney, p. 273.

7. Georges Gusdorf, "Conditions and Limits of Autobiography," trans. James Olney, in *Autobiography*, ed. Olney, p. 30.

8. See Mehlman, *A Structural Study of Autobiography*. Each autobiographer that Mehlman has selected for study seeks in one way or another to transcend what each sees as the constraints of a form dictated by historical consciousness.

9. "In France the applied linguisticians are now disavowing the applicability of their categories to literary criticism; at a recent seminar of European University French departments held in Poland, there was general agreement that the literary critical resources of pure structuralism had been exhausted." See A. T. H. Levi, "1: The Renaissance and After," *Times Literary Supplement*, 14 December 1979, p. 140.

10. Bruss, *Autobiographical Acts*, p. 165.

11. Ibid., p. 6.

12. Ibid., p. 93.

13. Spengemann, *The Forms of Autobiography*, p. 77.

Chapter 1

1. Sartre, *What Is Literature?* p. 16.

2. Jakobson, *Essais de linguistique générale*, p. 33.

3. Langer, *Feeling and Form*, p. 217.

4. Bruss, *Autobiographical Acts*, p. 2.

5. Ibid., p. 17.

6. Gombrich, *Art and Illusion*, p. 29.

7. Frye, *The Educated Imagination*, p. 29.

8. Gombrich, *Art and Illusion*, p. 301.

9. Ibid.

10. Frye, *The Educated Imagination*, p. 37.

11. Langer, *Feeling and Form*, p. 292.

12. Vaihinger, *The Philosophy of "As If,"* p. 208.

13. Ibid., pp. 12–13; his italics.

14. Olney, *Metaphors of Self*, p. 31.

15. Jerome S. Bruner, "Myth and Identity," in *Myth and Mythmaking*, ed. Murray, p. 279.

16. Langer, *Feeling and Form,* p. 254.

17. Ibid., p. 257.

18. Jung, *Memories, Dreams, Reflections,* p. 22.

19. Ibid., p. 311.

20. Forster, *Aspects of the Novel,* p. 34.

21. Todorov, *The Poetics of Prose,* p. 111.

22. Georges Gusdorf, "Conditions and Limits of Autobiography," trans. James Olney, in *Autobiography,* ed. Olney, p. 42; his italics.

23. Propp, *Morphology of the Folktale,* chaps. 1 and 3.

24. Campbell, *The Hero with a Thousand Faces,* p. 30.

25. Newman, *Newman's "Apologia,"* p. 99.

26. Jung, *Memories, Dreams, Reflections,* p. 3.

27. Russell, *The Autobiography of Bertrand Russell,* p. 3.

28. Sontag, *Against Interpretation and Other Essays,* p. 30.

29. Cornford, *Thucydides Mythistoricus,* p. 134; his italics.

30. Ibid., p. 135.

31. Northrop Frye, "New Directions from Old," in *Myth and Mythmaking,* ed. Murray, p. 117.

32. Jung, *Archetypes and the Collective Unconscious,* p. 38; his italics.

33. Woolf, *The Waves,* p. 189.

34. Dorothy V. White, *The Groombridge Diary,* p. 51.

35. Ibid., p. 65.

36. White, *Mark Rutherford's Deliverance,* p. vii.

37. Proust, *Remembrance of Things Past,* 2:109–10.

38. Ibid., 2:8; my italics.

39. Newman, *Verses on Various Occasions,* pp. 56–57.

40. *Newman's "Apologia,"* p. 135.

41. Ibid.

42. Ibid., p. 105.

43. Newman, "The Last Years of St. Chrysostom," p. 166.

44. Ibid.

45. Ward, *The Life of John Henry Cardinal Newman,* 2:21.

46. Ibid., p. 24.

47. *Newman's "Apologia,"* pp. 99–101.

48. Ibid., p. 133.

49. Ibid., p. 134.

50. Ibid., p. 135.

51. Ibid., p. 136.

52. Moore, *Confessions of a Young Man,* p. 185.

53. Woolf, "De Quincey's Autobiography," p. 136.

54. De Quincey, *Autobiography,* 1:316.

55. Bruss, discussing the failure of De Quincey's formal autobiography, feels that autobiography was an "artificial and shabby" alternative to "impassioned prose," that De Quincey was happier with the lyrical form that could be apprehended intuitively rather than rationally understood. See *Autobiographical Acts,* pp. 93–126, 172.

56. Jack, "De Quincey Revises his Confessions," p. 142. See also Salaman, *The Great Confession.*

57. *Paradise Lost,* bk. 1, ll. 20–21, in *The Poetical Works of John Milton* (Oxford: Clarendon Press, 1952), 1:54.

58. De Quincey bears comparison here with both Wordsworth and Dickens, who also find Eden in childhood and the country and see the city as dark and evil. De Quincey distinguishes himself, however, by

the fact that his decision rather than the city is bad. It is not just that the world exists outside Eden but that he himself now recognizes the magnitude of his original sin.

Chapter 2

1. "Fern Hill," in *Dylan Thomas, Collected Poems, 1934–1952* (London: Dent, 1952), pp. 159–61.

2. Eliot, *The Mill on the Floss*, p. 301.

3. See D. C. Phillips and Mavis E. Kelly, "Hierarchical Theories of Development in Education and Psychology," in *Stage Theories of Cognitive and Moral Development: Criticisms and Applications* (Cambridge, Mass.: Harvard Educational Review, 1978), p. 174.

4. Lévi-Strauss, "The Structural Study of Myth," pp. 81–106.

5. Leach, "Lévi-Strauss in the Garden of Eden," p. 392.

6. For this and the following creation stories, see: Beier, *The Origin of Life and Death*; Dickins, *Runic and Heroic Poems of the Old Teutonic Peoples*; Drahomaniv, *Notes on the Slavic religio-ethical legends*; Grey, *Polynesian Mythology*; Griffith, *Hymns of the Ṛgveda*; Leach, *The Beginning*; Long, *Alpha*; Macdonell, *The Vedic Mythology*; Sturluson, *The Prose Edda*.

7. Thomas Traherne, *Centuries of Meditations*, ed. Bertram Dobell (London: Published by the editor, 1908), p. 158.

8. Dickens, *Great Expectations*, p. 3.

9. Gosse, *Father and Son*, p. 28.

10. For this reason, perhaps,

memory tends to cling less tenaciously to grief or pain than to happiness. Ruskin, deliberately recalling in *Praeterita* only those things that gave him pleasure, omits to mention his marriage! "Since my memory calls up only pleasant objects," writes Rousseau, "it acts as the happy counterpoise to my fearful imagination, which makes me foresee nothing in the future but cruel disasters." See *The Confessions*, p. 261.

11. Ruskin, *Praeterita*, p. 8.

12. Greene, *Journey Without Maps*, p. 120. Greene's journey is notable in this context both for the fact that it takes place without maps and for his search specifically for himself among the tribes of West Africa.

13. Ibid., p. 277.

14. Cobb, *Ecology of Imagination in Childhood*, p. 89.

15. "The Schoolboy," in *Songs of Innocence and Experience* (New York: Avon Books, 1971), p. 131.

16. "Ode: Intimations of Immortality from Recollections of Early Childhood," in *The Poetical Works of Wordsworth*, rev. ed. Ernest de Selincourt (London: Oxford University Press, 1904), p. 460.

17. Coveney, *The Image of Childhood*, p. 53.

18. Ibid., p. 240.

19. Jean Starobinski describes Rousseau's work as containing two significant "tonalities," the elegiac and the picaresque. In the elegiac mood being noted here, Rousseau, "by his imagination and at will . . . fixes in writing a moment of his life in which he longs to hide. . . . the old era that Rousseau is trying to re-

capture in writing is a lost paradise." See "The Style of Autobiography," trans. Seymour Chatman, in *Autobiography*, ed. Olney, p. 82.

20. Pater, *Marius the Epicurean*, p. 14.

21. Eliot, *The Mill on the Floss*, p. 292.

22. Curious to know whether J. M. Cohen had taken irresistible liberties with his translation here in order to alert English-speaking readers to the familiar paradigm, I turned to the French. Rousseau's phrasing is identical: "J'entrais avec sécurité dans le vaste espace du monde." See *Les Confessions*, p. 48.

23. Philippe Lejeune suggests that Rousseau is more interested in the myth of the four ages of man than in that of paradise lost. He explores the first part of the *Confessions* as a progressive degradation from the age of gold to the ages of silver, brass, and iron. As we shall see with the metaphors that we have yet to examine, the classical dimension does not contradict but, rather, enriches the connotations of the Christian myth. See *Le Pacte autobiographique*.

24. Christopher Milne, *The Enchanted Places* (New York: E. P. Dutton, 1975).

25. "Hyperion," bk. 3, ll. 86–91, in *The Poetical Works of John Keats*, ed. H. W. Garrod (London: Oxford University Press, 1956), p. 241.

26. Gosse, *Father and Son*, p. 16.

27. Aksakoff, *Years of Childhood*, p. 230.

28. Gosse describes his discovery as interesting in part because of its inevitability: "The recollection . . . confirms me in the opinion that certain leading features in each human soul are inherent to it, and cannot be accounted for by suggestion or training. In my own case, I was most carefully withdrawn, like Princess Blanchefleur in her marble fortress, from every outside influence whatever, yet to me the instinctive life came as unexpectedly as her lover came to her in the basket of roses." See *Father and Son*, pp. 27–28.

29. Aksakoff, *Years of Childhood*, p. 132.

30. Leigh Hunt, exchanging his cap for a hat, finds he has now "a vague sense of worldly trouble, and of a great and serious change in [his] condition." His father arrives to take him away, and he notes, with some self-mockery, that "We, hand in hand, with strange new steps and slow / Through Holborn took our meditative way." See *The Autobiography of Leigh Hunt*, p. 107.

31. Pater, *Marius the Epicurean*, p. 14.

32. Gorky, *My Childhood*.

33. Ibid., p. 193.

34. Ibid., p. 203.

35. Ibid.

36. Ibid., p. 233.

37. Dickens, *Great Expectations*, p. 186.

38. De Quincey, *Autobiographic Sketches*, pp. 27–51.

39. Ibid., p. 27.

40. Ibid., p. 35.

41. Woolf, "De Quincey's Autobiography," p. 135.

42. De Quincey, *Autobiographic Sketches*, p. 44.

43. Ibid., p. 41.

44. Hudson, *Far Away and Long Ago*, p. 17.

45. Ibid., p. 32.
46. Ibid., p. 285.
47. Ibid., p. 292.
48. Ibid., pp. 293–95.

Chapter 3

1. Mead, *Coming of Age in Samoa*, p. 74.
2. Piaget and Inhelder, *The Psychology of the Child*, p. 130.
3. S. N. Eisenstadt, "Archetypal Patterns of Youth," in *Youth*, ed. Erikson, p. 26.
4. Inhelder and Piaget, *Growth of Logical Thinking from Childhood to Adolescence*, pp. 343–46.
5. Bettelheim, *Symbolic Wounds*. Winding passages and deep caves describe descent into the underworld, which will be studied in the next chapter.
6. Eliade, *The Quest*, pp. 113–14.
7. Propp, *Morphology of the Folktale*, chap. 3.
8. Campbell, *The Hero with a Thousand Faces*, p. 30.
9. Henderson, *Thresholds of Initiation*.
10. Underhill, *Mysticism*.
11. Toynbee, *A Study of History*, 3:259.
12. Frye, *A Study of English Romanticism*, p. 37.
13. Beebe, *Ivory Towers and Sacred Founts*, p. 299.
14. Ehrenzweig, *The Hidden Order of Art*, bk. 2, pt. 4, p. 171.
15. Todorov, *The Poetics of Prose*, p. 62.
16. Ibid., p. 63.
17. Ibid., p. 135.
18. Ibid.
19. Ibid., p. 139.

20. Weston, *From Ritual to Romance*, chap. 9.
21. Frye, *The Secular Scripture*, p. 157.
22. Frye, *Fables of Identity*, p. 166.
23. Describing the intimate mixture of the elegiac and the picaresque in the *Confessions*, Jean Starobinski suggests that Rousseau's autobiography replicates his philosophy of history. According to that philosophy, man originally possessed happiness and joy; in comparison with that first felicity, the present age is a time of degradation and corruption. But man was originally a brute deprived of "light," his reason still asleep; compared to that initial obscurity, the present is a time of lucid reflection and enlarged consciousness. The past, then, is at once the object of nostalgia and the object of irony; the present is at once a state of (moral) degradation and (intellectual) superiority. See "The Style of Autobiography," in *Autobiography*, ed. Olney, p. 83.
24. Brinsley Macnamara describes George Moore out walking, "coming from or returning to his house and garden in Ely Place, where, I had been told, he was inventing the story of his life. The one that was later to appear as the work in three volumes entitled *Hail and Farewell.*
"The story about the story went that half Dublin was going to be in it as a set of characters. Nobody knew which half. The anxiety of those who felt they were going to be in it for certain was only equalled by the rising jealousy of those who felt he mightn't be going to put them in it at all. Mr. Moore walked, therefore,

with a slight air of suspense surrounding him as he went. People would see him smiling to himself, and wonder who he might be turning over in his mind for a character just at that moment." Quoted from W. T. Rodgers, *Irish Literary Portraits: W. B. Yeats, James Joyce, George Moore, George Bernard Shaw, Oliver St. John Gogarty, F. R. Higgins, Æ* (broadcast conversations with those who knew them) (London: BBC, 1972), p. 77.

25. Ibid., p. 76.

Chapter 4

1. 1 Corinthians 15:8 and 26, in *The New English Bible* (Oxford: Oxford University Press, and Cambridge: Cambridge University Press, 1970).

2. Frye, *The Secular Scripture*, pp. 111–12. See also Bettelheim, *Symbolic Wounds*, for his discussion of rituals of rebirth as commonly represented by caves and tunnels.

3. Ibid., p. 119.

4. Frye, *Anatomy of Criticism*, p. 192.

5. Homer, *The Odyssey*, trans. E. V. Rieu (Harmondsworth: Penguin, 1946), p. 168.

6. Nock, *Conversion*, chap. 11.

7. James, *The Varieties of Religious Experience*, p. 164.

8. Jung, *Memories, Dreams, Reflections*, pp. 32–33. This passage about self-discovery bears comparison with the lines that I quote from Saint Augustine on p. 152.

9. James, *The Varieties of Religious Experience*, p. 193.

10. *The Comedy of Dante Alighieri the Florentine: Cantica I, Hell*, trans. Dorothy L. Sayers (Harmondsworth: Penguin, 1949), canto 1, ll. 1–3.

11. James, *The Varieties of Religious Experience*, p. 193.

12. Ibid., p. 186.

13. *The Confessions of Saint Augustine*, bk. 8, p. 158. Cf. *The Prelude*, 11:306, and Newman's sickness in Sicily discussed in chap. 1.

14. As Garrett Stewart writes: "The tribulation of fever becomes the ultimate trial of imagination in Dickens, an ordeal of constructive suffering. . . . [I]n the creative trials of Dick Swiveller, Mark Tapley, and David Copperfield, of Esther, Arthur, Pip, and . . . of Eugene Wrayburn—Dickens seems to be saying, once and for all, that suffering *is* sovereign. It is often how we must pay our way for the 'poetry of existence.'" See *Dickens and the Trials of Imagination*, pp. 196–97.

15. Gosse, *Father and Son*, p. 123.

16. Compare this ritual with the sickness metaphor found in Dickens, Wordsworth, Newman, and Saint Augustine.

17. Nock, *Conversion*, p. 255.

18. Quoted in Nock, *Conversion*, p. 234.

19. Discussing literary devices, Susanne Langer makes the interesting comment that while use of recollection and hearsay provides an illusion of authenticity, it also has the effect of turning fact into fiction, "wherefore in actual life, a story becomes less convincing with each retelling." See *Feeling and Form*, p. 293.

20. *Treatise on Religious Affections*, quoted in James, *Varieties of Religious Experience*, p. 165.

21. See Olney, *Metaphors of Self,* especially pp. 247–50 for discussion of the mechanical and organic metaphors in Mill's *Autobiography.* His discussion does not preclude description of the central crisis as mythic in the two senses that I established earlier; both form and content meet the needs of the situation and become its metaphor.

22. Hardy, *The Life of Thomas Hardy,* p. 58.

23. Ibid., p. 330.

24. Stillinger, *Early Draft of John Stuart Mill's "Autobiography,"* p. 117.

25. Ibid., p. 13.

26. Ibid.

27. Ibid., p. 15.

28. Letter quoted in Stillinger, *Early Draft of John Stuart Mill's "Autobiography,"* p. 22.

29. It is interesting to compare the results of his rigor with the finer artistic results of an equal rigor exerted by Edmund Gosse in *Father and Son.*

30. Stansky, *John Morley,* p. 142.

31. Leavis, *Mill on Bentham and Coleridge,* p. 72.

32. *The Confessions of Saint Augustine,* bk. 8, p. 162.

33. Descartes presumably followed a similar route; his "History of my Mind" evolved into the *Discourse on Method.*

34. Leavis, *Mill on Bentham and Coleridge,* p. 71.

35. Dickens, *Hard Times for These Times* (New York: Scribner's, 1911), p. 238.

36. Ibid., p. 242.

37. *The Confessions of Saint Augustine,* bk. 8, p. 167.

38. Stansky, *John Morley,* p. 142.

39. T. S. Eliot, *The Wasteland,* pt. 1, ll. 62–63, in *Collected Poems, 1909–1962* (London: Faber and Faber, 1963), p. 65.

40. Letter quoted in Moore, "*Sartor Resartus* and the Problem of Carlyle's 'Conversion,'" p. 675.

41. Letter quoted in Tennyson, *Sartor Called Resartus,* p. 153.

42. The names, of course, suggest Doubting Thomas, the fires of hell, and the fiery furnace in which Shadrach, Meshach, and Abednego prove their righteousness.

43. Parallel with his Wordsworthian-Pauline conversion, Mark Rutherford's rebirth of hope is markedly similar to that experienced by Teufelsdröckh and to Mill's recovery from purposeless gloom after loss of faith in Benthamism. He records how, on one memorable morning, "on the top of one of those Devonshire hills, I became aware of a kind of flush in the brain, and a momentary relief such as I had not known since that November night. I seemed, far away on the horizon, to see just a rim of olive light low down under the edge of the leaden cloud that hung over my head, a prophecy of the restoration of the sun, or at least a witness that somewhere it shone" (*Ab.,* p. 47).

44. Cf. Wordsworth's London.

45. Vaihinger, *The Philosophy of "As If,"* p. 132.

46. C. P. Cavafy, "Ithaka," in *Six Poets of Modern Greece,* trans. and ed. Edmund Keeley and Philip Sherrard (London: Thames and Hudson, 1960), pp. 42–43.

Chapter 5

1. Misch, *A History of Autobiography in Antiquity*, 2:575.

2. Homer, *The Odyssey*, trans. E. V. Rieu (Harmondsworth: Penguin, 1946), p. 181.

3. *The Rime of the Ancient Mariner*, pt. 7, ll. 576–85, in *The Poems of Samuel Taylor Coleridge* (London: Oxford University Press, 1912), p. 208.

4. Quoted in Rousseau, *Les Confessions*, p. ix.

5. See White, *God and the Unconscious*, chap. 11, for discussion of the distinctions between analysis and confession. Not least, religious confession deals with the evil men *do*, analysis with the evil men *suffer*. Autobiographical confession does not need to observe such distinctions but trespasses on both territories. Rousseau, for example, describes both the wrongs that he committed, about which, presumably, he was able to exercise some choice, and the neuroses or compulsions from which he suffered as from components of his character.

6. As Thomas Carlyle remarks: "Literature is but a branch of Religion, and always participates in its character: however, in our time, it is the only branch that still shows any greenness; and, as some think, must one day become the main stem." See "Characteristics," in *Critical and Miscellaneous Essays*, 3:23.

7. It resembles, in this sense, the picaresque fiction. Tom Jones, for example, travels from sin to redemption. Similarly, Rousseau's *Confessions*, which is also picaresque, moves the narrator from original sin toward an always receding redemption.

8. Psalm 51:17. The Roman Missal recommends saying Psalm 50, the Miserere (Psalm 51 in the King James version here quoted), as a part of the act of contrition.

9. *The Confessions of Saint Augustine*, bk. 10, p. 196.

10. Philippians 2:11.

11. Revelation 3:5.

12. Quoted in Rousseau, *Les Confessions*, p. xxxi.

13. *The Rime of the Ancient Mariner*, pt. 7, ll. 610–17.

14. Cf. the Preface to Goethe, *The Sufferings of Young Werther*: "And you, good soul, who feel the same anguish as he, derive comfort from his sufferings, and let this little book be your friend." Rousseau and Mark Rutherford also demonstrate this confessional tendency to reach out from the depths of private experience to help an anonymous soulmate and to plead for identification.

15. Psalm 51:13.

16. *The Confessions of Saint Augustine*, bk. 1, p. 8.

17. *Petrarch's Secret*, p. 21.

18. *The Confessions of Saint Augustine*, bk. 10, p. 205.

19. De Quincey, *Autobiography*, 1:14.

20. *The Confessions of Saint Augustine*, bk. 2, p. 24.

21. *Petrarch's Secret*, p. 192.

22. Bunyan, *Grace Abounding*, p. 185.

23. Ibid., p. 101.

24. Moore, *Confessions of a Young Man*, p. 185.

25. Ibid., p. 1.

26. *The Confessions of Saint Augustine*, bk. 4, p. 60.

27. Ibid., bk. 4, p. 69.

28. Ibid., bk. 10, p. 227.

29. Ibid., bk. 11, p. 243.

30. Ibid., bk. 5, p. 87.

31. Newman's sickness in Sicily, of course, derives its literary if not its psychological spirit from metaphors like these.

32. *The Confessions of Saint Augustine*, bk. 3, p. 52.

33. James Hogg, *The Private Memoirs and Confessions of a Justified Sinner* (New York: Chanticleer Press, 1947), p. 229.

34. Goethe and Carlyle and, to a lesser extent, Hale White, all use this device of double identity within the text to create dialogue and narrative tension.

35. *Petrarch's Secret*, p. 165.

36. Ibid., p. 190.

37. Bruss describes Bunyan as "performing an act which was still relatively rare in England." See *Autobiographical Acts*, p. 33. *Grace Abounding*, in her analysis, depends explicitly and anxiously on Scriptural texts but demonstrates considerable tension between the archetype and the personal experience.

38. Bunyan, *Grace Abounding*, pp. 64–65.

39. Ibid., pp. 67–68.

40. Ibid., p. 26.

41. *Rousseau Juge de Jean-Jacques*, p. 247.

42. Quoted in Rousseau, *Les Confessions*, p. xxiv.

43. Spengemann equates Rousseau's transition from what he calls historical to philosophical autobiography with Saint Augustine's transition from part 1 to part 2 of his *Confessions*. Both autobiographers, of course, exercise a profound influence on their successors.

44. Gill, "The Nude in Autobiography," p. 74.

45. "Never for a moment in his life could Jean-Jacques have been a man without feelings or compassion, an unnatural father. . . . I will be content with a general statement that in handing my children over for the State to educate, for lack of means to bring them up myself, by destining them to become workers and peasants instead of adventurers and fortune-hunters, I thought I was acting as a citizen and a father, and looked upon myself as a member of Plato's Republic" (*The Confessions*, p. 333). Yet this same compassionate philosopher refers earlier to his difficulties in persuading Thérèse to part with her babies. He overcomes her tears, however, and each "inconvenience" is "removed" to the Foundling Hospital "by the same expedient."

46. Les Charmettes is also Eden. Unlike the other episodes, however, in which Rousseau "returns" temporarily to Eden, Les Charmettes clearly doubles as assumption into paradise.

47. Rousseau, *Les Rêveries du Promeneur Solitaire*, p. 109.

48. Ibid.

49. Beebe, *Ivory Towers and Sacred Founts*, p. 49.

50. *The Autobiography of Johann Wolfgang von Goethe*, 2:214.

51. Ibid., p. 217.

52. Frye, *Anatomy of Criticism*, p. 307.

53. Shumaker, *English Autobiography*, p. 84.

54. *The Autobiography of Johann*

Wolfgang von Goethe, 1:305.

55. Gabriel García Márquez, *One Hundred Years of Solitude*, trans. Gregory Rabassa (New York: Avon, 1971), p. 383.

Conclusion

1. Liam Hudson, "Viewpoint," *Times Literary Supplement*, 25 January 1980, p. 85.

2. Ehrenzweig, *The Hidden Order of Art*, bk. 1, pt. 3, pp. 95–168.

3. White, *Mark Rutherford's Deliverance*, p. vii.

4. Martineau, *Harriet Martineau's Autobiography*, 1:157.

5. Spengemann, *The Forms of Autobiography*, p. xvii.

6. David J. DeLaura, "The Allegory of Life: The Autobiographical Impulse in Victorian Prose" (paper delivered at meeting of Victorian Studies Association, Vancouver, B.C., 8 October 1977).

7. Georges Gusdorf, "Conditions and Limits of Autobiography," in *Autobiography*, ed. Olney, p. 46.

8. Ibid.

9. Muir, *An Autobiography*, p. 158.

10. Ibid., p. 192.

Selected Bibliography

Primary Sources

Aksakoff, Serge. *Years of Childhood*. Translated by J. D. Duff. London: E. Arnold, 1916.

Augustine, Saint. *The Confessions of Saint Augustine*. Translated by Edward B. Pusey. New York: Random House, Modern Library, 1949.

Boswell, James. *Boswell's London Journal, 1762–1763*. Edited by Frederick A. Pottle. New York: McGraw-Hill, 1950.

Bunyan, John. *Grace Abounding to the Chief of Sinners*. Edited by Roger Sharrock. Oxford: Clarendon Press, 1962.

―――. *The Pilgrim's Progress from This World to That Which Is to Come Delivered under the Similitude of a Dream*. London: SCM Press, 1947.

Butler, Samuel. *The Way of All Flesh*. Harmondsworth: Penguin, 1947.

Carlyle, Thomas. *Sartor Resartus: The Life and Opinions of Herr Teufelsdröckh*. Edited by Charles Frederick Harrold. New York: Odyssey, 1937.

De Quincey, Thomas. *Autobiographic Sketches*. Boston and New York: Houghton Mifflin, 1876.

―――. *Autobiography from 1785 to 1803*. Vols. 1 and 2 of *The Collected Writings of Thomas De Quincey*, edited by David Masson. Edinburgh: Black, 1889.

―――. *Confessions of an English Opium-Eater in Both the Revised and the Original Texts with Its Sequels "Suspiria De Profundis" and "The English Mail-Coach."* Edited by Malcolm Elwin. London: Macdonald, 1956.

Dickens, Charles. *Great Expectations*. New York: Scribner, 1911.

―――. *The Personal History of David Copperfield*. New York: Scribner, 1911.

Eliot, George. *The Mill on the Floss*. London: Blackwood, 1901.

Freud, Sigmund. *An Autobiographical Study*. Translated by James Strachey. International Psycho-analytical Library, edited by Ernest Jones, no. 26. London: Hogarth Press and the Institute of Psycho-analysis, 1950.

Goethe, Johann Wolfgang von. *The Autobiography of Johann Wolfgang von Goethe (Dichtung und Wahrheit)*. Translated by John Oxenford. New York: Horizon Press, 1969.

―――. *The Sufferings of Young Werther*. Translated by Harry Steinhauer. New York: Norton, 1970.

Gorky, Maxim. *My Childhood*. Translated by Ronald Wilks. Baltimore: Penguin, 1966.

Gosse, Edmund. *Father and Son: A Study of Two Temperaments*. Harmondsworth: Penguin, 1949.

Greene, Graham. *Journey Without Maps*. New York: Viking, 1936.

Hardy, Florence Emily. *The Life of Thomas Hardy, 1840–1928*. London: Macmillan, 1962.

Hazlitt, William. *Liber Amoris and Dramatic Criticisms*. London: Peter Nevill, 1948.

Hudson, W. H. *Far Away and Long Ago: A History of My Early Life*. London: Dent, 1918.

Hunt, Leigh. *The Autobiography of Leigh Hunt*. London: Cresset Press, 1949.

Joyce, James. *A Portrait of the Artist as a Young Man*. New York: Viking, 1964.

Jung, Carl Gustav. *Memories, Dreams, Reflections*. Recorded and edited by Aniela Jaffé. Translated by Richard and Clara Winston. New York: Random House, Pantheon, 1963.

Martineau, Harriet. *Harriet Martineau's Autobiography*. 3 vols. London: Smith, Elder, 1877.

Mill, John Stuart. *Autobiography of John Stuart Mill*. New York: New American Library, 1964.

Moore, George. *Confessions of a Young Man*. Edited by Susan Dick. Montreal: McGill-Queen's University Press, 1972.

———. *Hail and Farewell*. 3 vols. London: Heinemann, 1933.

Muir, Edwin. *An Autobiography*. London: Hogarth, 1954.

Newman, John Henry. *John Henry Newman: Autobiographical Writings*. Edited by Henry Tristram. London: Sheed and Ward, 1955.

———. "The Last Years of St. Chrysostom." In *Essays and Sketches*, edited by Charles Frederick Harrold, 3:157–232. London: Longmans, 1948.

———. *Letters and Correspondence of John Henry Newman: During his Life in the English Church: With a Brief Autobiography*. Edited at Cardinal Newman's request by Anne Mozley. 2 vols. London: Longmans, 1891.

———. *Loss and Gain: The Story of a Convert*. London: Burns and Oates, 1848.

———. *Newman's "Apologia Pro Vita Sua": The Two Versions of 1864 and 1865: Preceded by Newman's and Kingsley's Pamphlets*. Edited by Wilfrid Ward. London: Oxford University Press, 1913.

———. *Verses on Various Occasions*. London: Longmans, 1912.

Pater, Walter. *Marius the Epicurean*. London: Dent, 1934.

Petrarch's Secret or the Soul's Conflict with Passion: Three Dialogues between Himself and Saint Augustine. Translated by William H. Draper. London: Chatto and Windus, 1911.

Proust, Marcel. *Remembrance of Things Past*. 12 vols. Translated by C. K. Scott Moncrieff. London: Chatto and Windus, 1960–66.

Rousseau, Jean-Jacques. *The Confessions*. Translated by J. M. Cohen.

Harmondsworth: Penguin, 1953.

———. *Les Confessions.* Edited by Jacques Voisine. Paris: Éditions Garnier Frères, 1964.

———. *Les Rêveries du Promeneur Solitaire.* Edited by Robert Niklaus. 2d ed. Manchester: University of Manchester, 1946.

———. *Rousseau Juge de Jean-Jacques: Dialogue.* London: N.p., 1880.

Ruskin, John. *Praeterita: Outlines of Scenes and Thoughts Perhaps Worthy of Memory in My Past Life.* London: Rupert Hart-Davis, 1949.

Russell, Bertrand. *The Autobiography of Bertrand Russell, 1872–1914.* New York: Bantam, 1968.

Trollope, Anthony. *An Autobiography.* Berkeley and Los Angeles: University of California Press, 1947.

———. *The Small House at Allington.* London: Nelson, n.d.

———. *The Three Clerks.* London: Oxford University Press, 1907.

Webb, Beatrice. *My Apprenticeship.* Harmondsworth: Penguin, 1971.

White, Dorothy V. *The Groombridge Diary.* London: Oxford University Press, 1924.

White, William Hale. *The Autobiography of Mark Rutherford.* Edited by his friend Reuben Shapcott. London: Hodder and Stoughton, 1913.

———. *The Early Life of Mark Rutherford (W. Hale White) By Himself.* London: Oxford University Press, 1913.

———. *Mark Rutherford's Deliverance: Being the Second Part of his Autobiography.* Edited by his friend Reuben Shapcott. London: Trübner, 1885.

Wordsworth, William. *The Prelude.* In *The Poetical Works of Wordsworth,* rev. ed. by Ernest de Selincourt. London: Oxford University Press, 1904.

———. *The Prelude.* A parallel text edited by J. C. Maxwell. Harmondsworth: Penguin, 1971.

Yeats, W. B. *The Autobiography of W. B. Yeats.* New York: Collier, 1965.

Secondary Sources: Critical, Theoretical, and General

Abrams, M. H. *Natural Supernaturalism: Tradition and Revolution in Romantic Literature.* New York: Norton, 1971.

Ariès, Philippe. *Centuries of Childhood: A Social History of Family Life.* Translated by Robert Baldick. New York: Knopf, 1962.

Baldwin, Kenneth Huntress, Jr. "Autobiography as Art: An Essay Illustrated by Studies of the Autobiographies of Henry Adams, Ernest Hemingway, and Vladimir Nabokov." Ph.D. dissertation, Johns Hopkins University, 1970.

Barfield, Owen. *Poetic Diction: A Study in Meaning.* Middletown, Conn.: Wesleyan University Press, 1973.

Barthes, Roland. *Mythologies.* Translated by Annette Lavers. New York:

Hill and Wang, 1972.

Beebe, Maurice. *Ivory Towers and Sacred Founts: The Artist as Hero in Fiction from Goethe to Joyce*. New York: New York University Press, 1964.

Beier, Ulli, ed. *The Origin of Life and Death: African Creation Myths*. London: Heinemann, 1966.

Berlin, Sir Isaiah. *John Stuart Mill and The Ends of Life*. London: Council of Christians and Jews, 1959.

Bettelheim, Bruno. *Symbolic Wounds: Puberty Rites and the Envious Male*. Rev. ed. New York: Collier, 1962.

Bloom, Harold, ed. *Romanticism and Consciousness: Essays in Criticism*. New York: Norton, 1970.

Booth, Wayne C. *The Rhetoric of Fiction*. Chicago: University of Chicago Press, 1961.

Borchard, Ruth. *John Stuart Mill the Man*. London: Watts, 1957.

Bottrall, Margaret. *Every Man a Phoenix: Studies in Seventeenth-Century Autobiography*. London: J. Murray, 1958.

Bruss, Elizabeth W. *Autobiographical Acts: The Changing Situation of a Literary Genre*. Baltimore: Johns Hopkins University Press, 1976.

Buckley, Jerome Hamilton. *The Triumph of Time: A Study of the Victorian Concepts of Time, History, Progress, and Decadence*. Cambridge: Harvard University Press, Belknap Press, 1966.

Burr, Anna Robeson. *The Autobiography: A Critical and Comparative Study*. New York: Houghton Mifflin, 1909.

Campbell, Joseph. *The Hero with a Thousand Faces*. Bollingen Series, no. 17. Princeton: Princeton University Press, 1949.

Carlyle, Thomas. *Critical and Miscellaneous Essays*. 5 vols. London: Chapman and Hall, 1899.

Clark, A. M. *Autobiography*. Edinburgh: N.p., 1935.

Cobb, Edith. *The Ecology of Imagination in Childhood*. London: Routledge and Kegan Paul, 1977.

Cockshut, A. O. J. *Truth to Life: The Art of Biography in the Nineteenth Century*. London: Collins, 1974.

Cornford, Francis Macdonald. *Thucydides Mythistoricus*. London: E. Arnold, 1907.

Coveney, Peter. *The Image of Childhood: The Individual and Society: A Study of the Theme in English Literature*. Rev. ed. Baltimore: Penguin, 1967.

Delany, Paul. *British Autobiography in the Seventeenth Century*. London: Routledge and Kegan Paul, 1969.

Dessalle-Régis. "Les Confessions de Saint-Augustin et de J.-J. Rousseau." *Revue de Paris* 5, no. 2 (1842): 27–44.

Dickins, Bruce, ed. and trans. *Runic and Heroic Poems of the Old Teutonic Peoples*. Cambridge: Cambridge University Press, 1915.

Drahomaniv, Mykhaïlo Petrovych. *Notes on the Slavic Religio-ethical Leg-*

ends: The Dualistic Creation of the World. Translated by Earl W. Count. Bloomington: Indiana University Press, 1961.

Dudek, Louis. *The First Person in Literature.* Toronto: CBC Publications, 1967.

Durrant, Geoffrey. *William Wordsworth.* Cambridge: Cambridge University Press, 1969.

Ehrenzweig, Anton. *The Hidden Order of Art: A Study in the Psychology of Artistic Imagination.* London: Weidenfeld and Nicolson, 1967.

Ehrmann, Jacques, ed. *Structuralism.* New York: Doubleday, 1970.

Eliade, Mircea. *The Quest: History and Meaning in Religion.* Chicago: University of Chicago Press, 1969.

Erikson, Erik H. *Childhood and Society.* 2d ed. rev. New York: Norton, 1963.

_____. *Identity: Youth and Crisis.* New York: Norton, 1968.

_____. ed. *Youth: Change and Challenge.* New York: Basic Books, 1963.

Forster, E. M. *Aspects of the Novel.* Harmondsworth: Penguin, 1927.

Fowler, Alastair. "The Life and Death of Literary Forms." *New Literary History* 2, no. 2 (1971): 199–216.

Freud, Sigmund. *The Interpretation of Dreams.* Translated by A. A. Brill. Rev. ed. New York: Macmillan, 1932.

Friedman, Alan. *The Turn of the Novel.* New York: Oxford University Press, 1966.

Frye, Northrop. *Anatomy of Criticism: Four Essays.* Princeton: Princeton University Press, 1957.

_____. *The Educated Imagination.* Toronto: CBC Publications, 1963.

_____. *Fables of Identity: Studies in Poetic Mythology.* New York: Harcourt, Brace and World, 1963.

_____. *The Secular Scripture: A Study of the Structure of Romance.* Cambridge: Harvard University Press, 1976.

_____. *The Stubborn Structure: Essays on Criticism and Society.* Ithaca: Cornell University Press, 1970.

_____. *A Study of English Romanticism.* New York: Random House, 1968.

Gill, W. A. "The Nude in Autobiography." *Atlantic Monthly* 99 (1907): 71–79.

Gillie, Christopher. *Character in English Literature.* London: Chatto and Windus, 1965.

Goldberg, Michael. *Carlyle and Dickens.* Athens: University of Georgia Press, 1972.

Gombrich, E. H. *Art and Illusion: A Study in the Psychology of Pictorial Representation.* 2d ed. rev. Princeton: Princeton University Press, 1961.

Gossman, Lionel. "The Innocent Art of Confession and Reverie." *Daedalus* 107, no. 3 (1978): 59–77.

Grey, Sir George. *Polynesian Mythology and Ancient Traditional History of the Maori as Told by their Priests and Chiefs.* Edited by W. W. Bird. Christchurch: Whitcombe and Tombs, 1956.

Griffith, R. T. H., ed. and trans. *Hymns of the R̥gveda.* Varanasi: Chowkhamba Sanskrit Series Office, 1963.

Hart, Francis R. "Notes for an Anatomy of Modern Autobiography." *New Literary History* 1, no. 3 (1970): 485–511.

Harvey, W. J. *Character and the Novel.* London: Chatto and Windus, 1965.

Henderson, Joseph L. *Thresholds of Initiation.* Middletown, Conn.: Wesleyan University Press, 1967.

Hernadi, Paul. "Historiography as Translation, Fiction, and Criticism." *New Literary History* 7, no. 2 (1976): 248–57.

Hirsch, E. D., Jr. *Validity in Interpretation.* New Haven: Yale University Press, 1967.

Holland, Norman N. *The Dynamics of Literary Response.* New York: Oxford University Press, 1968.

Houghton, Walter E. *The Art of Newman's "Apologia."* New Haven: Yale University Press, 1945.

Howarth, William L. "Some Principles of Autobiography." *New Literary History* 5, no. 2 (1974): 363–81.

Humphrey, Robert. *Stream of Consciousness in the Modern Novel.* Berkeley and Los Angeles: University of California Press, 1954.

Inhelder, Bärbel, and Piaget, Jean. *The Growth of Logical Thinking from Childhood to Adolescence.* Translated by Anne Parsons and Stanley Pilgram. New York: Basic Books, 1958.

Jack, Ian. "De Quincey Revises his *Confessions.*" *PMLA* 72 (1957): 122–46.

Jakobson, Roman. *Essais de linguistique générale.* Paris: Minuit, 1963.

James, William. *The Varieties of Religious Experience: A Study in Human Nature.* New York: New American Library, 1958.

Jung, Carl Gustav. *The Archetypes and the Collective Unconscious.* Translated by R. F. C. Hull. 2d ed. London: Routledge and Kegan Paul, 1969.

Kazin, Alfred. "Autobiography as Narrative." In *To the Young Writer,* edited by A. L. Bader, pp. 181–93. Ann Arbor: University of Michigan Press, 1965.

Kenner, Hugh. *The Counterfeiters: An Historical Comedy.* Bloomington: Indiana University Press, 1968.

Kermode, Frank. *The Sense of an Ending: Studies in the Theory of Fiction.* London: Oxford University Press, 1966.

Kris, Ernst. *Psychoanalytic Explorations in Art.* New York: Schocken Books, 1964.

Langer, Susanne K. *Feeling and Form: A Theory of Art.* New York: Scribner, 1953.

Leach, Edmund. "Lévi-Strauss in the Garden of Eden: An Examination of Some Recent Developments in the Analysis of Myth." *Transactions of the New York Academy of Science,* 2d ser., vol. 23, no. 4 (1961): 386–96.

Leach, Maria. *The Beginning: Creation Myths Around the World*. New York: Funk and Wagnalls, 1956.

Leavis, F. R., ed. *Mill on Bentham and Coleridge*. London: Chatto and Windus, 1962.

Lejeune, Philippe. "Autobiography in the Third Person." *New Literary History* 9, no. 1 (1977): 27–50.

———. *Le Pacte Autobiographique*. Paris: Éditions du Seuil, 1975.

Lesser, Simon O. *Fiction and the Unconscious*. Boston: Beacon Press, 1957.

Lévi-Strauss, Claude. "The Structural Study of Myth." In *Myth: A Symposium*, edited by Thomas A. Sebeok, pp. 81–106. Bloomington: Indiana University Press, 1958.

Lindenberger, Herbert. *On Wordsworth's Prelude*. Princeton: Princeton University Press, 1963.

Long, Charles H. *Alpha: The Myths of Creation*. New York: George Braziller, 1963.

Macdonell, A. A. *The Vedic Mythology*. Varanasi: Indological Book House, 1971.

Mandel, Barrett John. "The Autobiographer's Art: A Study of Bunyan, Gibbon, and Cowper." Ph.D. dissertation, University of Connecticut, 1966.

Matthews, William. *British Autobiographies: An Annotated Bibliography of Autobiographies Published or Written Before 1951*. Berkeley and Los Angeles: University of California Press, 1955.

Matthews, William, and Rader, Ralph. *Autobiography, Biography, and the Novel*. Los Angeles: William Andrews Clark Memorial Library, 1973.

Maurois, André. *Aspects of Biography*. Translated by Sydney Castle Roberts. New York: Appleton, 1929.

Mead, Margaret. *Coming of Age in Samoa: A Psychological Study of Primitive Youth for Western Civilization*. New York: Morrow, 1928.

Mehlman, Jeffrey. *A Structural Study of Autobiography: Proust, Leiris, Sartre, Lévi-Strauss*. Ithaca: Cornell University Press, 1974.

Meyerhoff, Hans. *Time in Literature*. Berkeley and Los Angeles: University of California Press, 1960.

Mink, Louis O. "History and Fiction as Modes of Comprehension." *New Literary History* 1, no. 3 (1970): 541–58.

Misch, Georg. *A History of Autobiography in Antiquity*. Translated by E. W. Dickes. 2 vols. London: Routledge and Kegan Paul, 1950.

Moore, Carlisle. "*Sartor Resartus* and the Problem of Carlyle's 'Conversion.'" *PMLA* 70, no. 4 (1955): 662–81.

Morley, John. *Rousseau*. 2 vols. London: Macmillan, 1915.

Morris, John N. *Versions of the Self: Studies in English Autobiography from John Bunyan to John Stuart Mill*. New York: Basic Books, 1966.

Murray, Henry A., ed. *Myth and Mythmaking*. New York: George Braziller, 1960.

Nicolson, Harold. *The Development of English Biography*. London: Hogarth Press, 1927.

Nock, A. D. *Conversion: The Old and the New in Religion from Alexander the Great to Augustine of Hippo*. Oxford: Clarendon Press, 1933.

Olney, James. *Metaphors of Self: The Meaning of Autobiography*. Princeton: Princeton University Press, 1972.

————, ed. *Autobiography: Essays Theoretical and Critical*. Princeton: Princeton University Press, 1980.

Pascal, Roy. *Design and Truth in Autobiography*. Cambridge: Harvard University Press, 1960.

Pattison, Robert. *The Child Figure in English Literature*. Athens: University of Georgia Press, 1978.

Peckham, Morse. *Beyond the Tragic Vision: The Quest for Identity in the Nineteenth Century*. New York: George Braziller, 1962.

Piaget, Jean, and Inhelder, Bärbel. *The Psychology of the Child*. Translated by Helen Weaver. New York: Basic Books, 1969.

Ponsonby, Arthur. *English Diaries: A Review of English Diaries from the Sixteenth to the Twentieth Century*. London: Methuen, 1923.

Poulet, Georges. *Studies in Human Time*. Translated by Elliott Coleman. Baltimore: Johns Hopkins University Press, 1956.

Praz, Mario. *The Hero in Eclipse in Victorian Fiction*. Translated by Angus Davidson. London: Oxford University Press, 1956.

Propp, Vladimir. *Morphology of the Folktale*. Translated by Laurence Scott. Austin: University of Texas Press, 1968.

Rader, Ralph W. "Literary Form in Factual Narrative: The Example of Boswell's *Johnson*." In *Essays in Eighteenth-Century Biography*, edited by Philip B. Daghlian, pp. 3–42. Bloomington: Indiana University Press, 1968.

Rinehart, Keith. "The Victorian Approach to Autobiography." *Modern Philology* 51, no. 3 (1954): 177–86.

Robbins, William. *The Newman Brothers: An Essay in Comparative Intellectual Biography*. Cambridge: Harvard University Press, 1966.

Salaman, Esther Polianowsky. *The Great Confession from Aksakoff and De Quincey to Tolstoy and Proust*. London: Allen Lane, 1973.

Salvesen, Christopher. *The Landscape of Memory: A Study of Wordsworth's Poetry*. London: E. Arnold, 1965.

Sartre, Jean-Paul. *What is Literature?* Translated by Bernard Frechtman. New York: Harper and Row, 1965.

Scholes, Robert, and Kellog, Robert. *The Nature of Narrative*. New York: Oxford University Press, 1966.

Shapiro, Stephen A. "The Dark Continent of Literature: Autobiography." *Comparative Literature Studies* 5, no. 4 (1968): 421–54.

Shumaker, Wayne. *English Autobiography: Its Emergence, Materials, and Form*. Berkeley and Los Angeles: University of California Press, 1954.

Sontag, Susan. *Against Interpretation and Other Essays*. New York: Dell, 1961.

Spacks, Patricia Meyer. *Imagining a Self: Autobiography and Novel in Eigh-*

teenth-Century England. Cambridge: Harvard University Press, 1976.

Spengemann, William C. *The Forms of Autobiography: Episodes in the History of a Literary Genre*. New Haven: Yale University Press, 1980.

Stansky, Peter, ed. *John Morley: Nineteenth-Century Essays*. Chicago: University of Chicago Press, 1970.

Stewart, Garrett. *Dickens and the Trials of Imagination*. Cambridge: Harvard University Press, 1974.

Stillinger, Jack, ed. *The Early Draft of John Stuart Mill's "Autobiography."* Urbana: University of Illinois Press, 1961.

Stock, Irvin. *William Hale White (Mark Rutherford): A Critical Study*. London: G. Allen, 1956.

Sturluson, Snorri. *The Prose Edda*. Translated by A. G. Brodeur. New York: American-Scandinavian Foundation, 1916.

Sturrock, John. "The New Model Autobiographer." *New Literary History* 9, no. 1 (1977): 51–63.

Tennyson, G. B. *Sartor Called Resartus: The Genesis, Structure, and Style of Thomas Carlyle's First Major Work*. Princeton: Princeton University Press, 1965.

Todorov, Tzvetan. *The Poetics of Prose*. Translated by Richard Howard. Ithaca: Cornell University Press, 1977.

Toynbee, Arnold J. *A Study of History*. 12 vols. London: Oxford University Press, 1934.

Underhill, Evelyn. *Mysticism: A Study in the Nature and Development of Man's Spiritual Consciousness*. London: Methuen, 1911.

Vaihinger, Hans. *The Philosophy of "As If": A System of the Theoretical, Practical and Religious Fictions of Mankind*. Translated by C. K. Ogden. New York: Barnes and Noble, 1935.

Walcutt, Charles Child. *Man's Changing Mask: Modes and Methods of Characterization in Fiction*. Minneapolis: University of Minnesota Press, 1966.

Ward, Wilfrid. *The Life of John Henry Cardinal Newman: Based on his Private Journals and Correspondence*. 2 vols. London: Longmans, 1927.

Weintraub, Karl J. "Autobiography and Historical Consciousness." *Critical Inquiry* 1, no. 4 (1975): 821–48.

———. *The Value of the Individual: Self and Circumstance in Autobiography*. Chicago: University of Chicago Press, 1978.

Weston, Jessie L. *From Ritual to Romance*. New York: Doubleday, 1957.

White, Hayden. *Metahistory: The Historical Imagination in Nineteenth-Century Europe*. Baltimore: Johns Hopkins University Press, 1973.

White, Victor. *God and the Unconscious*. London: Collins, 1952.

Woolf, Virginia. "The Art of Biography." In *The Death of the Moth and Other Essays*, pp. 119–26. London: Hogarth Press, 1942.

———. "De Quincey's Autobiography." In *The Common Reader*, 2d ser., pp. 132–39. London: Hogarth Press, 1932.

———. *The Waves*. London: Hogarth Press, 1955.

Index

Æ. *See* Russell, George William
  [pseud. Æ]
Aeneas, 122, 138–39, 141, 146,
  157, 169, 171, 173
Aksakoff, Serge, 7, 79, 92–96, 100,
  101
Augustine, Saint, 4, 8, 9, 88, 141;
  conversion, 152, 153–54, 161–
  62, 165, 179, 190; confession,
  174, 175, 176, 177, 178–85,
  186, 191

Blake, William, 76–77
Bunyan, John, 9, 115, 170, 175,
  176, 177, 178–81, 183–85, 186
Butler, Samuel [Ernest Pontifex], 15,
  23, 24, 32, 193

Carlyle, Thomas, 8, 12, 18, 32, 111,
  135, 147, 200, 201, 211 (n. 34);
  and Wordsworth, 112, 150, 163,
  165, 167, 209 (n. 44); journey,
  112–18, 126, 127, 146; conversion, 115–16, 137, 163–66, 169;
  and Mill, 150, 155, 163–67
Childhood, 7, 60–61, 68–103
  passim, 178, 179, 180, 184–85;
  Blake, 76–77. *See also* Rousseau,
  Jean-Jacques; Wordsworth,
  William
Coleridge, Samuel Taylor, 155
Confession, 4, 8–9, 12, 41, 170–95
  passim, 200, 210 (n. 5). *See also*
  De Quincey, Thomas; Psychology; Rousseau, Jean-Jacques
Conversion, 4, 8, 12, 26, 39, 107,
  116, 137–67 passim, 169, 170,
  172, 174, 176, 177, 179, 194,
  199. *See also* Myth: descent into

underworld; Newman, John
  Henry: *Apologia*; Newman, John
  Henry: sickness in Sicily; Rousseau, Jean-Jacques; White, William Hale

Dante Alighieri, 115, 117, 140, 141,
  157, 181
De Quincey, Thomas, 6, 7, 41, 79,
  97, 98–100, 181, 191, 199, 200;
  and Edenic paradigm, 59–65, 83;
  confession, 175, 176–77, 178,
  186
Dickens, Charles, 15, 65, 73, 76, 97,
  98, 99, 141, 153, 164, 191, 193

Eden. *See* Paradise
Eliot, George, 68, 79–80, 193
Epic, 5, 7, 8, 86, 170, 171, 177,
  199. *See also* Hero

Fiction, 3–7, 9, 12, 20, 28, 59, 66–
  67, 83, 97, 112, 131, 163, 182,
  192, 193, 194, 202; contingent
  reality, 7, 16, 24, 34, 66, 120,
  130, 167; virtual events, 14–15,
  19; theories of, 14–23, 41, 109–
  10, 208 (n. 19); inevitability of,
  14–67 passim; Vaihinger's "as if,"
  18, 66, 67, 167. *See also* Metaphor; Myth; Narrator
Folktales, 23, 41, 107, 170, 177
Formalism, 10
Freud, Sigmund, 99

Goethe, Johann Wolfgang von, 9,
  115, 147, 173, 191–93, 210 (n.
  14), 211 (n. 34)
Gorky, Maxim, 4, 7, 79, 96–98, 100

Gosse, Edmund, 73, 80, 89, 94, 142–43, 206 (n. 28)
Greene, Graham, 75

Hardy, Thomas, 56, 147, 191, 202
Hero, 39; epic, 5, 8, 62, 65, 107, 108, 114–15, 127, 133–35, 138, 168, 171, 172; as narrator, 8, 24, 32, 111, 133, 171, 189; picaresque, 127, 128. *See also* Narrator
Hudson, W. H., 4, 7, 74, 79, 100–102
Hunt, Leigh, 68, 95, 206 (n. 30)

Journey, 4, 7–8, 12, 98, 103, 104–36 passim, 137, 146, 147, 170, 172, 194, 195, 199, 200, 202. *See also* Conversion; Epic; Metaphor: of journey; Myth: descent into underworld
Joyce, James [Stephen Dedalus], 4, 20, 23, 24, 75, 193
Jung, Carl Gustav, 19–20, 30, 140, 194

Keats, John, 86–87, 88

Lawrence, D. H. [Paul Morel], 23, 75

Madonna, 181–82, 189–91
Maturity. *See* Conversion
Memory, 3, 7, 14, 52, 53, 54, 74–76, 79–81, 83–84, 85, 86–88, 90–91, 100, 102, 120, 125, 129, 130, 131, 132–34, 205 (n. 10). *See also* Childhood; De Quincey, Thomas; Moore, George
Metaphor, 5, 9, 10, 16–19, 20, 23, 27, 32, 62, 122, 147, 151, 168, 170, 196–97, 199–202; of journey, 4, 7–8, 104, 105, 106, 107–8, 109, 110, 111, 113, 114, 135, 167, 170; of Eden, 4, 69, 74, 76,

96; for narrator, 23–40 passim; of conversion, 116, 137, 138, 139, 147, 156, 165, 166, 199; of confession, 170, 177, 178, 181, 182, 193–95. *See also* Carlyle, Thomas; Jung, Carl Gustav; Myth

Mill, John Stuart, 197, 199; conversion of, 4, 8, 146, 147–56, 169; and Carlyle, 150, 155, 163–67; and Wordsworth, 150, 155–56, 159–61, 162, 163, 165, 167
Montaigne, Michel de, 11, 187
Moore, George, 7, 24, 33–40, 59, 66, 67, 74, 75, 111, 112, 169, 200; journey, 8, 131–35; Eden, 78, 81; confession, 170, 176, 177–78, 180
Myth, 5, 8, 9, 11, 17, 18–20, 39, 76, 167, 169, 177, 196, 199–202; creation, 7, 66, 68–72, 88, 138, 139, 170; descent into underworld, 8, 137–39, 146, 156, 157–59, 169, 171, 172, 194; as narrative pattern, 22–23, 40, 41, 48, 51, 58, 66, 67, 76, 77, 83, 96, 99, 102–3, 105, 106, 108, 109, 111, 112, 116, 119, 129, 146, 159, 169, 177, 194–95, 196, 200; Lohengrin, 36, 37; Messiah or Christ, 36–37, 40, 48, 108, 139; Siegfried, 37, 38, 40, 135; golden bough, 122. *See also* Jung, Carl Gustav; Metaphor

Narrative patterns. *See* Metaphor; Myth
Narrator, 6, 8, 19, 21, 22, 23–40 passim, 67, 81, 109–10, 111, 125, 126, 127, 131–34, 146, 166, 171, 189, 194, 200; third-person, 24–33, 179, 182; first-person, 33–40, 200; Carlyle's editor, 112, 114, 116–18, 124, 126, 127, 165; Rousseau's unreliability, 131

Newman, John Henry, 66, 98, 199;
sickness in Sicily, 4, 6, 41–48,
211 (n. 31); *Apologia*, 42, 43, 47,
50, 52, 55–59; sense of mission,
48–51; journal, 51–56; Saint
Chrysostom, 53

Odysseus, 109, 114, 118, 138–39,
141, 146, 157, 168, 169, 170,
171, 172, 173, 195
Oxford movement. *See* Religion

Paradise, 3–4, 12, 42, 49; lost, 61–
65, 68–74, 78–79, 81, 82–103
passim, 104, 130, 189, 202; as
myth, 61, 68–74, 76, 95–98,
137, 146, 170, 189, 194, 195;
original sin, 64, 82. *See also*
Childhood; Metaphor; Myth:
creation
Pater, Walter, 79, 96
Paul, Saint, 26, 39, 138, 141–45,
176, 177, 179, 209 (n. 43)
Petrarch, 9, 176, 177, 178, 181,
182–83, 185
Pre-Raphaelites, 33–34
Prophecy, 108, 146, 147, 162, 167
Proust, Marcel, 33, 37–38, 193
Psychology, 5, 169, 170; and metaphor, 7, 8, 9, 10, 19, 107–8, 147,
196, 197–99, 201; of childhood,
7, 68, 88, 94, 103, 104; of youth,
7, 105, 107, 135, 172; of conversion, 8, 48, 137, 140–41, 145,
147, 153, 166–67; of confession,
8–9, 170, 173, 178, 186, 188,
191, 193–94, 210 (n. 5); psychoanalysis, 77, 193, 202

Quest. *See* Epic; Journey

Rasselas, 94
Religion, 5, 7, 9, 91, 104; White,
26–32, Irish Catholicism, 36–37,
39, 40; Oxford movement, 42;

43, 51, 55, 57, 58; English
church, 49, 51, 54; Catholic
church, 55, 56, 134, 170, 172–
73, 174, 176, 185, 188, 189;
Rousseau, 189–90. *See also* Confession; Conversion
Rembrandt, 17
Romantic literature, 11, 77, 108,
111, 147, 193, 196, 202
Rousseau, Jean-Jacques, 11, 12, 13,
98, 111, 112, 132, 169, 170, 181,
197, 200; childhood, 3–4, 68,
76, 77, 78, 79–80, 82–83, 86,
87, 89, 92, 94, 178, 187; journey,
8, 127–31, 135–36, 147, 199;
confession, 9, 170, 171, 173,
175, 176, 177, 178, 180, 185–
91, 210 (n. 14); memory, 75, 79–
81, 83–84, 85; conversion, 141–
42, 185, 189–90; as a father,
188, 211 (n. 45); and elegiac
mood, 205 (n. 19); four ages of
man, 206 (n. 23); philosophy of
history, 207 (n. 23)
Ruskin, John, 17, 75
Russell, George William [pseud. Æ],
3, 5, 35, 36, 37, 133
Rutherford. *See* White, William
Hale

Sociology, 7, 9, 104, 106
Structuralism, 10, 17, 69–70

Teufelsdröckh. *See* Carlyle, Thomas
Thucydides, 22, 41, 42
Trollope, Anthony, 15, 193

White, William Hale, 24–33, 36, 40,
59, 66, 67, 201, 211 (n. 34); conversion, 26, 143–44, 209 (n. 43);
confession, 174, 183, 192, 210
(n. 14)
Wordsworth, William, 8, 12, 20, 75,
111, 135, 147, 166, 200; and
White, 26, 209 (n. 43); on child-

hood, 68, 72–73, 76, 77, 78, 83, 86–94, 100, 159; memory, 75, 80, 86–88; and Carlyle, 112, 150, 163, 165, 167, 209 (n. 44); and journey, 119–27 passim, 137, 146; and conversion, 137, 155–63, 199; and Mill, 150, 155–56, 159–61, 162, 163, 165, 167

Yeats, William Butler, 5, 35, 36
Youth. *See* Journey